Daddy Was the

Black Dahlia

Killer

Janice Knowlton
with Michael Newton

POCKET BOOKS

New York   London   Toronto   Sydney   Tokyo   Singapore

An *Original* Publication of POCKET BOOKS

POCKET BOOKS, a division of Simon & Schuster Inc.
1230 Avenue of the Americas, New York, NY 10020

ISBN: 0-671-88084-5

First Pocket Books printing August 1995

10 9 8 7

POCKET and colophon are registered trademarks of Simon & Schuster Inc.

Cover photos courtesy of Janice G. Knowlton

Printed in the U.S.A.

ON SUNDAY, GEORGE MAKES HIS FIRST ATTEMPT TO DUMP THE BODY.

He wraps Beth's remains in a heavy blanket, and puts her in the trunk of the La Salle. He takes Jan with him as cover. How suspicious can a man look to the world, out riding with his daughter on the Sabbath?

At the Seal Beach fishing pier, Jan watches as her father flings the bisected corpse into the ocean, waiting for the tide to do the rest.

Beth foils him at the last. Her body doesn't sink. The lower half falls into the shallow water at his feet and waffles in the surf. Some trick of buoyancy propels the body's top half to the surface.

Defeated! Mad frustration mounts in George, vented in a string of curses as he pulls the corpse from the surf. "Get your ass up that beach," he demands of Janice, "and keep your eyes open!"

George looks around and has a sudden inspiration. He carries the bundled, severed corpse to an open room near the picnic area, used for cleaning fish. . . .

Back at the car, George puts the blanket-wrapped remains in the trunk. "This is our little secret," he says to Janice. "You can never tell your mother any of this or I'll kill you, you little bitch, do you hear me?"

* * * *

ABOUT THE AUTHORS

JANICE KNOWLTON is a professional singer and publicist. She has appeared on *Hard Copy, Larry King Live,* and *Sally Jessy Raphael.*

MICHAEL NEWTON, author of *Hunting Humans, Serial Slaughter, FBI Most Wanted,* and *Silent Rage,* has been called "one of the most important true crime journalists in America" (*Coast Book Review*).

This book is dedicated to my therapist Jim Frey and all the other victims of child abuse, past and present. Especially to those who died of their abuse and cannot tell their stories.

How did I get here? Somebody pushed me. Somebody must have set me off in this direction and clusters of other hands must have touched themselves to the controls at various times, for I would not have picked this way for the world.

—Joseph Heller

Contents

CONTENTS

Authors' Note

The thoughts and quoted dialogue come from a variety of sources including the recollections of Jan and others who participated in the conversations or who observed them or took notes, from public documents, published sources and other written accounts.

Every heinous crime impinges on the lives of countless persons, innocent and otherwise: surviving victims, witnesses, fringe players, and accomplices who may or may not comprehend their role in the events as they unfold. With that in mind, we have changed the names of certain real-life characters to shield the innocent, including the authors, from harassment. Pseudonyms within the text are marked with an asterisk the first time they appear. Changed names aside, no literary license has been taken in the form of composite characters. There is no need to dramatize or fabricate. The truth is grim enough.

Preface

What's in a name?

The world, and then some. Fame and fortune to a handful; on the flip side, notoriety and death. Sometimes the bright side and the dark go hand in hand. Courageous pilots flying bomber missions over war-torn Europe lift their unit's nickname from a film by Howard Hughes; back home, forgotten after V-E Day, they keep the name and trade their bombers in for Harley-Davidsons—Hell's Angels rolling on to infamy. Another band of veterans in Pulaski, Tennessee, decide to call their boozing club the Ku Klux Klan; they put on silly costumes for amusement, and the rest is history.

In Hollywood the name game is refined to a peculiar art form. Norma Jean Baker is dying on the vine, but fans go wild for Marilyn Monroe. Frances Gumm soars over the rainbow as Judy Garland. Annemarie Italiano hits the marquee as Anne Bancroft. Lucy Johnson charms America, and a series of famous husbands, as Ava Gardner. Frederick Austerlitz and Tula Finklea seem lighter on their feet, somehow, when they waltz together as Fred Astaire and Cyd Charisse.

How many residents of modern-day Los Angeles, accosted on the street, could readily identify Beth Short? A few old-timers and police buffs might recall the name, but most would draw a blank and shrug the question off as insignificant.

Now mention the sobriquet. Watch them come alive with morbid curiosity. Not only in L.A., but in Manhattan and Miami, Paris and Palermo, Tel Aviv and Tokyo.

Everyone knows the Black Dahlia.

Immortalized in newsprint and novels, teleplays and feature films, the twenty-two-year-old aspiring actress now occupies a niche in modern folklore that she coveted but never managed to attain in life.

Hers was a quirky sort of fame. Obsessed with Hollywood, she never did a screen test that we know of, never even scored a cameo or silent walk-on in the cheapest features coming out of Warner Brothers, RKO, or Metro-Goldwyn-Mayer. When fame crept up on Beth, it came well armed and took her absolutely by surprise. No script to study, nothing in the way of lines or makeup.

All she had to do was die.

And what a death it was, trussed up and mutilated by a madman, beaten with a hammer, finally cut in half and driven to a vacant lot where she was dumped in the weeds like so much rubbish. It was the final insult in a life where nothing lived up to the expectations of a would-be starlet, closing out Beth's show before it ever had a chance to run.

Today, in a society where random killers surface in the headlines on an average of one a week, Beth's murder would be relegated to a footnote in the daily press, assuming it got any play at all. Los Angeles in 1947 was a different world, though, and the mutilation-slaying of a beautiful young woman generated front-page stories for a month, a record still unbroken after nearly half a century of riots, scandals, global warfare, flights to outer space, and the assassination of a president.

The name has magic. Although Beth Short was forgotten almost from the moment she was publicly identified, the Dahlia still commands our rapt attention, drawing countless gawkers to the field where she was found, compelling scores of desperate men and women to confess participation in the crime. Pathetic bids for brief, vicarious association with a dead girl's notoriety, regardless of the cost. Gray lives of such incalculable tedium that death row shines by contrast, holding out the promise of at least one tarnished moment in the sun.

The Dahlia lives, unscathed by passing decades and the butcher's blade. She blooms at night, a dark, exotic blossom redolent of sex and mystery. By synchronicity or sheer coincidence, she has transcended death. A mythic flower, cast in ink and amber, she will never fade.

So it has always been with famous crimes and criminals. If Jack the Ripper's mocking notes to Scotland Yard had been signed "John Doe," the case would be forgotten now; no author would have wasted five minutes speculating on a plot by Masons, princes of the realm, or Russian spies to slaughter London prostitutes. Who can remember Arthur Flegenheimer, as compared to the notorious Dutch Schultz? The troops of Bugs Moran, mowed down by Al Capone in old Chicago, would be lost amid the general carnage of the Roaring Twenties if they had not met their fate on Saint Valentine's Day. Detroit's chaotic "Purple Gang," annihilated to a man by the mid-1930s, was still so colorful that newsmen stubbornly applied the name to other thugs a generation later, selling papers on the strength of a nostalgic fantasy.

We know Beth Short today because her epithet and the circumstances of her death combined to forge a legend out of flesh and blood. In spite of all she suffered in her final hours, she owes us more, somehow, for keeping her alive in memory. The Dahlia had been ten years in her grave before a British author misstated new, unheard-of mutilations and his story wormed its way into the hazy realm of "common knowledge." There is nothing, so it seems, that Beth will not endure for her public.

Best of all, for those who trade in myths, the crime remains unsolved. It is, to paraphrase one self-styled expert on the case, like an exciting-looking birthday gift, the wrapping still intact. Anticipation triumphs over drab reality. What child, expecting special toys, has not been disappointed by a package filled with socks or underwear?

The truth is like that sometimes—bland, mundane, one size fits all. In other cases, though, if we search long and hard enough, an answer may eclipse the question, so expanding upon a timeless riddle that our view of human nature is forever changed.

The mystery of Beth Short's murder has been unresolved for almost half a century . . . until today.

It should not be supposed that a solution to the case was preordained, by any means. There are no diaries locked up in a dusty hope chest, no death-bed confession from a suddenly remorseful killer desperate to settle his account for Judgment Day. The Dahlia's slayer was not born again, but he left tracks for those with eyes to see.

He also left a living witness in the bosom of his family, and thereon hangs this tale.

A native Californian, I grew up with an awareness of the Dahlia murder, vague impressions gleaned from anniversary columns in the press, short chapters in the kind of crime anthologies that place a premium on gore at the expense of accuracy, lurid novels, and a TV movie of the week where Efrem Zimbalist Jr., as real-life homicide detective Harry Hansen, spent more time chewing his cigar than chasing leads. If asked, I would have said I knew all about the case.

In fact, I was completely ignorant.

I did not know, for instance, that the Dahlia's brutal death was only one of several homicides committed by a ruthless predator who roamed between the East Coast and the West for over thirty years, destroying lives wherever he touched down. I had no inkling that the Dahlia's story was merely the tip of a deadly iceberg, exposure of which would unravel a grisly tale of serial murder from the "good old days" before that term was coined—much less understood—by criminologists.

The revelation came about, as such things often do, by accident. A coffee break, the television tuned to Jerry Springer's talk show out of Cincinnati. No top-heavy strippers or lesbian nuns this morning; the topic was serial murder, and I sat down to watch with a kind of proprietary interest, having published five books on the subject in as many years.

The first guest was a woman in her sixties, hunched and gray, describing how her mother had practiced birth control by drowning newborn infants in the kitchen sink and planting them out back in unmarked graves. One of the woman's sisters, rescued from a similar demise, sat in to verify the tale. Police were at a loss for a response, since the offending parents were deceased . . . and did it really matter, after all this time?

Next up was Janice Knowlton, bright, attractive, and articulate. She faced the cameras squarely, and her tale transcended the mundane. She knew who killed the Dahlia and at least ten other victims, many of them in Los Angeles, a few in Massachusetts. She had tracked the killer's movements back to his childhood and documented his every step from census records, maps, family interviews, police reports, and clippings from a dozen daily papers. Under questioning, she was persuasive and unshakable.

The details of our meeting are irrelevant. It is enough to say that I approached the case with healthy skepticism and became convinced that Jan had solved not only Beth Short's murder but also a string of pattern homicides that span three thousand miles and thirty years. Los Angeles police know better, they insist, because Jan's evidence—which they refuse to study, falling back instead on garbled media reportage—"does not coincide" with evidence concealed for the past forty-seven years in their secret files.

This from the same police department that organized a whipping bee for so-called Communists in 1930 and protected outlaw gambling casinos well into the 1950s; that harassed and spied on local residents for over twenty years, then "lost" the crucial files in 1991 when that surveillance was exposed; that filed a positive ballistics match in the murder of Robert F. Kennedy after testing the wrong gun;

and that, in 1991 alone, paid out $10 million to resolve brutality complaints from citizens of color in Los Angeles. So much for objectivity.

What follows is the story of a recreational assassin and his selected victims, the Black Dahlia among them—a classic murder mystery whose time has come. It is a story of survivors, too, though they are few in number. The very fact of their survival testifies to something in the human spirit that, no matter how abused or beaten down, may yet emerge triumphant in the end.

This book could not have been prepared without Jan Knowlton's help and Herculean research, undertaken as a step toward long-delayed healing, plus access to the journals she compiled while working on a different book (*Renaissance House,* forthcoming) for survivors of incest and family trauma. Likewise, it would not exist without the efforts of our agent, Nancy Yost, at Barbara Lowenstein Associates. Jan's sister Prudence, despite some misgivings, performed a near-heroic feat of research, delivering more than one hundred handwritten pages of family history. Others who provided valuable assistance in the search for truth include Special Agent John Douglas, chief of the FBI's Investigative Support Unit in Quantico, Virginia; Sergeant Bill McComas, Los Angeles County Sheriff's Department, Homicide Division; Michele Bringier, Los Angeles County Coroner's Department; Lieutenant John Welter, San Diego Police Department, Homicide Division; Sergeant Roger Boram, San Diego County Sheriff's Department; Detective Sergeant Richard Urbanowicz, Salem Police Department; Cherry Goodman, senior deputy coroner, Orange County Coroner's Office; Richard Rodriguez, supervising deputy, Orange County Coroner's Office; Dr. Judy Suchey, California State Univeristy–Fullerton; Bill Hurd, editor of the *Claremore* (Oklahoma) *Daily Progress;* Anna Christensen, Orange County Archives; Dave Frasier, reference librarian at Indiana University; Carol Carbee, Claremont (New Hampshire) School Administrative Unit 6; Barbara Wright, Essex Agricultural and Technical Institute, Hawthorne,

Massachusetts; Jack Smith, *L.A. Times;* Donna Bendix, Skil Corporation; Rob Veneski, *Fresno* (California) *Bee;* Bradley Kuhlman of *The Jerry Springer Show;* Colonel Jim Ammerman; Jim Frey; Bill Nash; Thad Stefan; Valerie Reynolds; Rolf Larsen; Bill Welsh; Arthur Barton; Joe Jasgur; Bob Marshall; Willard Hanzlik; Carol Tibaldi; Vincent Carter; Sue Peterson; Mary Rabkin; Milo Speriglio; Tina Milburne; Lawrence Hemeon; Will Fowler; Mike Rothmiller; Anthony Summers; Velma Jackson; Louis Thiebert; Shirley Hyatt; Carl Conrad; Edwin Hall; Mary Shinnerer; Professor Harry Francisco; Dean and Carley Huguenin; Laurie Jacobson; Marrianne Wells; Betty Plunkett; Nathan Cohen, Irene Hoffland; Caroline Nay; and various reference librarians in Los Angeles, Orange, and San Diego counties.

To all of these, and to those who asked for anonymity to spare themselves embarrassment or further pain, my heartfelt thanks. For those who stand by the opinion that a dead man's memory should be inviolate, regardless of his crimes against humanity, a quick reminder that the human herd cannot afford to nurture lethal parasites. Selective silence is the breeding ground of evil, degradation, and despair.

In Beth Short's case, the silence has been drawn out long enough.

Michael Newton

Introduction

AS I STOOD BESIDE MY MOTHER'S COFFIN IN SALEM, MASSA-chusetts, in July 1989, I studied her lovely features. She was seventy-five when she died, and when I saw her last, the previous Christmas, she was so ill that I knew she would not live much longer. Though I had already started remembering that my father had molested me, I could not tell my mother. She had slipped even further behind the veil of denial that protected her. I had described her once as "fey," and years later read the old definition of that word: "fated to die, dying, appearing to be under a spell."

The cosmetic magic of the funeral home had transformed my mother into a woman much younger than her years. She looked as young as I'd remembered her in 1947, when I was ten. My niece, Elizabeth, stood next to me, sobbing and trying to summon the courage to kiss her grandmother good-bye.

To help Elizabeth, I forced myself to lean forward and press my lips against my mother's cold forehead. Unconsciously I was repeating a kiss I'd placed on the brow of a dead woman named Elizabeth when I was ten.

Then I placed next to my mother in her coffin a silver dollar my father had given me when I was twenty-two.

Though I did not know it then, my mother's death would free me to live. Not just to exist but to remember and come fully alive. It was a devastating process, yet my therapist, Jim Frey, assured me that I would recover. I clung to that hope, expressing it in a poem, "You'll Return":

> Hidden wounds, like hidden shrapnel,
> scrape against my soul,
> fraying, splaying, tearing
> till they leave a gaping hole.
>
> Through that hole I journey,
> first downward into hell,
> barely hearing someone whisper,
>   "You'll return. All will be well."

In November 1989 I moved into a small apartment with an enclosed garage. For some reason, I dubbed it Reality Cottage. Like the hundreds of other items, people, and places I'd collected unconsciously, Reality Cottage, the garage, and the neighborhood were memory aids. But I would not know that until I remembered that they represented, for me, a similar neighborhood in nearby Westminster, where I saw my father murder Elizabeth Short in the enclosed garage next to our cottage.

The visual memories that came to me beginning in 1988 explained, and eventually dissolved, the disembodied terror that had nearly destroyed me in 1986. Back then I was bedridden with the physical and psychological symptoms of complex post-traumatic stress syndrome.

Mercifully, there were times when I could move about, and it was during those recesses that I investigated to corroborate my once-repressed memories. A survivor friend, Marrianne Wells, whom I'd met in a support group, often accompanied me as I searched for the places I'd been taken to as a child. When the shock of finding the site of some horrible childhood torture reduced me to a shaking, shivering, disoriented child, Marrianne would take over, driving me home. These spontaneous regressions were embarrassing, and I wanted to hide forever in my apartment. But I hadn't named it Reality Cottage for nothing.

Old friends, new friends, even strangers, helped me as I did my detective work. And once a week I kept my appointment with Jim Frey, who gave me the strength to go on. Some call Jim's kind of support "re-parenting," and I suppose that word fits. I do know that my trust in him enabled my inner child selves to come forward and tell their secrets.

I had Jim, and I met with a couple of support groups weekly, but I needed more help as the avalanche of memories was unleashed. That aid came in the form of an old friend, Lloyd Battista, who gave me the telephone number for his beeper. He probably anticipated an occasional emergency call, but Lloyd became my night-and-day life support. He pulled off of freeways and rushed to pay phones to call me back. He left meetings—meetings that were critical to earning his own living as an actor and writer— and entered my nightmare world as I sobbed descriptions of my personal holocaust into his ear.

I don't know how he endured it, emotionally or financially. I do know Lloyd's steadfast loyalty helped me bear the hell of remembering. Secrets must be told or they remain secrets. It's written that "to every thing there is a season . . . a time to keep silence and a time to speak." Amnesia—silence—was once my only defense. Now I was in another season. I had to speak or die. And I needed to be heard.

Eventually I had gathered sufficient documentation to realize that certain law enforcement officials must have known that my father murdered Elizabeth Short, and yet he had been allowed to go free, to continue raping and murdering, for another fifteen years. That cover-up continues to this day.

To the pain of learning that I had been subjected, even in my infancy, to my father's molestation and beatings was added the pain of learning that certain law enforcement

3

officials had also betrayed me, my battered mother, and my abused siblings.

There were times when I wanted to die, but I couldn't destroy the new life within me. During therapy in 1986, a counselor recorded that I had told her I felt like a ten-year-old just waking up and that I didn't want that child any more than my parents had.

Now I welcomed her and she inspired me to go on. So did the stories told by other survivors of child abuse—and of the Holocaust.

When Michael Newton expressed interest in writing this book, he too became part of my healing process. Because memory is stored and debriefed by association, I recalled more details as I shared my story with Mike. His patience, kindness, and objectivity helped me walk through another year of hell.

Gradually, as I felt and safely expressed all the emotions connected to the traumas—terror, rage, grief—my senses came alive as well. Colors became more vivid. Especially green and fuchsia. Friends found it amusing that I would point out bright flowers blossoming in quite average gardens. I'd stop in my tracks and study erupting buds on the branches of the peach tree outside my apartment. Automobiles of the 1930s and 1940s suddenly appeared on the streets, though my friends told me they'd never disappeared.

To protect me from life-threatening shock, my mind had shut off certain sights, sounds, even scents, that might have caused me to recall the trauma.

Eventually I opened the curtains and let light into Reality Cottage, risking what I called "beauty shock." I'm still uncomfortable with red roses, for reasons explained in the book. But a white rosebush now grows in my patio garden, and I anticipate and love each new bloom.

By the time this book is published, I'll be fifty-eight years old. Because of the horrors—in particular, the murders—I witnessed as a child, I split off from myself at various stages of development, in a defense mechanism called dissociation. Author Susan Griffin describes this phenomenon clearly: "When there is death, time seems to stop, as if perhaps, in stopping, the dead could be called back into life, or events could be erased before sinking irrevocably into knowledge."

Though I tried, I never could call my father's victims back to life. With this book I bless them and let them go.

And, in my late fifties, I embrace and integrate my inner child, attempting to describe that process in my poem, "Together":

> The sun's rays warm my old skin
> just as they warm the young.
> The sunset thrills these old senses,
> an old song newly sung.
>
> The child in me, who always hid,
> walks forward in my being,
> and the older I politely retires
> to let her do the seeing.
>
> Together we live in the same body,
> together we share this space,
> considerate, kind, tolerant,
>   looking out of the very same face.

> Janice Gail Knowlton, Anaheim, California

1

Thirty-ninth and
Norton

*Most parents don't worry about a daughter until she
fails to show up for breakfast. Then it is too late.*

—Frank McKinney Hubbard

WEDNESDAY, JANUARY 15, 1947, WAS A GRAY DAY IN LOS
Angeles. After four weeks of southern California winter the
wind that ruffled tall grass on the vacant lots of Norton
Avenue was cool enough to nip at unprotected ears and
ankles. A drab sky hid the sun and threatened rain.

That very sky, in fact, had been a topic of debate
throughout Los Angeles in recent weeks. The city's modern
freeway system was still on the drawing board, a futuristic
dream as yet unrealized, but many residents were already
concerned about airborne pollution, that foul blend of
vehicle exhaust and factory waste that some local wag had
christened "smog." The *L.A. Times* was interested enough
to give the problem front-page coverage for three days
running, self-styled experts offering pronouncements on the
causes and potential solution to dirty air.

This morning, though, it simply looked like rain, and even
that would be unlikely if the wind kept up. By noon, with
any luck, the clouds might break and give Los Angeles a

glimpse of sun. If it was warm enough, and if one was unemployed or cutting class, a quick run to the nearest beach would be in order. That was one great thing about Los Angeles: no matter where you lived, the ocean wasn't far away.

Proximity was one thing; opportunity was something else. There would be no trip to the beach for Betty Bersinger that Wednesday, not with housework and an active three-year-old to occupy her time. Sometimes she thought her husband, John, was lucky, going off to work each morning with a nice hot breakfast underneath his belt. He paid the bills, of course, but it was Betty who maintained their smallish home on Norton, in the 3700 block just north of Coliseum. It was Betty who kept young Anne out of mischief all day long.

Or tried to, anyway.

At twenty-five, Betty Bersinger had the same aspirations, concerns, and complaints as most other white middle-class housewives in postwar Los Angeles. She was luckier than some: her husband's income was high enough to put them in a house instead of a cramped apartment. Little Anne, thank heavens, was a healthy, happy child, but anything could happen to a three-year-old. Childhood vaccinations for measles and crippling poliomyelitis were still years in the future, and there was also crime to think about. You only had to read the papers—tennis star Bill Tilden facing nine months on the road gang for molesting one of his young students—and it made you wonder what L.A. was coming to.

Still, Leimert Park was relatively safe, all things considered. Nothing frightening had ever happened there, and Betty had no reason to believe it ever would.

Today she was concerned with shoes—specifically a pair of Anne's that needed to be repaired. Near ten o'clock, she and Anne set off walking south on Norton, headed for a shop where Betty knew she could get the work done at a decent price. Anne walked beside her mother as they were crossing Coliseum, watching out for traffic, but the next block south on Norton Avenue was typically deserted. The construction boom had failed to reach this stretch of vacant lots where neighbors dumped their trash and where overheated teenage lovers parked by night. Amid the uncut grass and weeds, a passing glance could pick out broken bottles, rusted cans, and cardboard cartons melting from exposure to the elements.

Anne skipped ahead, enjoying the adventure of their outing. She was several yards in front of Betty when she stopped and pointed to an object lying in the weeds, close by the sidewalk.

"Mommy, lookit!"

Betty thought it was a broken mannequin at first. A closer look proved otherwise, and she could feel her breakfast coming back up in a sour rush of bile. She swallowed hard to keep it down and grabbed her daughter's hand, putting Anne in motion with a sharp tug, fairly dragging her along.

She had to find a telephone—but first, she had to think.

As Betty Bersinger was racing home, Bill Nash set off from Grayburn Avenue, two blocks away, to take his four-door Plymouth ragtop on a shake-down cruise. A thirty-eight-year-old captain with the Los Angeles Fire Department, Nash had changed the Plymouth's sparkplugs that morning, with marginal help from neighbor Roy Preston, and a leisurely run through Leimert Park would see the job done. Ten minutes, give or take, and he would have the whole day to relax.

With Preston riding shotgun, Nash drove south on Grayburn to Thirty-ninth Street, turning right, to the west, then right again and rolling north on Norton. The last leg of his short trip home. Across the street, beyond the west-side curb, Nash thought he saw a statue lying in the weeds.

A *statue?*

"What the hell . . . ?"

Nash parked the Plymouth and got out. Preston fell into

step beside him as he crossed the street. Up close they saw that the "statue" was a woman's body, stone-cold dead . . . and worse.

She had been cut in half.

The first thing that impressed Nash, after that, was the enormous smile that seemed to stretch across the woman's face.

The second was a clump of grass protruding from the lips of her vagina, like a bookmark.

"Jesus Christ."

Roy Preston's face had lost its color; he could barely catch his breath. Nash helped him to the car and set a new speed record for the drive back home to Grayburn, where he phoned in news of his discovery to the police.

Outside, he found Roy Preston slumped against the Plymouth, looking old and gray. "I'm going back," Nash said. "You wanna come?"

No answer from his neighbor. Preston had his hands full, throwing up his breakfast onto Nash's lawn.

An operator at the Los Angeles Police Department's University Division took the first call at 10:35 A.M. A woman's voice, all trembling apprehension, told the operator of "a drunk man lying in the weeds" on Norton Avenue, between Thirty-ninth and Coliseum. Betty Bersinger made no mention of a homicide as she attempted to divorce herself and her family from any further contact with the pallid object lying in the field. She rattled off her home telephone number on request, then caught herself and cradled the receiver before the operator could ask her name.

A drunk passed out on Norton Avenue was no emergency, but crime was slow that Wednesday morning in the University Division. Patrolmen W. E. Fitzgerald and F. S. Perkins were dispatched to the scene. They cruised along the block in their radio car until they spotted one bare foot protruding from the grass.

Above the foot, a naked calf.

Above the calf, a snow-white thigh.

Above the thigh . . .

Two-way radios were relatively new in L.A. squad cars, having made their debut farther east. The system made for swift responses from the field in an emergency, but there were also drawbacks. Anyone who bought a simple monitor could eavesdrop on police calls and even beat detectives to a crime scene. Reporters for the daily papers were among the first to learn the trick.

James Richardson, city editor of the *Los Angeles Examiner,* was busy at his desk when he received police reporter Bill Zelinsky's call about the discovery of a murder victim on Norton Avenue. Determined to scoop the *Times,* Richardson dispatched every news hawk and photographer available to blanket the scene.

Sid Hughes was the first to call Richardson back. "It's a pip," he declared.

The naked woman had been laid out on her back, arms raised above her head, legs splayed, as if the body had been posed deliberately to shock. She might have been attractive once, but it was difficult to tell, the pale face slashed and battered out of shape. Both breasts were marked by knife wounds, and a deep slash ran between the victim's navel and her pubic thatch. Between the severed torso and its lower half, a foot or so removed, grass sprouted up like a surrealistic cummerbund.

It was clearly too much for a pair of patrolmen to handle, and a desperate call went back to LAPD Homicide. Captain Jack Donahoe, in charge of the unit, reached out for his two best detectives to nail down the scene and decide what remained to be done.

Detective Harry Hansen—with twenty-one years on the job and eleven in homicide—had already seen one corpse that morning, an elderly man dead of natural causes in a rooming house at Sixth and Rampart, four miles due northwest of Thirty-ninth and Norton as the vulture flies. Hansen and his partner, Finis Brown, were questioning the landlord, waiting for the coroner to put in an appearance, when Donahoe reached them by telephone with news of the grim discovery on Norton Avenue. "It sounds bad," he warned them.

Bad, and then some.

Hansen and Brown were on the scene by 11:05 A.M. It only took a glance at the discarded corpse to tell them this was something special, and they called for backup: lab men, extra suits and uniforms, photographers, an ambulance— the works. Patrolmen blocked the street off to civilian gawkers, but the press was out in force, collecting quotes and photographs. Most of the photos were unprintable, the statements from detectives and technicians rife with speculative nonsense, but the newsies didn't care. They had a three-ring circus on their hands, and they were veterans at milking tragedy for all that it was worth.

It was a brisk five-minute walk from Grayburn back to Thirty-ninth and Norton, but police and sundry rubber- neckers were on hand before Bill Nash arrived. He moved around the fringes of the growing crowd, approached one of the uniforms to tell his story, and was hustled back across the street.

So be it.

Walking home, Bill Nash reflected that the cops would be in touch when they were ready. Meanwhile he had work to do.

He had to hose the vomit off his lawn.

A haze of confusion settled on the case from the begin- ning, with the first report from Betty Bersinger that brought patrolmen searching for a "drunk man in the weeds." Once L.A. newsmen got involved, mistakes and fabrications multiplied and were immortalized in print. By Wednesday afternoon, Los Angelenos "knew" the victim found at Thirty-ninth and Norton was a teenager, perhaps as young as fifteen years of age; one of her breasts had been cut off and several teeth knocked out; she had been dead from eight to fourteen hours by the time her body was discovered; and she had been tortured fiendishly for two or three days prior to death, the greater part of that while she was dangling upside down.

One minor problem: none of it was true.

Detectives at the scene must take their share of blame for the distortions that have passed into history as fact. Lieutenant Paul Freestone moved in to take charge of the scene after Hansen and Brown called for help. He was trailed by a small army of investigators, none of them bashful when it came to granting interviews. Depending on the local paper of your choice, the "principal investigators" on the case were variously named as Brown and Hansen, Jack McReadie, Marty Wynn, and L. M. Baughn. Ray Pinker, chief of LAPD's crime lab, was on hand to sift the evidence, with police science technician Lee Jones at his elbow. Overall, some 250 detectives and patrolmen fanned out from the vacant lot, accosting passersby and ringing door-bells in search of useful information.

Back at the crime scene, police were meeting their first dead end in the case Lieutenant Freestone called "the most brutal example of a sex crime I have ever seen." For starters, they were looking at a dump site, not a murder scene. The small amount of blood in evidence—described in some reports as "one small drop"—would clearly not accommodate the theory of a woman bludgeoned, slashed, and cut in half where she was found. There *was* enough blood to reveal a partial footprint, almost certainly the killer's, but police could never quite decide if they were looking at a heel or a toe, a man's shoe or a woman's. Skid marks in the gutter indicated that a southbound car had stopped abruptly near the site, but attempts to trace the make of tire led nowhere. Finally, Lee Jones reported finding several "hairs" or "bristles" on the victim's body. He gave conflicting statements to the press, suggesting they were from a scrub brush used to wash the corpse or possibly loose fibers from the floor mat of a car.

One thing investigators could agree on was the killer's skill at carving meat. Bisection of the corpse had been "a clean job," they declared, "with the killer probably using a sharp butcher knife and possibly a small saw." Ten days later, a police psychologist—acting on false information that none of the victim's internal organs were damaged—told the *Daily News* that "only a nurse, a medical student, or a doctor" could have performed such "precise" and "meticulous" surgery.

Of such unfounded off-the-cuff remarks are legends born. In fact, as we shall see, the truth was bad enough.

Establishing the young Jane Doe's identity was job one with investigators assigned to the case. They struck out at Missing Persons, where the closest match—Diana Heaney, missing from her Lynwood home since mid-October 1946—was squelched by Chief Paul Kerr of the Lynwood police. Another hopeful lead that Wednesday morning was a paper-wrapped bundle of clothing and trinkets found by Alvin McCloskey near his used-car lot on West Adams Boulevard. Inside the bundle, homicide detectives found a woman's dress and underwear, a scarf, a pair of alligator shoes, a hairbrush, toiletries, and a musical powder box that played "Comin' through the Rye" when its lid was raised. Before the day was out, a laundry mark inside the dress led officers to Cora Bryant, alive and well on East Forty-sixth Street, where the package had been stolen from her car.

Strike two.

Interrogation of neighborhood witnesses was another washout. The nearest house on Norton Avenue stood a hundred yards from the crime scene, and residents had grown accustomed to watching strangers dump their trash on vacant lots in the 3900 block. One neighbor recalled seeing a Ford sedan parked near the site around 6:30 A.M., but several pedestrians had passed the spot two hours later without noticing a corpse. Could it be that the killer was bold enough to make his drop in broad daylight?

One of Freestone's uniforms eventually got around to Grayburn Avenue and roused Bill Nash. When Nash recounted his discovery of the body, the patrolman looked surprised. He made a note and told Nash that detectives would be calling back.

The rest is silence. Forty-five years later Nash had given up on waiting for their call.

Grasping at straws, perhaps attempting to relieve anxiety among their home-grown readers, L.A. journalists began at once to speculate that Jane Doe was a foreigner, possibly a war bride recently abandoned in Los Angeles. A spokesman for the coroner's office described her as "a peasant type with heavy thighs." Homicide detectives suggested that her "extremely bad teeth" were the mark of an alien, "a condition typical of young Australian or British women." If any war brides took offense or felt an urge to let the coppers check their pearly whites, no record of the challenge has survived.

With nothing else to go on, Captain Donahoe announced that LAPD would be checking the alibis of all known sex offenders in the city. Detectives would be poring through the files of Dr. Paul DeRiver, a police psychiatrist who had examined every head case jailed by L.A.'s finest in the past ten years. It was a dirty, time-consuming job, but someone had to do it, in the hope of stumbling onto a psychopath whose rage at women had surpassed the detonation point.

Jane Doe's fingerprints were taken at the county morgue, but once again detectives drew a blank. Their victim had not been arrested in Los Angeles, but there were other sources for a fingerprint I.D. The Federal Bureau of Investigation, for example, boasted of its vast print collection, 104 million subjects in all, neatly filed and cross-referenced in Washington, D.C.

Ray Pinker's team needed the help. They rolled a second set of prints and sent it off by airmail to the FBI in Washington, with a request to speed up the matching process as much as possible.

It would be helpful, the police and journalists agreed, to have a photo of the victim they could publish, show around the neighborhood, in restaurants and beauty shops, hotels, saloons. Unfortunately, all of the crime scene photographs displayed a battered, mutilated death mask that was unsuitable for publication and useless as a tool for tracking down Jane Doe's identity. That afternoon an artist on the staff of the *Examiner,* one Howard Burke, prepared a likeness of the victim as he thought she might have looked, without the gashes and contusions. Burke came fairly close, but his efforts turned out to be a waste of time.

On Wednesday night a pair of homicide detectives stopped by the *Examiner* office to pick up a copy of Burke's sketch. Assistant managing editor Warden Woolard drew them into a conversation about the set of fingerprints they had dispatched to Washington, pointing out that severe midwestern storms had grounded most flights to the Atlantic seaboard. Days might be lost, unless . . .

All generosity—and with one eye on a scoop—Woolard offered the use of his paper's Soundphoto equipment, permitting detectives to wire a set of Jane Doe's fingerprints from L.A. to Washington. Granted, the FBI's fingerprint bureau was closed for the night, but Woolard was not above pulling some strings. A telephone call to Ray Richards, head of the Washington bureau for all the Hearst papers, routed FBI technicians from their beds and had them standing by when the prints were transmitted—the first time prints had ever been transmitted in a manner that is now routine.

Even at that, the first attempt went nowhere. Jane Doe's prints arrived in Washington too blurred for any accurate comparison with Bureau files. Photographer Russ Lapp was summoned to provide enlargements of the fingerprints, and this time they were readable.

The FBI is justly proud of its success at matching fingerprints in record time, and this was no exception. Suddenly the severed corpse from Thirty-ninth and Norton had a name and personal history. She was Elizabeth Ann Short, age twenty-two, born in Hyde Park, Massachusetts, on July 29, 1924. The FBI had filed a copy of her fingerprints when she was hired as a civilian clerk in the post exchange at Camp Cooke, near Lompoc, California, in the midst of World War II.

Jane Doe had been transformed into a young, attractive woman with a life, a family. Presumably there had been friends; police would take for granted the existence of at least one enemy.

Having identified their victim, the detectives' next task was to find out who had murdered her. And, almost as an afterthought, they might discover why.

Short of a surprise eyewitness or a confession from the slayer, Dr. Frederick Newbarr was the Homicide Division's next best hope of finding out exactly what Beth Short had suffered in her final hours. With any luck, the killer might have left some traces of himself behind—a bit of skin beneath a fingernail, a smear of semen that would yield his blood type.

Something.

Dr. Newbarr was the chief autopsy surgeon for the county of Los Angeles, a post that today would carry the title of chief medical examiner. Selected to assist him on the short postmortem was Dr. Victor Cefalu, Newbarr's "number two" around the county morgue.

By January 16, 1947, so many stories had taken root around Beth Short—many of them wholly false but clinging stubbornly to life for decades, magnified and mangled in translation—that the stark, official language of the autopsy report should finally bear witness to the truth:

Office of the County Coroner

I performed an autopsy on Elizabeth Short on January 16, 1947, at the Los Angeles County Coroner's mortuary and found the immediate cause of death: hemorrhage and shock due to concussion of the brain and lacerations of the face.

Examination:

The body is that of a female about 15 to 20 years of age, measuring 5′5″ in height and weighing 115 lbs.

There are multiple lacerations to the midforehead, in the right forehead, and at the top of the head in the midline. There are multiple tiny abrasions, linear in shape, on the right face and forehead. There are two small lacerations, ¼″ each in length, on each side of the nose near the bridge. There is a deep laceration on the face 3″ long which extends laterally from the right corner of the mouth. The surrounding tissues are ecchymotic and bluish purple in color. There is a deep laceration 2½″ long extending laterally from the left corner of the mouth. The surrounding tissues are bluish purple in color. There are five linear lacerations in the right upper lip which extend into the soft tissues for a distance of ⅛″. The teeth are in a state of advanced decay. The two upper central incisors are loose, and one lower incisor is loose. The rest of the teeth show cavities.

Upon reflecting the scalp there is ecchymosis in the right and upper frontal area. There are localized areas of subarachnoid hemorrhage on the right side and small hemorrhagic areas in the corpus callosum. No fracture of the skull is visible.

There is a depressed ridge on both sides and in the anterior portion of the neck, which is light brown in color. There is an abrasion, irregular in outline, in the skin of the neck in the anterior midline. There are two linear abrasions in the left anterior neck. There are two depressed ridges in the posterior neck, pale brown in color. The lower ridge has an abrasion in the skin at each extremity.

The pharynx and larynx are intact. There is no evidence of trauma to the hyoid bone, thyroid or cricoid cartilages, or tracheal rings. There is a small area of ecchymosis in the soft tissues of the right neck at the level of the upper tracheal rings. There is no obstruction in the laryngotracheal passage.

There is an irregular laceration with superficial tissue loss in the skin of the right breast. The tissue loss is

18

more or less square in outline and measures 3¼″ transversely and 2½″ longitudinally; extending toward the midline from this irregular laceration are several superficial lacerations in the skin. There is an elliptical opening in the skin located ¾″ to the left of the left nipple. The opening measures 2¾″ in a transverse direction and 1¼″ in a longitudinal direction in its midportion. The margins of these wounds show no appreciable discoloration. There are multiple superficial scratches in the skin of the left chest on the anterior wall. There is a healed scar in the skin of the right lower posterior chest at the level of the ninth rib which measures 3¼″ in length and its direction is diagonally to the right. Crossing this scar are three scars which appear to be healed suture scars. There are four small superficial lacerations in the skin of the lower chest on the left side close to the midline. There is no discoloration at the margins. There are superficial linear lacerations in the skin of the left upper arm on its external aspect. There is a double ridge around the left wrist close to the hand. The fingernails are very short, the thumbnail measuring ⁵⁄₁₆″ in length and the fingernails measuring ³⁄₁₆″ in length. There are superficial lacerations and scratches in the skin of the external surface of the right forearm. There is a double ridge depressed around the right wrist. The fingernails are very short, the thumbnail measuring ³⁄₁₆″ in length and the others ⅛″ in length. The palmar surfaces of both hands are somewhat roughened but no firm calluses are seen.

The organs of the chest are in normal position. The left lung is pink in color and well aerated. The right lung is somewhat adherent due to fairly firm pleural adhesions. The lung is pink in color and well aerated. There is a calcified thickening of the ninth rib on the right side in the midscapular line. The heart shows no gross pathology.

The trunk is completely severed by an incision which is almost straight through the abdomen severing the intestine at the duodenum and through the soft tissue of the abdomen, passing through the intervertebral disk between the second and third lumbar vertebrae. There is very little ecchymosis along the tract of the incision. There is a gaping laceration 4¼" long which extends longitudinally from the umbilicus to the suprapubic region. On both sides of this laceration there are multiple superficial lacerations. There are multiple crisscross lacerations in the suprapubic area which extend through the skin and soft tissues. No ecchymosis is seen.

There is a square pattern of superficial lacerations in the skin of the right hip. The organs of the abdomen are entirely exposed. There are lacerations of the intestine and both kidneys. The uterus is small, and no pregnancy is apparent. The tubes, ovaries, and cul-de-sac are intact. The labia majora are intact. There is an abrasion which extends through the lower half of the labia minora and the margin shows some bluish discoloration. Within the vagina and higher up there is lying loose a piece of skin with fat and subcutaneous tissue attached. On this piece of loose skin there are several crisscrossing lacerations. Smears for spermatozoa have been taken.

The anal opening is markedly dilated and the opening measures 1¼" in diameter. The mucous membrane is brown throughout the circumference of the opening. There are multiple abrasions, and a small amount of ecchymosis is seen at the margin. The laceration of the mucous membrane extends upward for a distance of ½". At a point about 1" up from the anal opening there is a tuft of brown curly hair lying loose in the anal canal. The hair corresponds in appearance to the pubic hair. Smear for spermatozoa has been taken.

There is an irregular opening in the skin on the anterior surface of the left thigh with tissue loss. The opening measures 3½" transversely at the base and 4" from the base longitudinally to the upper back. The laceration extends into the subcutaneous soft tissue and muscle. No ecchymosis is seen. There is a ridge in the skin of the lower right thigh, anterior surface, located 5″ above the knee. There is a diagonal ridge in the skin of the upper third of the right leg which is light brown in color; extending down from this point there are three light brown depressed ridges. There is a circular ridge around the left lower leg and also a diagonal depression ridge just below this area. The skin of the plantar surface of the feet is stained brown.

The stomach is filled with greenish brown granular matter, mostly feces and other particles which could not be identified. All smears for spermatozoa were negative.

/s/ Frederick D. Newbarr, M.D.
Chief autopsy surgeon,
in association with Victor Cefalu, M.D.
Asst. Chief autopsy surgeon

The several references to the absence of ecchymosis—that is, bruising due to seeping blood in wounded tissue—are especially significant. Such bruises form only when living tissue is assaulted. Simply put: the dead don't bruise or bleed to any great degree. If Dr. Newbarr's findings are correct, only Beth Short's head and facial wounds were suffered while she lived, and these are listed as the cause of death. What followed afterward, as grisly as it was, can hardly be described as torture, since the victim was, in fact, already dead. Extreme dilation of the anal passage likewise indicates postmortem sodomy or penetration by a foreign object, when the lifeless sphincter muscle was beyond contracting to its normal size.

The Newbarr autopsy effectively debunks a host of "facts" about Short's death that have become enshrined in newsprint through the years. Her teeth, while loose, were not punched out or broken off. Her skin displayed no burns from cigarettes or any other source. Her breasts were not sliced off, nor did the killer clip one earlobe as a grisly souvenir. No words or cryptic letters had been carved into her flesh. Her genitals were not deformed or "infantile," and so would not explain a would-be lover's sudden homicidal rage.

For all his meticulous notes, however, Dr. Newbarr was not above holding an ace up his sleeve. He made no mention of the grass removed from Beth's vagina. Furthermore, the piece of fatty skin recovered from the same location matched the gouge mark on her thigh, and it spoke of a great deal more than "several crisscross lacerations."

That flap of skin was decorated with a stylish rose tattoo.

The grass, the tattooed skin, its final resting place, and the peculiar tuft of pubic hair removed from Beth Short's violated rectum would be held back from the press, a means of weeding out the cranks who fed on headline cases, offering advice, a morsel of explosive "evidence," perhaps a false confession—anything to grab the spotlight for a moment and relieve the quiet desperation of their lives.

A case like Beth Short's always draws a few nuts out of the woodwork.

This time, though, the usual parade of crazies would become a stampede.

The young and once-attractive woman who could generate such passion from her killer and from a host of total strangers would, in different circumstances, have enjoyed the show. From adolescence, she was drawn to Hollywood as to a magnet, convinced that she could replicate the small-town-girl-makes-good cliché. In fact, she never cracked the big time, never even scratched the surface in a town whose heart is brass, not gold. It took an ugly twist of fate to make Beth Short a household name. Instead of posing on a stool at Schwab's, she was discovered in a vacant lot at Thirty-ninth and Norton, all used up and thrown away.

The middle child of five, all girls, Beth Short had seen her parents separate when she was six years old. Her father, Cleo, put a continent between himself and his family, trusting distance to absolve him of responsibility. Beth's mother, Phoebe, did her best to keep the family together, but the Great Depression came along in 1929 and times were hard. In those days, little boys looked up to bandits waging hit-and-run guerrilla war against the banks and railroads. Little girls were more inclined to wish upon the stars that shone from Tinsel Town.

It took Pearl Harbor to reverse the nation's economic slump. By that time, Beth had seen enough of Medford, Massachusetts, and environs. After dropping out of school in 1942, she drifted to Miami where she waited on tables and cultivated an attraction to the men in uniform who thronged a nearby army air force base. In time, her father grudgingly supplied the money for a one-way ticket to Vallejo, California, but their father-daughter reunion was a grim mistake. Beth failed to make the cut as her father Cleo's live-in cook and maid, and their final parting was marked by bitter words that neither would recant.

The war was going strong by now, and Beth was as drawn to servicemen as she was to fame and fortune in the movies. For a time, she settled near Camp Cooke and worked as a civilian clerk in the PX. G.I. admirers voted Beth their "Cutie of the Week," but flirting with the soldiers also had its downside. One of Beth's dates belted her around. Some said he threatened murder in an effort to restrain her roving eye. A flying squad of Santa Barbara cops arrested Beth in late September 1943 while she was killing time in a café with two young soldiers and a girlfriend. There was liquor on the table and she was underage for drinking, but a lenient judge in juvey court released her on condition that she leave the state.

Back home in Massachusetts, things were much the same. Beth waited on tables at a small café in Cambridge near the Harvard campus, but the young men of the Ivy League did not compare, in her eyes, to the pilots, sailors, and marines who had enlisted to defend the nation with their lives. In time she started drifting west again, making a pit stop in Chicago, then homing irresistibly on southern California.

Moving toward her death.

Once homicide detectives had a name to work with, they were able to chart Beth's movements during the last months of her life. Cleo Short had moved south from Vallejo to Los Angeles, but her father was useless to investigators. Beth, as he recalled, "spent all her time running around when she was supposed to be keeping house for me. I made her leave." Four years without a word until his daughter turned up dead, and he was satisfied to let it go at that.

Between mid-July and early August 1946, detectives learned that Beth had lived in Long Beach. She moved from there to a hotel on North Orange Drive in Hollywood. Two roommates split the rent with her, but it was still a trifle high, and Beth was gone by late October. Mid-November found her still in Hollywood, sharing an apartment on North Cherokee with seven other girls at a dollar a night, but even that rent seemed exorbitant, and Beth slipped out the back door on December 5, one step ahead of manager Juanita Ringo's flat demand for cash. Three days later, in the San Diego suburb of Pacific Beach, she moved in with Elvera French and occupied French's guest room until January 8, the day a young man known as Red came by to pick her up. Their destination was Los Angeles. Beth's time was running out.

It was in Long Beach that she earned the epithet which, ironically, deprived Beth of her final claim to fame. Two reporters, Jack Smith of the *Daily News* and Bevo Means of the *Herald-Express,* would quarrel about who got there first, but it makes no real difference in the scheme of things. A Long Beach druggist, mobbed by newsmen, reminisced about Beth's stunning looks, the way she styled her jet-black hair, the all-black outfits she adopted as a trademark. One of her admirers tagged her "the Black Dahlia," and it stuck.

The label was a godsend to the tabloid headline writers in a case that cried out for glamour to accentuate the gore.

Police were interested in Red, the last man known to have seen Beth Short alive. Elvera French recalled a telegram that had come for Beth on January 7, and reporters tracked a copy down. It read: "Be there tomorrow afternoon late. Would like to see you. Red." Investigators found a motel in Pacific Beach where Beth and her companion had spent the night of January 8. The motel registration card gave up a license plate number that led to Robert Manley, age twenty-five, residing in the L.A. suburb of Huntington Park. Red wasn't home on Saturday. His job as salesman for a pipe-clamp company had taken him to San Francisco with a partner, Harry Palmer, but his wife expected Manley home on Sunday night.

Jack Donahoe decided he could wait.

Meanwhile, a friend recalled that Beth had stored a trunk at L.A.'s Union Station. When she failed to make her storage payments, someone had packed the trunk off to a local warehouse, and detectives found it there. Inside were clothes, a stack of photographs of Beth with boyfriends in and out of uniform, and several dozen letters penned by young men she had dated through the years. Their tone, coupled with interviews of friends around the country, painted Beth as a romantic who exaggerated—even fabricated—her relationships with men and who sometimes surprised brief acquaintances by talking about love and matrimony. She was frequently rejected, but she saved the letters anyway, like milestones on her search for Mr. Right.

Police staked out Harry Palmer's home on Mount Royal Drive and pounced on Sunday night when Robert Manley dropped his partner off. After being taken into custody, Manley readily admitted meeting Beth in San Diego on December 15. To him, their short-lived fling had been a test "to see if I was still in love with my wife." Still mulling that one over on the night of January 8, he picked Beth up and drove her to a cheap motel. Along the way she showed him scratches on both arms, inflicted by a jealous boyfriend she described as "an Italian with black hair." That night, at the motel, a take-out dinner turned Beth's stomach, and she spent the night in misery, dividing her time between the bathroom and a chair while Manley slept alone.

On Thursday morning, late, they set off for Los Angeles.

Beth claimed to have a meeting scheduled with a married sister from Berkeley, with whom she hoped to spend some time rent-free. Near one o'clock she dropped some bags off at the Greyhound depot, and Manley drove her from there to the Biltmore Hotel, where she was supposed to meet her sister in the lobby. At 6:30 P.M., tired of waiting, Red bade the Black Dahlia adieu and went home to his wife.

High hopes among the homicide detectives had begun unraveling as Manley told his tale. The salesman's alibi checked out from January 10 through January 15, and Harry Hansen found a doorman at the Biltmore who recalled Beth leaving by herself near ten o'clock on January 9. A polygraph examination finally erased all doubt, and Manley was released on Monday afternoon.

Detectives followed Manley's tip and checked the Greyhound depot, where they came up with two suitcases and a hatbox checked by Beth on January 9. The contents were familiar: clothing, photographs, another stack of letters to and from selected paramours. From Manley and the Biltmore doorman, homicide investigators had a fair description of the outfit Beth had worn the last time she was seen alive: a collarless black suit, a frilly white blouse, black suede shoes, nylon stockings, white gloves, a full-length beige coat, and a large plastic purse with two handles.

All of which was worthless in the absence of a lucky break.

For once, police could not complain about a dearth of witnesses. If anything, they had too many—some of value, others well meaning but hopelessly confused, plus a growing fringe of mental cases, crass attention-seekers, and malignant parasites. Bartenders, cabbies, bus drivers, and waitresses began to surface from L.A. to San Diego, each with sightings of the Dahlia to report. Some of them claimed to have seen Beth, even spoken to her, in the late-night hours of Tuesday, when detectives knew she was already dead. A comment overhead in passing, scraps of arguments remembered from a tavern or a hotel lobby, took on new significance for those who spilled the story out. It seemed important, in the climate of the time, to have known Beth Short, to present some evidence of having passed her on the street or glimpsed her on the far side of a crowded room.

The worst of these insistent "witnesses" were those who fastened on the case for covert motives of their own. Around L.A., a rash of landlords pointed fingers at tenants they were anxious to evict. Astrologers worked overtime to glean the killer's name from Beth Short's horoscope. An aging psychic told police the slayer would be caught within a week if Beth was buried with an egg in one hand "like they do in Alabama." A photographer suspected he would find the killer's likeness on Beth's retina, if homicide detectives let him take an eyeball home. Around the city, women telephoned complaints of husbands, boyfriends, and casual pickups brandishing knives, threatening to dish out "the same thing the Black Dahlia got." Some of the offending males were booked on charges of assault, but none was tagged for murder.

And by Friday afternoon, the first of the confessions had begun.

James Richardson knew all about the cranks and crazies. From his city desk at the *Examiner* he had been keeping track of each new lead and each snafu in the investigation. Richardson's reporters had, in fact, been more successful than police in tracking evidence: Beth's luggage, Robert Manley's address, the immortal epithet, interviews with friends and relatives.

But the story was running out of steam.

By Wednesday, January 22, it was obvious to Richardson that there was little more to say about Beth Short. Her life and loves had been subjected to the kind of microscopic scrutiny reserved in modern times for presidential candidates, but none of it had led anywhere. Without dramatic new developments, the case would be another nine-day wonder, banished to the inside pages and forgotten altogether in another week or so.

As if on cue, the switchboard operator passed a call on to Richardson. A man's voice, calm, anonymous: "Is this the city editor?"

"Yes."

"What is your name, please?"

"Richardson."

"Well, Mr. Richardson, I must congratulate you on what the *Examiner* has done in the Black Dahlia case."

Richardson frowned. "Thank you."

"You seem to have run out of material," the caller said.

"That's right."

Soft laughter in the newsman's ear. "Maybe I can be of some assistance."

"We need it," Richardson admitted, trying to suppress a shiver as the mocking chuckle was repeated.

"I'll tell you what I'll do," the caller said. "I'll send you some of the things she had with her when she . . . shall we say . . . disappeared?"

Hands trembling, Richardson scrawled "Trace this call" on a scrap of paper and passed the note to his assistant on the city desk. At once his aide picked up another telephone and started muttering instructions to the switchboard operator.

"What kind of things?" asked Richardson.

"Oh, say, her address book and her birth certificate and a few other things she had in her handbag."

"When will I get them?"

"Oh, within the next day or so. See how far you can get with them. And now I really must say good-bye. You may be trying to trace this call."

"Wait a minute!" Richardson demanded, but a dial tone was now humming in his ear.

Across the desk, his assistant was leaning forward, curious. "What was it, Jim?"

"I think I just talked to the Dahlia's killer," said Richardson.

Two days later he was sure.

On January 24, Beth Short was laid to rest in Oakland's

Mountain View Cemetery, plot 66, grave 913. It was an odd choice for a Massachusetts native murdered in Los Angeles, but she had relatives in Berkeley, just across the bridge, and Phoebe Short was in town to see her daughter off. Beth's father couldn't find the time or energy to travel north. If anybody missed him at the graveside ritual, it didn't show.

On Saturday morning, Los Angeles postal inspectors intercepted a parcel wrapped in plain brown paper, postmarked the previous day and reeking of gasoline. The address, clipped from newspapers and pasted on, read: "Los Angeles *Examiner* and other Los Angeles Newspapers. Here is Dahlia's belongings. Letter to follow."

Opened in the presence of police, the package contained Elizabeth Short's birth certificate from Suffolk County, Massachusetts; her Social Security card; a claim check for the luggage already recovered from the Greyhound depot; a Western Union telegram concerning disposition of her trunk at Union Station; several photographs of pilots; a membership card in the Hollywood Wolves Club; a newspaper wedding announcement for Army Air Force Major Matt Gordon, with the bride's name scratched out; and a diary with "Mark M. Hansen" and "1937" printed in gold leaf on the cover. The diary was chock full of names and telephone numbers, mostly of men, but one page had been ripped out.

LAPD's crime lab verified that Beth's belongings had been washed in gasoline, as if to wipe out any telltale traces of the killer, but the effort was apparently in vain. The local press reported that a dozen or more "exceptionally clear" fingerprints had been lifted from the parcel and its contents. Whose they were remains a mystery; a copy of the prints was sent to Washington, but seven years would pass before they earned another mention, in Hank Sterling's *Ten Perfect Crimes*. By that time the "clear" fingerprints were allegedly smudged and useless, ruined by careless handling at the Los Angeles post office.

Undismayed by one more roadblock, Captain Donahoe remained optimistic. "This is the big push," he announced after a closed-door meeting with his staff. "Our men are fanning out now to bring in the killer."

Their first stop was a Carlos Avenue address, where homicide detectives questioned Mark M. Hansen. The middle-aged theater owner remembered Beth as one of several would-be starlets who had rented rooms from him in recent months. The diary-turned-address-book had been a gift from friends in Europe. Hansen had never gotten around to using it, and he suspected Beth had stolen it before she left his home. There was no evidence connecting Hansen with the murder, and detectives scratched him off their list.

Matt Gordon, whose scratched-up wedding announcement was found among Short's effects, was another dead end. He had been photographed with Beth and had corresponded with her for a time, but there appeared to be more fantasy than fact in her belief they were engaged. If nothing else, his marriage to another woman proved the point, and besides, Gordon had been killed in 1945 while flying with the U.S. Army Air Force from a base in India.

Detectives went on working their way through the list of names and numbers, all without result. They heard more anecdotes about Beth's life in Hollywood—her failed romances, her dreams of stardom, and her apparent promiscuity—but none of it produced a suspect they could charge with any crime. Department spokesmen were reduced to speculating on the killer's mental state, informing newsmen that the package pointed toward "an egomaniac" who "still lurked near the scene of the crime."

On January 26 a woman's purse and black suede shoe were found at a garbage dump in the 1800 block of East Twenty-fifth Street. Robert Manley swore the items were Elizabeth's, and detectives took him at his word, but the information shed no fresh light on the case.

That Sunday night a postcard addressed to the *Examiner* was mailed in downtown Los Angeles. In lieu of cutting and pasting, the nameless correspondent had written in bold block letters, in ink: "Here it is. Turning in Wed., Jan. 29, 10 A.M. Had my fun at the police. Black Dahlia Avenger."

Monday also brought a second note, this one addressed to the district attorney's office. The envelope bore a typewritten address, above which the sender had scrawled the cryptic notation "Sorry, Greenwich Village, not Cotton Club." Inside, another message, its letters clipped from newspapers and magazines, declared "Dahlia killer cracking—wants terms."

It was a hopeful sign, and plainclothes officers staked out the *Examiner* building on Wednesday morning, ready to strike if the suspect put in an appearance. They were wasting their time, and the clock was striking 1:00 P.M. when Donahoe received his last typewritten envelope, another paste-up message tucked inside. "Have changed my mind," the letter read. "You would not give me a square deal. Dahlia killing was justified."

It was the final straw. Ray Pinker's team could find no fingerprints on any of the recent notes, and Captain Donahoe's detectives were forced to content themselves with speculation on the author's "monstrous ego and fiendish sense of drama." Barring an arrest, at least they could insult the man who had made them look like fools.

Beth's killer never turned himself in to police, but others did. By the end of January, confessing to the Dahlia murder had become a cottage industry around Los Angeles, with an occasional contestant weighing in from Texas, New Jersey, and even overseas. At least sixteen confessions had been recorded and discounted by the end of 1947, more than double that within a decade. At last count, more than fifty self-styled "suspects" had come forward with false confessions, but they invariably ran aground on fine points of the mutilations, which had been held in confidence by members of the LAPD Homicide Division. None could place the grass and flap of tattooed skin in Beth's vagina or recall the knot of pubic hair inserted in her rectum.

Still, they tried.

From Utah, one determined entrant in the Dahlia sweep-stakes made the drive to L.A. three times over, sulking when investigators shook their heads and sent him home. A mental case whom detectives called "Confessing Tom" still holds the record—four confessions to the murder without a single hit on any major point of evidence—but he was not the strangest of the lot.

In San Diego, where Short spent the last month of her life, a veteran of the Women's Army Corps said she dismembered Beth for stealing her fiancé; hours later she recanted, swearing that she had "made the whole thing up." Police agreed, but each confession had to be checked out. A lesbian from Oakland put a new spin on the case in 1950, telling the police she went berserk when Beth Short left her for another woman. Less than two weeks later, homicide detectives had their hands full with a new confession from Max Handler, ultimately cleared despite his knowledge of Beth's favorite hangouts and his past employment with a firm whose business card had been found among the Dahlia's effects. In January 1956, Manhattan dishwasher Ralph von Hiltz admitted having cut up Beth's corpse, but told investigators she was murdered by "a friend"; detectives never got their hands on Mr. X, but they were able to discount von Hiltz's confession on the grounds that details of the Dahlia's mutilations did not match his account.

For just a moment, at the end of January 1947, there was hope. On January 31, the *Daily News* reported that investigators expected the case to "break wide open before night-fall." Anonymous "other sources" confided that "a woman was the central figure" in the mystery.

That evening, Norris Stensland, chief of detectives for the Los Angeles County Sheriff's Department, was flanked by reporters as he emerged from a meeting with Jack Donahoe. Asked if a soldier or sailor had murdered Beth Short, he replied: "If you asked me if it was a woman you'd be closer to it."

Captain Donahoe also made a show of confidence. He

told reporters that "Stensland has given us as good a lead as we have had on this case." Detectives from the University Division were "expecting developments within an hour or an hour and a half."

On Saturday, February 1, *Daily News* subscribers read the headline "Dahlia Case Runs into Stone Wall." Captain Donahoe's optimism had evaporated overnight, replaced by vague assertions that his men were looking for a murder site "somewhere outside the city limits of Los Angeles." By February 3, the hot new lead had been dismissed as "flimsy" in the press, its details never aired.

And there, for all intents and purposes, the matter rests. Detectives Brown and Hansen kept on grilling the "suspects" who surfaced through the years, pathetic men and women driven by a craving for publicity, until retirement rolled around and younger men inherited their dusty files. No member of the LAPD team would ever hint—as Scotland Yard has done with Jack the Ripper—that the case was ultimately settled out of court.

But there was never any doubt that someone knew the killer.

Someone *always* knows.

2

Still Small Voice

Children begin by loving their parents. After a time they judge them. Rarely, if ever, do they forgive them.

—Oscar Wilde, *A Woman of No Importance*

IT IS DIFFICULT, PERHAPS IMPOSSIBLE, TO UNDERSTAND THE TER-
ror secondhand. We can describe a mugging or an auto crash
to total strangers and we have a common frame of reference,
even if our words do not convey the full enormity of fear
and pain. We have all seen twisted wreckage on the roadside, all tuned in to the late-night TV news and caught a
glimpse of sullen thugs in handcuffs, ambulance attendants
carting shrouded victims away from a crime scene across
pavement slick with blood.

But few of us have felt the terror.

This terror can strike at any time, without a moment's
warning, triggered by a fragment of music on the radio, a
taste, an odor—anything at all. It brings convulsions,
dizziness, and loss of breath. Blind, screaming panic. Fear
so overpowering that death is sometimes viewed as a relief.

The terror paralyzes, cripples, incapacitates.

If you are driving on the highway when it strikes, you
clutch the wheel and pray that you can make it to the
shoulder without killing anyone, yourself included. Walking
down the street in broad daylight, your legs betray you, and
your lungs feel starved for oxygen. Pedestrians cannot resist

doing a startled double take. Some stop and stare. Most turn away.

If the attacks repeat themselves, increase in frequency, your life grinds to a screeching halt. Old friends can't bear the wounded, dazed expression on your face. You are a freakish curiosity to strangers. Your physician runs a battery of tests and comes up empty, recommending therapy. The therapist, in turn, is lost without some conscious trauma to dissect and exorcise.

A vicious spiral, turning in upon itself. A grinding wheel.

The terror has no deadline. It can wait.

Its chosen victim isn't going anywhere.

A respite of days or weeks, and you allow yourself to hope. The worst is over now. You've made it. Understanding takes a back seat to relief. If you can live through *that,* it stands to reason you can live through anything.

Or maybe not.

It only takes a heartbeat to demolish false security. The madness comes back stronger than before, no rhyme or reason to it. Screaming in the middle of a fever dream.

The simplest task becomes impossible.

A human life implodes.

The answers come belatedly. Too often they are never found at all.

In the spring of 1986, Jan Knowlton seemed to have her life on track. A Massachusetts native, forty-nine years old, she had performed as a professional singer on both coasts by the time she was twenty-five. Once married and divorced, she had settled in California's Orange County by 1973, moving on from an executive secretarial job at Disneyland to found her own public relations firm, performing on the side in a one-woman show called *Broadway Plus.* In public and in private, Jan was known for her confidence, professional experience, and easy charm.

If she was not Most Likely to Succeed, at least Jan must have seemed Least Likely to Collapse, but there were dark, subconscious forces stirring in her life that she had yet to recognize.

The great unraveling began, as near as we can determine, with unexplained depression, anxiety, and panic attacks in late 1981. The melancholy worsened after April 1983, when Jan's pet dog was euthanized following surgery to remove a benign tumor. During the operation, Bamse's liver was damaged, and the vet made it clear that Jan's only option was to end her pet's suffering.

The vet didn't think it was in Jan's or Bamse's best interest for Jan to be present during the injection that ended the dog's life. So after it was over, Jan saw Bamse lying dead on the narrow examining table. She pleaded with the vet to cover the long incision in Bamse's stomach.

That incision haunted Jan's waking moments, as did her decision to take the vet's advice and leave the body with him—to abandon Bamse without a funeral or burial. Skeet and Elsie Wilson, an elderly couple who were acting caretakers in Jan's apartment complex, came by after hearing of Bamse's death, to leave a floral bouquet and sympathy card. They had "adopted" Jan and her dog and grieved with her. In retrospect, Jan realized that the informal funeral they provided helped save her sanity.

In July 1985, Jan sought help from a psychotherapist, but the sessions were fruitless, since Jan had no memories of any trauma or disturbance that would help explain her plight.

By autumn 1985, Jan had developed physical problems to complement her emotional distress. In late October, while performing a self-examination to monitor a small fibroid growth in her uterus, Jan discovered a new, larger mass near her bladder. On November 11, her gynecologist, Dr. Susan Murphy,* performed ultrasound tests and recommended surgery, warning Jan that the growth seemed "too hard to be a fibroid." Jan requested a second opinion, and Murphy directed her to a colleague, Dr. Thomas Westlake.* Unknown to Jan, and in defiance of her request for independent review, Dr. Murphy wrote to Westlake that Jan's test results displayed a "fibroid appearing" uterus. Murphy also expressed concern about the possibility of an "adnexal mass"—that is, a malignancy—although a Dr. Chin, who analyzed the test results at Hoag Hospital, disputed that portion of her diagnosis.

Dr. Westlake met with Jan for the first time on November 18. His report on that meeting records his "impression"— unsupported by further ultrasound tests—that the uterine mass was benign but should still be removed. Westlake recommended a total abdominal hysterectomy with bilateral salpingo-oophorectomy—in other words, the surgical removal of the uterus and both ovaries. He would prescribe the same procedure for his own sister, he told Jan. She would be "better off" without her ovaries, since she was "rapidly approaching menopause." Believing that her life might be in jeopardy and that the drastic treatment was required to save her, Jan agreed. Dr. Murphy, meanwhile, instructed Jan to find a new gynecologist because "You chose a male surgeon."

Jan was admitted to Long Beach Memorial Hospital on Monday, November 25, and Dr. Westlake operated the following day. Lab analysis torpedoed all fears of cancer, reporting a mass of benign leiomyomas—fibroid tumors of the uterus—their size "consistent with a twenty-week pregnancy." Furthermore, according to the hospital pathologist, "Both ovaries appeared to be normal."

Jan later learned the entire surgery was unnecessary.

One depressing aftereffect of the operation was the large keloid scar that bisected Jan's abdomen, gathered into a pucker of flesh at one end. Unsightly and painful, the scar showed no signs of fading, and Jan reported it to Dr. Westlake's nurse.

"If we'd known you form keloid scars," the nurse said, "we could have treated it differently, with steroid cream."

Jan was furious. "Why in the hell didn't you ask?" she demanded.

No answer.

Jan was discharged from Long Beach Memorial on Sunday, December 1, with a prescription for replacement hormones aimed at compensating for the loss of healthy ovaries. Dr. Westlake prescribed 1.25 mg of Premarin (estrogen extracted from the urine of pregnant mares) on the first twenty-five days of each month, with 10 mg of Provera, on days sixteen through twenty-five.

It seemed to work. Jan's life returned to normal.

For a while.

In April 1986, Jan recognized the warning signs of black depression creeping back into her life. The change accompanied her shift from Premarin to a generic form of estrogen, but no one in the medical establishment had warned her that the two drugs might have different strengths or side effects. Likewise, she had not been informed that hysterectomies are often followed by depression—in 85 percent of all cases, according to the Pennsylvania-based Hysterectomy Educational Resources and Services.

Jan was alone and groping in the dark.

Accustomed to pushing on, Jan continued with her public relations practice and singing. She was temporarily heartened by an invitation to sing "America the Beautiful" for Barbara Bush, the wife of the vice president.

Then the terror struck in June without apparent cause, which simply meant Jan did not yet recognize her problem. News reports at that time were full of stories about Marla Hanson, an aspiring model whose face had been mutilated by a pair of mercenary thugs on orders from a spiteful would-be lover, but the New York case had no more bearing on Jan's life than news from outer space.

Or did it?

On July 31, Jan took her problems back to Dr. Westlake. His report of that date reads as follows:

> The patient comes in today for follow-up examination. Physically, she is great. Her estrogen is well estrogenized. She is not having any hot flashes, but she · is having severe depression. She is convinced it is due

to hormones. I doubt it, from looking at her vagina. I gave her 2 cc of Delestrogen anyway. She is seeing a psychologist, and she is on a couple of drugs.

I suspect that she is one of these rare patients who cannot absorb estrogen from the G.I. tract. These symptoms only started two months ago, [although] she was operated on about nine months ago. She is taking conjugated estrogen now, and she was taking Premarin before. The possibility exists that she is not absorbing the conjugate. On the other hand, her vagina is well estrogenized.

Our plan is to see her again in one months [*sic*] time.

In fact, far from being "physically great," Jan was already suicidal. She states, for the record, that Dr. Westlake did not perform a blood test to see if her estrogen was "well estrogenized." Instead, he relied on a visual examination of her vagina and let it go at that. Westlake clearly recognized potential problems in the switch from Premarin to a generic brand of estrogen, but took no steps to switch Jan back. Neither did he refer Jan to an endocrinologist for confirmation of his "suspicion" that she was not absorbing estrogen properly through her gastrointestinal tract. He did not even record the names of the medications Jan was on, referring to them offhandedly as a "couple of drugs."

Before leaving Dr. Westlake's office on July 31, Jan received a massive estrogen injection, boosting her level to an incredible 4,075 pg/ml, without compensation from natural progesterone. A normal high for estrogen in post-hysterectomy patients is around 100 pg/ml. Once again, Jan was not warned that estrogen adrenalizes human beings, much less that adrenaline is thought to be the central factor in repressing—or unleashing—painful and traumatic memories.

Jan deteriorated rapidly after the injection, losing her health and business. She stopped taking hormones, but found no relief from the antidepressant. Hiding in her home, she was visited by a friend, Don Koleff, who reported to his wife, May, that he feared Jan would die. "Her eyes look dead," he said.

By September 1986, Jan's terror intensified and persistent thoughts of suicide defied the medication. Her alcoholic stepmother dismissed Jan's problem as a case of Jan "being dramatic," but her friends were visibly concerned, and Jan's therapist had reached the point of threatening to commit her to an institution if she did not seek help on her own.

Daily, Jan fought the urge to commit suicide to end her agony. Her friends, Alma and Bill DeSmith watched helplessly as she disintegrated mentally and physically, still hoping the Desyrel would take effect. Word came from one of her sisters in the East that a different antidepressant, imipramine, had worked for her. Having read that blood relatives often benefited from the same medication, Jan asked her psychiatrist to prescribe it. She did, continuing the Desyrel as well, but it was too little too late.

Another concerned friend, Joan Bergeron, aghast at Jan's rapid deterioration, invited her to sleep over the last few days of September. Perhaps the combination of the drugs and her mind's struggle to push down the memories had caused serious memory lapses that made Jan a potential danger to herself and others.

"You left the gas jets on, put food in the dishwasher instead of the cupboard," Joan told her later. "And when I saw you get into your car, I was scared you'd crash."

Jan remembered one car trip. It was about September 27, 1986, when she drove to the cemetery where her father and Kevin were buried under the marker that read "Father and Son, Together Always." The cemetery was closed, but Jan's rapid weight loss enabled her to squeeze in through a narrow opening in the fence.

She knelt at the grave sobbing and pleading, "Don't take me with you. You have Kevin. You don't need me."

On Monday, September 29, Jan presented herself at an Orange County hospital which she describes, in retrospect, as "the county mental Dumpster." Her first impression was of a dingy corridor that led her to a claustrophobic waiting room. Wallpaper torn and sagging. Yawning gaps in the acoustic ceiling panels. Most of the damage had been caused by a recent heavy rain, but all Jan saw through swollen, teary eyelids was the bottom of the barrel.

She made her way through paperwork and interviews, received a sedative, and heard herself pronounced "acceptable for hospitalization." Surrendering her daily medication at the nurse's station, Jan was shown to a cramped room with two other patients. Supportive telephone calls from several friends on the outside had a counterproductive effect, making Jan feel even lonelier and more helpless than before.

The staff served up some bad news after supper. Jan's antidepressant and sedatives, prescribed three months earlier, were being discontinued until further notice so that the staff could evaluate her true condition. By this time, Jan was a self-taught expert on prescription drugs and their side effects. She understood the danger of abruptly discontinuing antidepressants, but the staff had no interest in a patient's "uninformed" opinion.

They left Jan in tears, which degenerated into hysteria as the night wore on. Unable to sleep or even lie still, she roamed the murky hallways, weeping, moaning, finally screaming out to God, her family, and her friends for some relief. The staff ignored her until she made her way back to her room. An orderly peered in at that point, shined a flashlight in her eyes, and closed the door behind him as he left without a word.

The next day a nurse told Jan that she had been observed in her nocturnal rambling, but no steps were taken to help her because the staff "wanted to see what she would do." Jan felt a rush of sudden fury, but she kept it locked inside.

First lesson: this was not a place to let your anger show.

The staff let Jan "adjust" on Tuesday, exempting her from everything but daily rounds. In most hospitals, the physicians make their rounds from room to room, but Orange

County's mental facility took a different approach, routing patients from their cubicles and having them troop past a psychiatrist's file-laden desk. When several had briefly described their emotional state, Jan voiced concern about the sudden termination of her daily medicine.

"I'm upset," she explained, "because they won't give me my medication, and it's dangerous to stop it abruptly."

The doctor dismissed her concern out of hand.

Second lesson: complaints to the staff were a grand waste of time.

She slept that night, if only for a little while.

On Wednesday morning Jan was summoned to the hospital director's office. Apprehensive, feeling like a schoolgirl being sent to the principal, she feared a scolding for her "outburst" during Tuesday's rounds. It struck her that she had been stripped of all power and denied even the privilege of defining her own personality.

In the office Jan confronted the doctor, leaning over his desk and pointing at her own face. "Can't you tell by my eyes that I'm sane?"

The doctor stared back coldly. "No."

An icy chill swept over Jan. She realized, at last, that she was well and truly caged.

"I hear you were very upset last night, screaming and crying," the doctor said. "What was that all about?"

"You said I should express what I was feeling," Jan replied. "If I felt suicidal, I should tell someone."

"But you carried on a bit dramatically, didn't you?" Much later Jan would find a notation in her file: "Histrionic, dramatic, and theatrical."

"That was the way I felt," Jan said, defensive. "I was terrified."

The doctor's tone was patronizing. "Didn't you carry it to extremes?"

She glimpsed the one escape hatch open to her. Absolute capitulation meant forgiveness. "Yes," she said, "I guess so. I feel a little sheepish."

The doctor looked satisfied, settling back in his chair to

discuss Jan's problem. She explained her belief that the hysterectomy and subsequent hormone treatments had caused her condition. The psychiatrist agreed that hormonal imbalance could alter emotions, but he suspected there was more at work in Jan's case than a glitch in chemistry.

A brief summation of Jan's childhood led the doctor to remark that she had never matured.

"But I've supported myself since I was eighteen," Jan told him. "Paid all my own bills . . ."

"A teenager can hold a job and pay bills," the doctor said. "That doesn't mean he's mature."

"What is maturity?"

He shrugged. "If you don't know, I can't explain it to you."

Catch-22.

From the cryptic interview, Jan proceeded to occupational therapy. With several arts and crafts to choose from, she leaned toward drawing. Later, thumbing through a copy of her file, she would discover this notation: "Patient chooses a project, completes it swiftly, and then sits quietly, looking into space with a sad expression."

Jan's opinion of the institution was not improved by her conversation with a new arrival that first afternoon. The latest patient was a rape victim and a self-described manic-depressive. A recent suicide attempt had prompted relatives to place her in the hospital.

"I'm sure they'll help you here," Jan said. "Then you'll get better and never have to go through this again."

The young woman looked blank. "Oh, this is my third time," she said.

Despair.

Jan pictured herself racing out of the hospital, running across the parking lot to Highway 39, and flinging herself into traffic. Instead she found a mental health worker and poured out her fears. She was cautioned to avoid involvement with her fellow patients, bearing in mind that each of them had problems that would skew evaluation of another's plight.

"Why don't you just go back to bed?" the aide suggested. "You'll feel better tomorrow, you'll see."

Three weeks of tomorrows, in fact, made no difference. When Jan checked out of the hospital on Tuesday, October 22, with a referral to outpatient care, she was still suicidally depressed. Her social worker recognized Jan's silent resistance to the notion of ongoing treatment.

"Jan," she said, "if you go home and lie down, you'll never get up. Do you hear me?"

Jan heard.

Back on the street, Jan visited her general practitioner and accepted her advice to resume hormone treatment. She was so hormonally depleted by this time that when a county psychiatrist put her back on imipramine, her mood was elevated within days.

Jan found some compassion in the form of a county counselor named Lupe,* who spoke to her about getting in touch with her "inner child." Long after her trauma memories returned, Jan obtained the counselor's records and read these notations about her response to being reminded of her childhood:

> November 7, 1986: continues to express fear and anxiety and discussed feeling like a child and not wanting that part of herself any more than her parents did.
>
> November 14, 1986: states she feels she has been asleep since age ten and just now is awakening with suicidal ideation.

Another clue to the memories would emerge three years later—a drawing Jan made at the request of the inpatient psychiatrist. She had chosen to sketch herself and her father. The psychiatrist noted that "The female figure is herself in the mid-twenties and the male is in the mid-thirties. The female's facial expression is open, friendly, and a desire for contact. In contrast, the male's expression is closed."

Jan recalls she drew herself dressed in black, as she had been the last time she saw her father, about August 1962. And in her mid-twenties, close to the age Elizabeth Short was when she was murdered.

Yet she drew her father not at the age of his death, fifty, but at the age he was when he murdered Elizabeth Short—thirty-five.

Within weeks Jan seemed "as good as new," but her improved appearance was only part of the healing process. Step two was education, and it began by accident.

Browsing for discount Christmas presents at a close-out sale, she lingered at the bookshelves. One title in particular leaped out at Jan: *The Castrated Woman* by Naomi Miller Stokes. Its subtitle clinched the sale: *What Your Doctor Won't Tell You about Hysterectomy.* On page 120 she read that "Contemplation of suicide is common with hormone deprivation or imbalance in both sexes. All things seem tragic, all people hateful. Inappropriately administered hormones can be tantamount to a death sentence."

Jan reviewed the book's medical references in wonder. This was scientific fact, not high-flown theory. It was documented to the nth degree, hard data readily available to gynecologists and surgeons but seldom mentioned to prospective candidates for hysterectomy.

Jan felt like shouting from the rooftops. She was vindicated at a single stroke, her "histrionic" fears backed up by scientific fact with the turn of a page. Still, there was more to learn before she began to strike back.

Jan telephoned a longtime friend in Manhattan, a successful endocrinologist with a Fifth Avenue practice. He listened to Jan's list of problems and asked, "What hormones did your doctor put you on?"

"Premarin and Provera," Jan replied, "but I changed to generics in April because a druggist said they were the same."

"Good God!" the doctor blurted out. "They're not the same at all. They probably weren't passing through the blood-brain barrier."

"What?" Jan was confused. "What does that mean?"

"Never mind," her friend said. "Just stay on those hormones from now on."

A few days later, Jan got through to Dr. Albert Frost,* at Mercy Hospital's sleep disorders lab in Chicago. The call was prompted by Dr. Frost's appearance on a TV talk show, where he discussed the variations between original patented drugs and generics. Once again Jan told a thumbnail version of her story, this time to a total stranger.

"Are you back on Premarin now?" Frost asked.

"Well, no," Jan said. "My doctor thought I might do better on Ogen."

"But weren't you doing all right until you switched to the generic?"

"Yes," said Jan.

"Then I suggest that you return to Premarin and not take chances," Frost responded. "Good luck."

Jan made the switch, but she also read voraciously on hysterectomy and hormones, finding time and time again that doctors knew the risks and complications. Most of them, it seemed, were loath to share that crucial knowledge with their patients. Worse, a growing mass of literature stated flatly that many—perhaps most—hysterectomies were medically unnecessary. According to those critical sources, misdiagnosis, negligent malpractice, and greed were responsible for thousands of needless operations in America each year. Dr. Norman King Beals, a local physician specializing in hormone replacement therapy, told Jan that less than 5 percent of the 673,000 hysterectomies performed in 1983—the last year with available records— were dictated by medical necessity.

Jan checked her file—benign fibroids, healthy ovaries— and knew that one of those unnecessary surgeries was hers.

Armed with a wealth of statistics and heretical opinions from doctors courageous enough to speak out in the face of official silence, Jan organized SHE—the Society for Hysterectomy Education. From Dr. Benjamin Spock came a note of congratulations on Jan's "wisdom and courage in organizing SHE. The medical profession will feel the impact, even if they don't admit anything."

Indeed, the silence from some medical quarters was deafening. Jan's written complaints on her own case were roundly ignored by the American Medical Association and the California Board of Medical Quality Assurance. Others, however, were listening. In March 1987, Jan appeared on June Cain Miller's television program, from Anaheim, and local bookings multiplied, climaxing with an appearance on the national *Hour Magazine*. In February 1988 the latter program earned Jan a mention in *McCall's* magazine. Within a year after her breakdown, Jan's literature was being solicited by the Orange County Mental Health Department and by several psychiatrists in private practice.

Granted, there were some embarrassing moments for Jan as she pursued her new crusade. Publicity was one thing, she acknowledged in January 1988, but "It was another matter to publicly announce that I was a patient in a county mental facility as a result of the surgery." As for the odds against her, she informed the *Orange County Register* on March 21, "Frankly, I've found the medical profession is practically unimpeachable. They don't feel they're accountable to anyone."

There was no easy answer, nothing in the way of swift solutions. Jan was making progress, gaining national attention for her cause, but she had other problems to cope with.

And once again, increasingly by early 1988, those problems threatened to consume her life.

By September 1987, Dr. Norman Beals was treating Janice as a patient. Beals prescribed a larger daily dose of estrogen than she was used to, with a supplement of steroids. Unknown to Janice, and perhaps to Beals as well, the mixture was a cocktail with potential for a major jolt to any memories repressed from childhood onward.

They would not appear just yet, but they were coming.

From that point on, there was nothing Jan could do to head them off.

Sporadic bouts of terror resumed by Christmas, peaked after New Year's, and mounted to a fever pitch in February. Dr. Beals gave Jan her last injection on March 6, and three weeks later she was seated in the office of a new psychiatrist, Dr. Sarah Mensik,* recommended by Jan's latest general practitioner.

With twenty-twenty hindsight, Jan describes Dr. Mensik as "a crazy lady shrink," more interested in promoting her own radio show than in the welfare of her patients. Blood tests revealed that Jan was overestrogenized, but Dr. Mensik prescribed *more* estrogen with a side order of antidepressants. Jan's terror increased, estrogen blocking the antidepressant . . . whereupon Dr. Mensik boosted that dosage as well. Through it all, she discussed Jan's case in public, on the airwaves, with an audience that spanned Orange County and the L.A. basin. "Now I know she did it deliberately," Jan says, "so I'd be forced into the hospital, giving her income and ensuring that hospital officials would keep her treatment program going."

Harsh words, but that is exactly what happened in May 1988. Jan was admitted briefly to La Palma Intercommunity Hospital, near Knott's Berry Farm, under suicide watch for life-threatening depression. Dr. J. Younger found Jan "alert, oriented times three," although her "judgment was, at times, idiosyncratic (e.g., when asked what she would do if there was smoke in a theater, she replied, 'Yell fire and get out')." Younger noted a "slight head-bobbing tremor which can be brought out by forward flexion of the neck," but noted with apparent satisfaction that Jan "hops well on either the left or the right foot." His final diagnosis was "benign essential tremor, mild."

A second physician, Dr. Abdelmalek, also found Jan "a very pleasant woman who relates very well," although "she doesn't want to live any more and would rather die." This doctor's diagnostic impression was "major depression with suicidal intentions, active." He accepted Jan's statement that the drug Tofranil relieved her depression on a temporary basis.

Reduced to living on disability checks by the time of her release, Jan signed up with Co-Dependents Anonymous, discovering through that group's twelve-step program that she had a tendency to let herself be used by unethical parent substitutes.

Jan knew she needed help, but she was running out of champions.

And she was running out of trust.

A friend referred Jan to Jim Frey in 1987, but Jan delayed making contact while she explored other options. A counselor specializing in marriage and family problems, with particular expertise in the field of child abuse, Frey operates from Orange County's Sophia Fellowship Christian Counseling Center. Despite word-of-mouth recommendations, Jan shied away from Frey at first, because the center's "Christian" label put her off.

By April 1989, however, she had nowhere else to go. Surgeons, psychiatrists, gynecologists, and general practitioners had done nothing to relieve her problem in four years of trial and error. Jan had been sedated and adrenalized, observed and psychoanalyzed, deprived of vital organs and subjected to replacement therapy, humiliated on the radio and in the local snake pits. All she had to show for it, so far, was a scar and an increasing fascination with the thought of suicide.

Jan kept her first appointment with Frey on Wednesday, April 12, 1989. Frey listed her presenting problem as "Depression, chronic anxiety, hyperalertness, insomnia, changeable moods, irritable, restless, and tremulous." Physical symptoms of Jan's illness included head and body tremors, labored breathing, aching joints, chronic fatigue, and an exaggerated startle response. Based on standard guidelines from the *Diagnostic and Statistical Manual,* Frey diagnosed Jan as suffering from post-traumatic stress disorder and dependent personality disorder. Her condition was "fragile and greatly impaired," with a strong potential for "implosion" through suicide. Prescribed treatment included weekly sessions of individual psychotherapy, with additional participation in group therapy for adult survivors of childhood sexual abuse and incest.

In the early days of therapy with Frey, Jan still had no coherent memories of physical abuse from childhood, other than a single beating by her father in her early teens and some incidents of cruelty involving family pets. Frey recognized the yawning gaps in memory that spanned Jan's life from infancy until her father's death in 1962, but his suspicion of a trauma long repressed was not enough to pierce the wall Jan had erected to contain her missing memories.

Ironically, it took a chain of deaths by natural causes to unleash Jan's memories of other deaths, decidedly unnatural, that formed the key to opening her past and airing out the charnel house of memory. Jan's mother died in July 1989, her stepmother in October, and a longtime friend who shared her father's given name a few days later, in the first part of November. Before the month was out, she had experienced the first of countless flashbacks to her childhood in the 1940s.

Riding in her father's car, along a quiet street in Massachusetts. Up ahead, a stranger in the middle of the street. The car accelerating on a dead collision course.

Her father's smile.

It was the first of several homicides that Janice would remember in the next four years, along with incidents of rape and other violence. Over time, as she recovered, bits and pieces of her shattered childhood, Jan came to realize that she had witnessed eight or nine sadistic homicides committed by her father, spanning twelve or thirteen years.

One of the victims was Jan's infant son, a child of incest.

Yet another was the subject of California's most infamous unsolved murder, dating back to January 1947.

Elizabeth Short.

The Black Dahlia.

Jim Frey evaluated the unfolding memories and pronounced them legitimate, entirely consistent with Jan's preexisting symptoms. The images recovered under therapy explained Jan's fear of cars and swimming, her relationships with domineering and abusive men, and her compulsion to collect random objects as mementos of a past that she could not recall.

Jan herself was more than happy to reject the flood of graphic memories. Her greatest fear—insanity—seemed preferable to the emerging truth. Reluctantly at first, and then with grim determination, she began to look for answers in the public record. Family documents and classic texts on memory. The annals of forgotten crimes.

Blood trails.

Jim Frey had no doubt that her memories were accurate, but Jan took some convincing. If she had indeed survived such trauma, how had she repressed it for so many years?

And why in God's name were the ghastly images returning now?

In essence, memory is a chemical process. Specific events, pleasant or painful, produce reactions in the human body, triggering the release of different hormones that spark physical sensations ranging from fatigue and hunger to excitement and arousal, or anxiety and fear. Those reactions, through a process barely understood by modern science, also store events away inside the brain as memories, which can be retrieved by stimuli called triggers. A familiar taste or smell. A flash of color. Sound. Sensation. Anything at all.

We are informed by experts that the human brain remembers everything. No memory is ever truly lost, except where trauma or disease destroys the crucial brain cells. Granted, certain individuals are more adept at memory retrieval than others, but even the involuntary process of forgetting is controlled by body chemistry.

Depending on the circumstances and the individual, some incidents are too traumatic for a given person to survive with sanity intact. Confronted with a waking nightmare—in the home or on a foreign battlefield—some individuals emerge as heroes. Others cut and run, disgrace themselves with cowardice, or simply lose their minds.

And some forget.

In World War I, the military doctors referred to this kind of trauma as shell shock. A generation later, in another global conflict, the condition was known as battle fatigue. Since Vietnam, the syndrome has had another name: post-traumatic stress disorder.

Bombs and tanks and troops are not required to generate the classic symptoms of post-traumatic stress. A tragic accident or a violent crime can do the same kind of damage. Increasingly, within the past two decades, psychotherapists have diagnosed PTSD among survivors of homes in which sexual abuse and violence have produced a toxic atmosphere of hatred, fear, and shame.

We know that many victims of abuse in childhood themselves become abusers later on: alcoholics, addicts, child-molesters, wife-beaters, career criminals. They act out symptoms of the trauma suffered in another time, when they were victims of abuse. With time and therapy, some members of the victim-victimizer class can be redeemed, while others are beyond the pale, fit only for confinement in a prison cell.

Another kind of victim locks the secret up inside and keeps it there, perhaps forever, hidden from the world. Some turn the fear and anger inward, on themselves, with self-destructive actions ranging from pursuit of damaging relationships to suicide. Still others show the world a normal face and deny that they were ever traumatized.

They manage to forget for years or decades. Now and then a rare survivor takes a secret to the grave.

But each and every one of them has scars.

Modern researchers tell us that stress and other trauma-linked emotions affect the brain primarily through hormones like adrenaline and cortisol, which trigger the flight-or-fight response to physical or psychological danger. Such changes are normally smooth, even routine, with the mind and body returning to normal when danger has passed, but persistent long-term fear can overactivate the hormones to the point where they dominate genetic regulation, in the words of author Ronald Kotulak, "like a band of terrorists." The "terrorized" genes, in turn, may produce aberrant networks and reactions: an epileptic seizure instead of a clear signal between cells; depression instead of happiness; sudden rage in place of reasonable compromise.

According to Christopher Coe, a psychologist at the University of Wisconsin, overactive stress hormones may produce physical brain damage by turning genes on and off at the wrong times, thus creating abnormal links between cooperating brain cells. This, in turn, explains the prevalence of learning disorders among abused children, as explained by Dr. Michael Merzenick, a neuroscientist at the University of California at San Francisco.

Genes thus abnormally triggered also leave memory traces of bad feelings associated with the particular trauma. Reinforced over time by additional stress, the memory trace takes on a life of its own, producing depression and other destructive reactions even without the specific trigger of a stressful incident to light the fuse. Dr. Dennis Charney, director of clinical neuroscience at the National Center for Post-Traumatic Stress Disorder, reports that a single incident of overwhelming terror can alter brain chemistry, making victims abnormally sensitive to adrenaline surges years after their traumatization. And women, it appears, may be even more susceptible to such damage than men.

Adrenaline is the hormone most conclusively linked to repression of traumatic memories. As a panic-induced adrenaline surge may help the brain file and forget painful incidents, so a later variation in the level of adrenaline available to "keep the lid on" may unleash disturbing flashbacks, mood swings, terror, and depression. Women, by virtue of their physiology, experience a decrease in adrenaline with menopause or when their body chemistry is altered via hysterectomy.

As explained by Dr. Arabella Melville in *Natural Hormone Health,* studies of the link between memory and the menstrual cycle reveal that women recall happy events more readily around the time of ovulation, while unpleasant memories dominate the premenstrual period, when estrogen levels are elevated and the hormone is converted to adrenaline. The rapid change in hormone levels also helps explain the prevalence of depression among hysterectomy patients and women passing through menopause.

After menopause or a hysterectomy, the hormone levels change, and memories surge forward from the murky past. Typically, as in Jan's case, they surface first as unexplained emotions, mood swings, and body memories—anything from nervous tics to full-blown seizures that may threaten life and limb. It may take months or years of cautious therapy to find out what is really going on, then years longer to sort the problem out and lay the ancient ghosts to rest. It is the reason some combat veterans still flinch when they hear a car backfire, and it causes some adult survivors of abuse to shrink away from a handshake.

A case in point is that of Marilyn Van Derbur Atler, who was Miss America in 1958. Raped repeatedly by her wealthy socialite father from childhood until her freshman year of college, Marilyn survived the trauma by unconsciously dividing herself into a smiling "day child" who brought home straight A's and starred on the high school swimming team, and a cringing "night child" who lay awake locked in a fetal position, praying that the next assault would be postponed. The abuse was six years behind her when Marilyn experienced her first conscious memory and told her fiancé about it, but years of therapy were needed to complete the picture, filling in the gaps.

There is a difference, though, between recalling a specific instance of abuse in childhood and constructing lurid tales of murder. Is it possible for ancient memories, unearthed through therapy, to prove a suspect's guilt beyond a reasonable doubt, as called for in a court of law?

By 1991 the crucial votes were in.

The answer was a loud, resounding yes.

* * *

The most famous case of repressed memory to date is certainly that of Eileen Franklin-Lipsker. At twenty-eight, in January 1989, Eileen was watching her eight-year-old daughter at play when she suddenly noted the resemblance of her own child to a former playmate, Susan Nason, who was raped and murdered in September 1969. From that brief flash of recognition sprang more detailed memories of Eileen's father, retired San Mateo fireman George Franklin, committing the murder while Eileen looked on, terrorized into silence by his threats. Before the odyssey of recollection was completed, Eileen knew that she had also been a victim of her father's sexual abuse and violence, beginning at the age of five.

Dr. Lenore Terr, professor of clinical psychiatry at the University of California at San Francisco, examined Eileen and explained her case to *Houston Chronicle* newsman Evan Moore. According to Dr. Terr, "Eileen fit into a pattern. If a child goes through one terrible event, they usually remember it with great clarity. But if it's a series of terrible events, they detach themselves. They walk away from the bad part. Because she'd been abused since the age of five, by age eight [Eileen] was able to shelve the bad parts. But it's all still there. Once she began remembering, she was able to form almost a complete scene over several months."

Furthermore, in Dr. Terr's opinion, "Repressed memories can be extraordinarily precise—far more detailed and specific than memories of ordinary events. Later, victims can remember what happened, how things looked, what was said."

Police in the vicinity had suspected George Franklin of Susan Nason's murder from day one, even photographing his visits to the child's grave, but they could never build a solid case until Eileen stepped forward with her newly resurrected memories. Despite denials from her father and a storm of controversy in the press, twelve jurors weighed the evidence and voted to convict George Franklin on November 30, 1990. Two months later he was sentenced to life imprisonment.

A similar case surfaced in Garfield, Pennsylvania, around the time of Franklin's California conviction. Twenty-year-old John Mudd was playing Trivial Pursuit with friends when another player cursed his girlfriend. Suddenly enraged, Mudd stepped back from the table, raised a chair as if to strike the bigmouth . . . and suddenly flashed back to age five, a wholly different time and place.

In that instant of memory, Mudd was transported to his parents' home in Wilkinsburg. He saw the family watching television, when suddenly the power failed. His father went downstairs to check the circuit box, and seven shots rang out. A moment later a man strode through the basement door. Mudd recognized him as the man he had earlier seen "trying to kiss my mother." Mudd identified the man as former neighbor Steven Slutzker, an illicit lover of Mudd's mother. Slutzker was charged with murder soon after the killing, but the charges were dropped for lack of evidence. By April 1991 a renewed investigation, based on Mudd's repressed memory, had produced charges of murder and criminal conspiracy against Slutzker and Arlene Mudd. The charges against the widow were dismissed three months later, but Steven Slutzker was convicted of murder on January 28, 1992, and sentenced to life in prison.

In each of these cases and in various civil suits, judges and jurors have recognized testimony on the subject of repressed memories as valid, admissible evidence. The accused and their apologists have insisted that trauma survivors are actually victims of "false memory syndrome," but the registered verdicts have been supported by higher courts on appeal.

Denial is tenacious, no less among the offenders than among the victims who have repressed the abusers' crimes, but truth emerges, given time.

Assuming one has time to spare.

By late November 1989, Jan Knowlton knew her father had committed several homicides, including the murder of the Black Dahlia, but knowing it and proving it were two entirely different matters. To validate her memories, and thereby save herself, Jan had to undertake a private odyssey through hell, reliving the events she had spent a lifetime trying to forget. She had to understand her father and his crimes; she had to know all about the life that had produced a monster cast in human form. Jan started at the beginning, years before her father's birth, in her attempt to find out how he had evolved.

It was a trip she would have given anything to cancel, but avoidance of the truth, once memories began to flow, was not an option. Neither could she relegate the task to others.

Jan would have to make the trek alone.

With any luck at all, she might survive.

3

New England Gothic

No man ever became extremely wicked all at once.

—Juvenal, *Satires*

THE PAST GIVES UP ITS DARKEST SECRETS GRUDGINGLY, BUT SOME details can be discovered more easily than others. In the good old days before the first computer was imagined, much less put on-line, most families kept records of their lives. The family Bible and a scrapbook said a good deal. If anyone was missing from the roster, he or she had been deleted for a reason. Best forgotten, all around.

The Bartons were respected by their neighbors, more or less. Harry lived on the outskirts of Cambridge, New York, five miles from the Vermont border, in Washington County. He came from God-fearing stock, but some among his neighbors disdained his choice of a mate. Ida May Orcutt was a child of white trash, they said, perhaps alluding to the strain of Indian blood in her family, dating back to the Iroquois Confederacy in colonial times. That aside, she was handsome and fertile, producing five children in rapid succession. Gladys Harriet was born in 1894, soon followed by Jesse, Jerome, Kenneth, and Elizabeth.

A telling incident occurred in the Barton household when Gladys was fifteen years old. One of her brothers died, and a physician was summoned to prepare the lad for burial. Mortuaries were frequently bypassed in those simpler times, and the doctor came prepared, with all his implements. Drafting the first child he saw—young Gladys—the physician handed her a bucket, stationed her beside the table where her brother's body lay, and proceeded to disembowel the corpse, scooping out handfuls of viscera and tossing them into the pail. Apparently he mistook Gladys for a neighbor, grasping his mistake only when a relative walked in on the grisly scene and identified Gladys as the dead boy's sister.

Ida May Barton died in her thirties, and Harry remarried. His second wife was a blue-eyed brunette named Viola, who gave him four more children: Arthur, Henry, Louise, and Loretta. By that time, however, Gladys was grown and off on her own, having settled in Beverly, Massachusetts, 130 miles from home. It was as far as she could travel to the east without a boat, and Gladys put down roots, determined to escape the stigma attached to half-breeds and white trash. She was reborn in Beverly, and if she sometimes put on airs, she was simply striving to succeed.

Removed from Salem by a mile-wide stretch of water, settled six years after Plymouth, Beverly had hosted one of America's last witch trials in 1693. Today it is better known as the home of the world's largest plant for manufacturing shoe-making machines. Ambitious residents of Beverly aspire to stylish homes in suburban Montserrat, Pride's Crossing, or Beverly Farms, where famed Supreme Court Justice Oliver Wendell Holmes maintained a summer hideaway with an ocean view.

George Franklin Knowlton lived in Beverly when Gladys got there, but he had been raised in Salem, one of thirteen children who could trace their roots to England, to solid Norman stock. Two Knowltons, stalwart brothers, had served under William the Conqueror, bearing arms in the Battle of Hastings. There was nothing to conquer in Massachusetts, though, and George spent his life working in machine shops, mostly at the huge United Shoe Machinery plant in Beverly.

In his spare time he sometimes stepped out in the evening, and so it was that he met Gladys Barton. A slender seventeen-year-old brunette in those days, she was pretty enough to catch George's eye and strong-willed enough to dominate the relationship from day one. It seemed like his idea when George proposed, and possibly it was. The newlyweds moved into a home on Cabot Street and stayed there until the house became crowded. With two kids underfoot and one more on the way, they moved to Winthrop Avenue in Rial Side, Beverly. It was the kind of house that Gladys could be proud of, and she helped support it by operating a beauty shop downstairs, expanding over time to run a chain of four salons.

If she had not arrived, at least there could be no denying she was on her way. She would make something of herself in Beverly. If necessary, she would re-create herself from scratch.

And family was not about to hold her back.

Gladys Knowlton was only eighteen when her first child, George Frederick, was born on June 28, 1912. A daughter, Myra,* followed two years later. Harold was next, the first of three boys born in Rial Side, but he died in infancy. Donald came along in 1919, followed by the baby of the family, Clifton—known as Babe—in 1921.

That was enough for Gladys. She took a separate bedroom after Clifton's birth, informing George that if he wanted sex, he was at liberty to seek it elsewhere. Never one to argue with the mistress of the house, George Senior took his business to a local prostitute, who charged him for the privilege of watching her disrobe.

Later he would find other outlets.

Sex aside, the Knowltons were a normal Massachusetts family, as far as anyone could tell. They kept a standing Sunday date with God at the Episcopal church. They were politically conservative, with all of the proper attitudes toward social issues of the day. Hard workers, in the bargain. George would never dominate United Shoe, of course, but Gladys was a dynamo, expanding from her small salon at home to open shops in Beverly Farms, in Lynn, and at the prestigious Somerset Hotel in Boston.

And at home on Winthrop Avenue, she ruled the roost. George Senior knew enough to stay out of her way, and the Knowlton children learned that lesson early on. Myra, the only daughter in the family, picked up all the "girl's work"—washing dishes, cleaning house—and while she usually kept her mouth shut in her mother's presence, she resented the chores so deeply that as an adult she adopted an almost slovenly approach to keeping house. She also passed the famous Barton temper on to yet another generation, but of that, more later.

It was somewhat different with the boys. They had their chores, of course, but men were not expected to keep house. They were the strong face of the family, competing for their daily bread and struggling to feed their loved ones in a cutthroat world. They needed grit, intelligence, ambition. Greed was perfectly acceptable too, as long as it was couched in Christian terms—at least on Sunday.

In her quest for perfection, Gladys was abrasive, hypercritical, and sometimes cruel to her children. She did not spare the rod or spoil the child—except, perhaps, Babe, who was her clear-cut favorite from birth. He was the fair-haired boy whom Gladys had been praying for through five deliveries, one death, the sweaty grapplings with her husband that she tolerated as a necessary evil. She had waited for the perfect son. To Uncle Arthur, with his prejudice against the swarthy Orcutts, Babe was "more like a Barton than the rest, even in appearance. He had more common sense."

To Gladys, Clifton's birth was proof, at least in part, that she had overcome her "taint." We know that she despised her half-breed, white-trash roots and sought to put that past behind her, bury the association under layers of "culture" and "respectability." Appearance was exalted over substance. In a few more years she would experiment with bleach and henna to disguise her raven hair, but in the meantime she concentrated on her children. They were a living testament to her achievement, never mind their father. Any one of them could shame her in the public eye and bring her down.

George Junior seemed to have the greatest potential for embarrassment. He bore the taint, and no mistake. With straight black hair and dusky skin, he might have been adopted from a tribal reservation rather than delivered by a proud white mother at the local hospital. Art Barton, visiting in Beverly when he was still a child, recalled the "Indian look" that set George Junior apart from the rest of the family. For Gladys, Georgie was a flesh-and-blood reminder of her dreaded "secret." All he needed was a feather in his hair, and Gladys supplied it.

They played a twisted shaming game on Winthrop Avenue, with Georgie cast as the receptacle of Glady's self-loathing. Even as a toddler he was taunted and belittled for his "Injun" looks—the tiny "redskin," dropped into the middle of a proud white family by mistake. A photograph of Georgie, taken at the age of eighteen months, speaks volumes of his plight. He stands alone, his back against the wall, a baby waiting for the firing squad. Tiny fists are clenched at his sides, baggy trousers tucked into his first pair of boots. Someone has crowned him with a "native" headband, feathers sprouting up like donkey ears on either side. His eyes are downcast, his pudgy face contorted. He is on the verge of tears.

One little Indian.

But it was all in fun. No harm intended, honestly.

We can but guess at what else happened to the Knowlton children while they were growing up on Winthrop Avenue. They all got whippings when they misbehaved, of course, but that was standard parenting procedure for the time. We know that George "went bad," but every clan had one black sheep, a rotten apple, recognized, with any luck, before it spoiled the lot. It happened in the best of families.

And yet it wasn't only Georgie who bore scars of life with Gladys. The results of physical and psychological abuse later became apparent in Myra's treatment of her own kids and the children of her siblings—treatment that strongly indicated replication of a personal experience. Her brothers are deceased today, their offspring mostly silent or deliberately forgetful, but it would be strange—unique, in fact—if only two of George and Glady's five children were victims of mistreatment.

Gladys had a motto when it came to discipline around the house. "I brought you into this world," she informed the tiny miscreants, "and I can send you back where you came from." One of them, at least, was listening. He would remember and repeat the warning to a future generation.

There was also sexual abuse at No. 7 Winthrop Avenue, though we are forced to speculate on its extent and nature. At least one grandchild was molested and survived to tell the world, and little Georgie's predilections demonstrate that he had picked up some unhealthy lessons on the home front by the time he started school in Beverly.

If anyone was spared, we may assume that it was Babe, the golden child, his mother's pride and joy. She had defied genetics to produce what she considered a perfect son, devoid of any half-breed characteristics. He could do no wrong.

George Junior, on the other hand, was trouble from the git-go. Short and swarthy, scarred by adolescent acne, he would reach his full growth in the neighborhood of five feet seven, trusting cowboy boots to add a few more inches. In addition to his unacceptable appearance, the boy was constantly in trouble—fighting, stealing, playing hooky. Based on observations from his adult years, we may assume that he took pleasure from abusing animals.

A psychopath in training.

As the twig is bent . . .

George grew up envious of Clifton and despised his youngest brother for the very fact of Babe's "perfection." Georgie knew that even if he bleached his hair, he would never be his mother's golden boy with rosy cheeks and flashing smile. He never had a prayer of graduating to the rank of Favored Son, and there was no point trying. Why waste effort on a hopeless cause?

But he could still command attention in the family.

A personal attack on Babe would never fly. George Junior lived in fear of Gladys and her righteous anger to his dying day. But there were other targets in the house and in the neighborhood. He only had to shop around. Reach out and touch someone.

And in the process, he could give his private rage some exercise.

By age nine or ten, George Junior had begun to torment smaller, younger children, gravitating toward the weak and helpless with a predator's sixth sense. Some of his acts were simple cruelty, a punch or shove without a ghost of provocation. Other incidents were sexual, as far removed from children "playing doctor" as a gang rape is from love.

Inevitably, given Georgie's reckless arrogance, adults found out.

There was no public dialogue on child abuse in those days. Families with an ounce of self-respect took care of their own problems quietly, to salvage their good names. If the object of abuse was a relative, so much the better. All concerned were automatically presumed to know what was best for the family. Another skeleton for someone's closet, back there in the dark, and if the bones kept rattling, parents might console themselves with the belief that it was "just a phase." Boys act that way sometimes, but they grow out of it.

And still, word got around.

Within the family there was a new unwritten law: You don't leave little children alone with Georgie. *Ever.* Something odd about that boy, make no mistake.

His closest friend in those days was a ruffian named Frederick Gardner Denno—Denno to his pals, the hated given names discarded—whom he met at school. The two boys didn't spend much time in class, though. Acquaintances recall that Georgie's parents had "a hard time keeping him in school." Denno had dropped out entirely by seventh or eighth grade and was well on his way to becoming a town character. George Junior never made it past his freshman year of high school, dropping out to work part-time and mostly to bum around. Another member of his circle was Carl Conrad, fellow dropout in his sophomore year, who worked with Denno at a local factory.

At quitting time, they prowled the streets, and Arthur Barton recalls that nephew George was "always in trouble with the law" for burglarizing stores, shoplifting, stealing anything that caught his eye. Most often Denno tagged along to help himself or simply to watch his young friend work. It was a shame to Gladys, but she knew exactly how to deal with scandal.

Sweep it out of sight.

Keep silent.

Wear a brave face for the family, and never let a stranger know what you were thinking.

Adolescent theft and child-molesting were a problem, granted, but the first step toward remediation, in the best of families, was to nip a scandal in the bud, before word got around and ruined everything.

In August 1928, with school about to start, somebody had the bright idea that Georgie, Carl, and Denno should take off for Maine and look for work in the potato fields. They had no cash to speak of, but they did have wheels—Carl's fifty-dollar Essex—plus a funnel, a rubber hose, and a red five-gallon can to hold any gasoline they "found" along the way. "We had no problem with gas," Conrad recalled more than sixty years later. "We just siphoned it out of other cars. We could not get it any cheaper."

As it turned out, digging spuds was *work,* and after several days of sweating while his back ached, Denno had a brainstorm: they should go to California, "following the sun." It wasn't hard to win his traveling companions over to the scheme, and they drove west in Conrad's Essex, sticking to the back roads like a band of Gypsies, living off the land.

They siphoned gas, stole eggs for breakfast, begged for their lunch and supper, and slept in the car or underneath the stars. Hard times were closing in, but none of them went hungry. Looking back, Carl recollects that "Denno with his comical look and Georgie with his innocent look were good at bumming food."

At one farmhouse, Denno charmed two elderly women with the sad tale of three brothers racing desperately for home before their ailing mother died. It was good for a home-cooked meal and two dollars in change, which they spent a few miles down the road. "The next town we came to," Conrad says, "we went to the movies, popcorn and all."

Stranded with an empty gas tank the next day, Denno flagged down a passing truck and told the driver all about his dying grandma. Touched, the trucker agreed to donate a gallon of gas, and Georgie siphoned off five gallons. He apologized for the "accident," but there was nothing he could do to make it right. Their funnel "only fit the Essex." Sorry.

Somewhere in the wilds of Pennsylvania, Georgie started acting homesick. Denno wasn't acting, as it happened: he had hurt his leg somehow, and now the knee was swollen to twice its normal size. They started back, drove steadily, and reached Beverly Hospital in the small hours of a late September morning. Filled with brotherly concern, they hoisted Denno from the car and left him on the steps outside.

"Within two days," said Conrad, "I had my old job back and stayed there for fifteen years. Later I heard Denno had water on the knee and that the kneecap was just hanging on. He went on and became a town character, had a series of tragic events in his life, and died some years back by his own hand. I am guessing now, but I hoped that Georgie went back to school."

Not quite.

In mid-December, George and Denno made their second

foray west. His first letter, undated and mailed from Philadelphia, reveals that they were not together long.

Dear Mother,

I am headed for California and a job. We made [it] here to Nellie's. With luck I hope to be there in 22 or 3 days. Do not worry about me this time as I will keep you posted as to where I am and how. I am getting along great and sleeping in good hotels at night.

George

P.S. The first day in Boston we made $3.65 helping people out of the snow and we slept in a hotel in Brockton. Denno went ahead at Boston and he is still ahead.

George later drifted back to Beverly, but not to stay. Spring found him on the road again, bound for Leeds Center, Maine, in Auburn's Adroscoggin County. Georgie's first letter home, dated May 12, 1929, suggests he was expected there.

Dear Mother,

I arrived here that same night at half past six. He was glad to have me back. I got a ride from Beverly to the turnpike then another to Newberryport [sic] then I got one to Portland and took the interurban to Lewiston. Was lucky enough to get a ride from Lewiston to the very door. Please send my clothes and if you will get me a couple of pairs of short socks to go with those linen knickers. Well, I'll tell a huge crowd I was glad to hit that feather bed that night. Will you ask Dad if he will send that harness as soon as he can, as I think I can sell it. Write soon.

Your Loving Son
George Frederick Knowlton

Three weeks later, on June 1, he found the time to write again.

Dear Mother,

I have not had the time to write before this. Milk mornings I did not get to town. I shot a hedgehog noon hour a couple of days ago and got 50¢ bounty on him. I have only one pair of stockings besides those I have on my feet. Will you please send the harness and those linen knickers and stockings to go with them for Sundays. Please write oftener even if I don't.

Your Loving Son
Geo. F. Knowlton

The farmwork played out in late summer, and Georgie found himself back in Beverly, feeling restless. He was picked up by police for hauling stolen items in a pickup truck, but wriggled out of it by blaming Denno. Soon thereafter, on a whim, he stole a horse and wagon and struck out for parts unknown. The sheriff ran him down, and he was packed off to the Essex Agricultural School at Middleton on September 3, 1929. It didn't take, and Georgie gave up on his last attempt at formal education five weeks later, bailing out of Middleton before he had received any grades. He was already shaping up as "a hard person," in Uncle Art Barton's words, while baby brother Clifton "had the smarts."

Two weeks after Georgie's abrupt departure from Essex Agricultural, the stock market crashed. Overnight, it seemed, thousands, then millions of Americans were thrown out of work. For countless men and boys, the answer to unemployment seemed to lie in aimless travel, drifting back and forth across the continent in search of jobs or handouts.

Long enamored of the highway, Georgie hardly needed an excuse to pack his grip and leave.

They know about recession and depression in suburban Medford, thirteen miles southwest of Beverly. Settled in 1630 and incorporated as a town in 1684, four years ahead of Beverly, the region lured farmers with the rich loam of its riverbanks, while fishermen were beckoned by the Mystic River's surging tides. The townspeople tried shipbuilding, but without success at first. A century of grueling economic hardship followed, till New England's rum and slave trade gave the area a new lease on life. In nothing flat, the fame of Medford rum and ships spread out to Europe, Africa, and Asia, circling the globe. The navigable Mystic offered yet another source of livelihood, with Medford merchants underselling their competitors in Boston to supply New Hampshire and Vermont with everything from chocolate and cod to gunpowder and steel. The Civil War finally doomed the shipyards, but a few distilleries hung on through the turn of the century. By the time the last one closed its doors for good in 1905, Medford was well on its way to becoming a blue-collar bedroom community for the workers who kept Boston's industries rolling.

That history meant nothing to Elizabeth Ann Short who was born, the third of five sisters, on July 29, 1924. The business of America was business in those days, with Calvin Coolidge piloting the steady ship of state. The ugly specter of depression had not materialized, except among the nation's farmers. Industry was doing fine, according to the latest news from Wall Street. Members of the Ku Klux Klan were prowling Middlesex and Essex Counties all that summer and the next, but Massachusetts Klansmen saved their threats for Catholics, and when the tough talk turned to rioting in nearby Burlington or Newton, the white knights found themselves outnumbered, stoned, and driven off the streets by raging Catholics who refused to submit to terrorism.

Back in Medford, if you felt inclined to worry, the cause was mostly personal.

Beth's parents never seemed to get along very well, although they kept producing children. Cleo Alvin Short built miniature golf courses for a living, riding the crest of a national fad that collapsed, like so much else, with the stock market crash of 1929. By early 1931 he had seen enough of his wife, Phoebe, and the girls—or some of them, at any rate. He took the oldest child, Virginia, with him when he left for California, running for his life and stopping only when another ocean barred his path. Virginia grew up on the West Coast and met her husband there. The couple moved to Berkeley and raised a family, while Cleo drifted back and forth between Vallejo and Los Angeles. He had a taste for liquor, working when he had to, to quench his thirst. As far as Cleo was concerned, his wife and daughters back in Medford had ceased to exist. If God had meant for fathers to support their children, he would have given every man on earth a private money tree.

The Great Depression was reality by 1931, and Phoebe Short had four mouths to feed. In time, despite her mom's best efforts, Beth displayed the symptoms of neglect. She was asthmatic, chewed her nails, and threw raging temper tantrums. More than anything, she dreamed of getting out—away from Medford, away from the Commonwealth of Massachusetts, away from New England.

Fame and fortune awaited her out west, in Hollywood. A child could see the magic, sitting in the darkness of a movie theater where giants laughed and cried, loved, sang and danced across the silver screen.

Beth knew the secret.

She had glimpsed her destiny.

On the morning of January 3, 1930, George Junior wired Gladys collect from Tucumcari, New Mexico: "Stranded here and need a little money. Please hurry. Waiting." In fact, while Gladys didn't know it at the time, he was in jail.

A second telegram came two weeks later, this time from Flagstaff, Arizona. It read: "Starting work first. Send clothes. Wire few dollars. Send clothes general delivery."

The same day, Georgie wrote a longer letter to explain himself.

Dear Mother,

I have met up with a young fellow from New Hampshire and he is working here. Him and I are sharing a cabin here and I start work the first of Febuary [*sic*] at $2.75 a day and board. My work will be about 4 miles away from the Grand Canyon of the Colorado. The is [*sic*] great country. Why I telegraphed for money is I need a pair of high shoes. My others are all gone. I know alot of people in this town and they are very nice. I have been to a couple of parties already.

A girl I got acquainted with is teaching me how to dance. I have clean shirts and things of my pardners to wear. He bought all the grub and we do our own cooking. The pimples on my face are all gone. We are having a dance here tomorrow night. My pardner is a peach. This is great country. I feel great but don't let anybody kid you about the west is tame. A cowpoke come in the other night and painted the town. I received that money from you when I was in New Mexico. The town [Tucumcari] is all Mexicans and the skunks wouldn't give me any place to sleep. In the jail there I couldn't get anything to eat for two days. That is why I telegraphed for money there.

But I need shoes now. There is three feet of snow here. I am wearing a pair of my pardners shoes but they are pretty small. I am getting a good job here. Will save up some money before I come home.

How is Babe an[d] Donald and the whole family? Please write. The address is Flagstaff, Arizona, General Delivery. I hope you send some clothes quick. Love to all.

Your Loving Son
George Knowlton

Six days later, on January 23, George Junior wrote again, with a slight change of plans.

Dear Mother,

I didn't keep on going because I like Arizona and I met a fellow here from home. Thanks for that money. I need clothes bad. I may go to California in the spring but I am going out on a ranch till then. I hope the house is nice and I hope Dad gets some good work. I cannot ride freights anymore because the brakemen here will throw you off, and cars cannot go because there's too much snow. It costs 20 dollars to ride from here into California. Maybe when I get that much I may go to Long Beach. You did not know that I got thrown of[f] a freight train and stayed in a hospitable [*sic*] with 3 broken ribs but I have got the tape off a long time ago. I wish I could be sending money home instead of asking for it.

> Your Loving Son
> George

As far as we can tell, George Junior did not make it to the West Coast on that occasion. When he wrote to Gladys next, on March 24, he made do with a penny postcard.

Dear Mother,
   I am coming home. Will be there about the 20th of April. When you write to me send the letters to Oklahoma City and send me a couple blankets and a piece of canvas so I won't freeze to death nights. Be sure and send them right away so they will be there when I do get there.

> George

Gladys spent twenty-two cents on an airmail letter to Georgie in Oklahoma City, but he never picked it up, and the envelope was returned to Massachusetts on April 7. Her firstborn's change of plans was noted in his next letter, undated and mailed from Halford, in northwestern Kansas.

Dear Mother and Dad,
   I had started home and Halford was on the highway so I dropped in on Bill. I asked Mildred if she knew me and she couldn't figure out who I was. But Bill looked up and said, Hello George. I am sorry I missed Mother's Day, but I was about 100 miles from any town during that week.
   I think I will stay here through the harvest. Bill has got me set up for the loading job at one of the wheat

elevators here [at] 5 dollars a day. I hope you don't miss me as much as I miss you. I know I didn't write much but I couldn't, and I didn't want to come looking like I did and have all the neighbors say well I told you he was a regular hobo. So when I come home I will look at least half way decent and have a few pennies. Bill's baby is seven years old now and pretty as a picture. Will you go to Carl Holstrom's and tell him to write and tell me why he didn't wait for me in Sayre, Okolohoma [sic]. Tell him I rode that immagrant [sic] car all the way into there. Will write soon.

Your loving son
George

Two months later, on June 6, there was another change of plans and scenery. This time the telegram came addressed to George Senior, from an army recruiting officer at Fort Logan, Colorado. The instructions were startling: "Wire government collect correct age your son George and your consent for his enlistment in the army."

In fact, Georgie had three weeks to go before his eighteenth birthday, and his passion for a uniform cooled off before the magic date arrived. On Wednesday, July 30, he cabled Gladys from Kansas City, Missouri: "Wire five dollars quick Western Union. Don't fail. Be home Tuesday."

Something apparently got lost in the translation, and Georgie sent a second urgent wire the following day: "Send money to Kansas City not Jefferson City. Waiting here."

The latest stipend from home got him as far as Cumberland, Maryland, where he ran out of steam and fell back on the kindness of strangers. On July 16, an agent for the Travelers Aid Society wired Gladys: "George F. Knowlton stranded in Cumberland. Shall we send him to his Uncle Ernest Bates in Philadelphia? Wire me Mr. Bates address collect."

No other records of George Junior's early travels have survived the intervening decades, but he often spoke about a ranch where he was once employed near Panhandle, Texas, the seat of Carson County.

And on rare occasions, with a trusted friend, he might discuss the first time that he killed a human being.

All we know about that homicide today is the account George Senior gave to Janice forty years after the fact, when she went home to see Gladys buried in 1971. According to his father, Georgie's victim was a black man, bludgeoned to death with a crowbar somewhere "in the South"—perhaps on a train, maybe not. George Senior did not specify a date or place, but he explained that Georgie was arrested by the local sheriff, then released into his father's custody on the assumption that the killing of a black man must have been "self-defense." George Senior kept the secret hidden from his wife, until one night when Georgie started talking in his sleep, and Gladys heard enough to make her fear he might someday be held accountable. Years later, when Jan discovered a box of her father's old letters in Beverly, Gladys was livid with fury.

"Don't you *ever* tell a soul about those letters," she commanded. "No one can *ever* know where he went in those days."

Unfortunately there appears to be no record of the homicide in question. Killings done in "self-defense" would not be marked as unsolved crimes or spared from systematic purges of police department files. A black man's death in 1930 did not rate headlines, and even if the case had been covered by the press, research would require a specific date. The FBI includes such states as Texas, Maryland, and Oklahoma in "the South" for purposes of crime reporting, but federal agents have no file on Georgie Knowlton in their archives. Many states are negligent in filing crime reports even today, and things were understandably much worse in the Depression. Even where we know the date and place of an arrest, as in New Mexico, no documents remain to indicate why Georgie was confined. We simply know that he was killing by the time he turned eighteen.

The nameless southern black man was his first victim.

He would not be the last.

4

"No Childhood Here"

> I cannot even plant a seed
> There is no time for growing
> I cannot even tell my need
> There is no time for knowing.
>
> I must be ready to move on
> To leave my toys and friends
> I cannot rest, I cannot play
> The fighting never ends.
>
> I cannot even ask for love
> My mother turned away
> My daddy's love is terrible
> And I'm too scared to play.
>
> There is no childhood here for me
> There is no place to hide
> It's like the pain that Jesus felt
> That made him glad he died.
>
> —Janice Knowlton, 1989

IT TAKES ALL KINDS, IN BEVERLY AS IN THE LARGER WORLD beyond. For every youngster cutting classes, learning to survive on guile and phony charm, there is another putting in the time with books and essays, faithfully completing chores at home. Most commonly, these two types move in different circles, but their paths may cross from time to time.

And sometimes opposites attract.

George Junior didn't know it yet, but he was on the verge of stumbling into love.

The story starts with trees. No special kind, just the sicklier the better. Kenneth Hatch could fix them—or at least explain his failures with scientific-sounding phrases. A professional tree surgeon, he came from the Worcester area sixty-odd miles west of Salem, but his work with ailing plant life often took him far afield. A run out to Beverly Farms was nothing special . . . until the day he met young Annie Larcom Standley.

If the facts are sparse on Kenneth Hatch's parentage, perhaps we know too much about that of his future bride. The name Larcom resulted from a maternal family link to Lucy Larcom, a poet best known for her memoirs, *A New England Girlhood,* published four years before her death in 1893. Annie's mother, Mary, died when Annie was a toddler. Her father, Rufus Standley, ran a livery stable, and he sent his only child to live with relatives, a quirky brother-sister act who occupied a stately home in exclusive Beverly Farms. Annie spent the rest of her young life there, in an atmosphere best described as eccentric. She grew up frail and timid, with the stature and demeanor of a frightened sparrow. Kenneth Hatch was just the opposite. At six feet two, he was large-boned and outspoken. His relationship with Annie, likewise, was the polar opposite of George and Gladys Knowlton's. He pampered her and treated her like a fragile child until the day he died.

What we now know of Kenneth Hatch suggests that his wife's childlike quality was probably the main attraction.

Annie gave her husband daughters, four in all, filling the house in Beverly Farms with little girls, which suited Kenneth fine. He didn't seem hung up on producing a son and thus perpetuating the male bloodline. Little girls were wonderful.

The first in line was Marjorie Lawrence, born at Beverly

Hospital on November 20, 1913. She was Daddy's pride and joy.

The Hatches were a Baptist clan, and Annie made a regular appearance at church every Sunday, but she shied away from any sort of crisis that involved her relatives or neighbors. Simple illness threw her into a panic, and funerals were far too grim for her to bear. When sickbed visitations were required, she begged off, claiming illness of her own, and little Marjorie would take her place at Kenneth's side. In some ways, wife and daughter had begun exchanging roles. And knowing Kenneth as we do today, it is impossible to say exactly where the line was drawn.

Whatever happened in that house, with one man and his troop of little girls, it happened quietly. There was no shouting, certainly no whippings of the sort that Georgie Knowlton would regard as standard fare. The Hatches never hit their children. They *explained,* sometimes in tedious detail, the difference between right and wrong.

And there were lessons by example.

Young Marjorie grew up with certain strengths—and weaknesses—atypical of other girls her age. She was a straight-A student, pretty, if a trifle overweight. Classmates remember her as courteous and shy, but she possessed a waspish tongue when roused to anger. She could skewer any target of her choice with verbal barbs and leave her victim wriggling in embarrassment. One of her daughters later described her as "a witch" when she waxed sarcastic.

Disgusted with her mother's frailty and the way in which it forced her to assume the adult role with Kenneth and her sisters, Margie sought to weed out any trace of weakness in herself. Still, there was one persistent failing she could never overcome. From puberty, she was attracted to the bad boys, smokers and drinkers, even though she neither smoked nor drank. It almost seemed that she was courting trouble.

A psychotherapist might find the straight-A student's yearning for a sleazy man instructive, in the light of modern knowledge. Was the woman-child rebelling against a home life that had stripped her youth away? Or was she simply looking for a man who measured up to Daddy when you glimpsed the soul behind his public face?

Ken Hatch was strict about protecting his young ladies. A prospective suitor found a double-barreled shotgun waiting for him when he came to call on one of Margie's sisters, and the young man beat a swift retreat. But Kenneth wasn't always there to man the barricades.

He missed the boat with Georgie Knowlton, and his oversight would cause no end of suffering for all concerned.

Abe Reles, once a heavy hitter for the syndicate in Brooklyn, sat down with a young D.A. in 1940 to explain the art of killing without conscience. "How did you feel when you tried your first law case?" he asked.

"I was rather nervous," the D.A. admitted.

"And how about your second case?"

The lawyer shrugged. "It wasn't so bad, but I was still a little nervous."

"And after that?" Reles asked.

"Oh, after that I was all right. I was used to it."

"You answered your own question," the triggerman said. "It's the same with murder. I got used to it."

And so did Georgie, given time.

More to the point, he *liked* it.

Another victim was one of Georgie's fellow workers at a Massachusetts foundry. Harsh words were exchanged, a punch was thrown, and Knowlton grabbed a shovel and swung it with deadly aim. Again, we have no date or name to pin the killing down, but he bragged about it sometimes, when he was in his cups, to friends and relatives he trusted.

"Self-defense," he said.

No charge, no record.

Beating men to death was fun for George Junior, no doubt about it, but it seems he felt that there was something missing. With a woman, he apparently decided, it would be much better. There were more things he could do, a greater range of feelings and reactions to examine.

Maybe next time.

At the moment he had stumbled into love.

We have no idea where or when he first laid eyes on Margie Hatch, but Georgie knew a challenge when he saw one. Denno and his other rowdy friends insisted it was hopeless. "She's a nice girl," they reminded George. "She wouldn't want a wild thing like you."

Marjorie later told her children that Georgie started to pursue her on a dare. He followed her to a night school typing class and crept into a back-row seat. A clown of sorts, he made so many wisecracks to the teacher and embarrassed Marge so badly that she quit the class.

Slick Georgie had her full attention now.

He asked her out, and she agreed to go. A real live bad boy on her doorstep. Kenneth left his shotgun in the closet, and Margie's sisters scrambled around to get their dainties off the wooden rack that stood beside an iron stove in the kitchen. Georgie smiled as he told them, "Aw, that's nothin' that I haven't seen before. I've got a sister."

They were a study in contrasts, Georgie and Marge. He was a boozer and a braggart, quick with his fists. She was quiet and serious most of the time, but not afraid to speak up for herself when he riled her. Georgie Knowlton was the only boy, the only man, Marge ever loved. He knew it, too, and played upon her weakness like a pro. One of his rare gifts was a puppy, christened Boo-Boo, that she cherished as a pet until the day George dumped it on the roadside in the middle of a desert, leaving it to die.

But she was hooked.

In September 1933, Georgie made an easy run across the state line to New Hampshire and came back with a marriage license in his pocket. "Marry me," he told her, "or you'll never see me again."

It was Margie's last real chance to save herself.

They drove to Plaistow, just across the state line, on September 24. Mahlon Keezer, the justice of the peace, performed the civil ceremony in a tiny flat behind his grocery store. With Kenneth Hatch and Gladys Knowlton to consider, plus the cost of setting up a home during the

Depression, George and Margie kept their wedding secret for the next six months. They stayed with their own families and consummated the relationship on dates until the truth came out.

George Senior was apparently the first to know, but there was little anyone could do about the marriage by that time. Marge never really felt at ease around her in-laws, viewing them in years to come as hypercritical, but they supported Georgie in his choice of a mate. George Senior even helped the newlyweds locate a flat on Cabot Street in Beverly, and threw in some secondhand furniture for good measure.

Home sweet home.

The honeymoon was over in a heartbeat.

Living with a man like Georgie Knowlton is as far removed from dating him as visiting the zoo is different from spending ten years naked in the jungle. One experience is tantalizing, an adventure, while the other bottoms out as life or death.

For Margie Knowlton, life with George became a waking nightmare, and it stayed that way for thirteen years. Abuse —including insults, rape, and battery—became a daily fact of life. George sometimes worked, typically in foundries, but his temper often cost him jobs, and he was sometimes fired for taking an unscheduled leave of absence when he felt like hunting deer. His poor working habits hardly mattered to Margie, since he spent most of any earned money on himself. He loved the nightlife and made no secret of his roving eye. The rent and other bills were frequently past due. If creditors were too insistent, Georgie found it easier to move than to pay his debts.

Marge had no household budget, in the normal sense. George kept food on the table, more or less, and she could save up for a housedress if she watched the pennies closely enough, but there was seldom anything left over. George might come home with a brand-new rifle or a set of tools, and he was never short of drinking money, but his bride knew all about depression on the home front.

Early in the marriage, Marge learned that George was cheating on her. The marginal discretion Georgie practiced in his killing never carried over to adultery. He was proud of his affairs, a strutting rooster. He seemed to believe that each new conquest proved his manhood, and it apparently made no difference to him if he had to pay for sex from time to time. In fact, he often bragged about the hot times he enjoyed with prostitutes.

Marge thought about repaying him in kind. She went out shopping, tried on dresses she could not afford, and talked about how sweet revenge would be. Each time, though, she returned the dresses to their hangers and went home alone. She never had the nerve to play her husband's game.

Or maybe she had too much class.

And then there was the baby to consider.

By the spring of 1934, Marge knew that she was pregnant. She was plagued by nausea the whole nine months, a pattern that repeated in her later pregnancies. George found her constant illness inconvenient. "Just my luck," he griped, "to have a wife who's always sick."

The pregnancy and illness did not stop him from slapping Marge around from time to time. On one occasion, at his parents' home, his sudden violence so infuriated sister Myra that she climbed up on the mantelpiece and threw herself on top of Georgie, pounding him with angry fists.

If Marge was hoping that a child would tame her husband, she had underestimated Georgie's selfishness. He celebrated David's* birth, of course—March 2, 1935—but only because he regarded it as one more badge of personal achievement.

And another mouth to feed.

The food was Marge's problem. George had other things to think about. His buddy Denno had departed Beverly for Melrose, eight miles distant. That meant extra driving time, new bars and new women, different foundries to investigate the next time George got canned for skipping work or fighting in the shop.

In early 1936 the Knowltons pulled up stakes on Cabot

Street and found a new place on Blaine Avenue. It was the first of many moves inspired by nagging creditors. The greedy bastards kept expecting George to pay his debts, for God's sake. What else could he do but run away?

By that time, Marge was feeling sick again. She had another baby on the way.

Janice Gail Knowlton was born at Beverly Hospital on January 8, 1937. It was a difficult delivery, and Marge spent two weeks recovering in the hospital. George took the baby home, and sister Myra, who had recently miscarried twins, volunteered as a wet nurse. She was none too gentle with the child that should have been her own, but that was life.

And life with George, by this time, was an ordeal that included infant sexual abuse.

Authorities are bitterly divided on the subject of what children may remember, even more so on the moment when they start remembering. Some experts swear that children have no memory at all before the age of four or five, a strange position that would seem to cancel out much of the normal learning process. Yet another school of thought maintains that children soak up everything from before birth, collecting first impressions in the womb and moving on from there. Devices have been patented for teaching foreign languages in utero, but we have yet to see hard evidence of their success.

The truth, perhaps, lies somewhere between the two extremes.

Jan Knowlton's early memories include an image of her father at cribside, jabbing his erection at her face.

We know that such things happen. Several thousand men are doing time around the country for molesting infants. Thousands more are on probation, some with dates for mandatory counseling, which will leave their records squeaky clean in one or two years' time. But those pathetic specimens were caught red-handed by adults. Their tiny victims cannot testify in court.

Do they remember? Do they *know?*

Marge Knowlton came home from the hospital a pale, emaciated woman. She was sick, off and on, for the next two years, beset by menstrual periods that were irregular, curiously frequent, and marked by heavy bleeding. She was also carrying a tapeworm, diagnosed belatedly, which helped to sap her strength.

And there was always George.

Another memory of Daddy's love, when Jan was roughly eighteen months of age: George standing over her, exposed, erect, intent on penetrating her. Marge screaming from the doorway, "Jesus, George, you'll kill her! She's only a baby!"

Relatives confirm that Margie briefly left her husband in the latter part of 1938. She could not stay away for long, though, because she had no money and her father did not want her children in his house. In time, George took her back. Forgiveness, or at least acceptance, was the order of the day.

In 1939 the family moved to Bartlett Street in Beverly, another dodge to throw the bill collectors off. It seemed to work. Two children and an ailing wife would be enough to put a crimp in most men's style, but Georgie kept up his rowdy lifestyle. If anyone suggested that he was neglecting things at home, he merely had to point at Marge, now pregnant with another child.

Daughter Evelyn* was born in late September. Georgie's house caught fire a short time later and the family moved in with his parents, pending relocation to another home. Young Janice was by then an active toddler—Marge sometimes called her Pillage, for the havoc she wreaked around the house—and she was picking up Georgie's coarse vocabulary. Gladys didn't know if she should laugh or scold her the first time Janice called her a "bish." In any case, she thought enough of Janice to insist that the two-year-old share her bed.

More memories of Gladys, fingers groping, probing in the dark. Impossible to prove, now that fifty years and more have passed. Impossible for Janice to ignore.

Ken Hatch, for his part, didn't mind a visit from the

grandkids now and then. He simply did not want them moving in to stay. His little girls were all grown up and married now with families of their own. He needed company, and it was a pleasure showing off his flower garden to little Janice. He showed her other things as well. If anybody heard her sobbing at the bottom of the garden or in Grandpa Kenneth's private bathroom, kept off-limits even to his wife, no one bothered to investigate. Who knows what makes a high-strung child burst into tears?

And Janice learned to go away.

Dissociation is the mind's escape hatch from unbearable reality. We may overdose on shock from time to time, and different victims cope with the experience in varied ways. Some die. A few emerge as monsters in their own right, causing trauma for a whole new cast of victims. Others learn to separate themselves and tuck the pain away, "forgetting" even as the flesh and soul are traumatized.

Repression and dissociation are established facts of life, though barely understood by modern medicine. Adrenaline and other hormones, triggered by emotional or physical sensation, clearly play a major role in triggering memories, but we are years away from comprehending the process. In the most extreme cases, when dissociation runs amok, dozens—or even hundreds—of alternate personalities may emerge from the psychic rubble.

All things considered, young Janice was lucky. She learned to survive without falling completely apart.

She learned to forget.

In 1940, George and Margie moved the kids to Wentzell Avenue in Beverly. It was another dodge, this one of short duration. Georgie's creditors were getting wise. A new technique was called for.

Near year's end he slipped across the state line to New Hampshire with the family in tow and put down temporary roots in Claremont, where he found a job with Ripley Brass. His wife was pregnant for the fourth time in six years, afflicted with the same near-constant nausea that had marked her other pregnancies. It seemed that she had barely recovered from Evelyn's birth, and now she had another baby on the way.

Georgie, of course, was no help at all. He worked when he had to, with time out for boozing and road trips. On Monday, February 17, he broke both ankles in an accident at Windsor, Vermont, ten miles northwest of Claremont. The circumstances are vague, but we know he was treated at Windsor Hospital and released. Weak ankles would plague him for the rest of his life, but the cowboy boots he always wore helped Georgie get around all right.

A third daughter, Prudence,* was born to George and Marjorie in Claremont on May 8, 1941. Marge took more time recovering from each successive birth, and Georgie groused about her poor health and about the way she "let things go" around the house on River Street. His son was old enough to be in school by now, but that could wait until the fall.

Certain random killers, we are told by FBI psychologists, are driven out in search of victims by increasing pressure in their private lives—an accident or illness, trouble on the job or in a marriage, the arrival of a child.

George Knowlton had it all. Five mouths to feed. A sickly wife. Sore ankles. Mounting debts that clamored to be paid. A job he barely tolerated at the best of times.

He was a walking time bomb, ready to explode . . . but he was also wise enough to move ground zero well away from home.

It was a maxim handed down through generations of survivors, going back to prehistoric times: You don't shit where you eat.

He had been lucky twice before, but this time he had something more ambitious on the drawing board. More satisfying. Self-defense would never wash for what he had in mind.

The predator was learning.

It was time to hit the road.

* * *

It is a hundred miles over open highways from Claremont down to Lynn and Salem, Massachusetts. Nothing to a driver with a heavy foot and one eye on the rearview mirror, watching out for patrol cars. Poke along at fifty and the drive can take two hours. Push yourself a little, you can shave it down to ninety minutes, maybe less.

If you've got family in the neighborhood, there's no great hurry heading back.

A friend of Frances Cochran once described the nineteen-year-old bookkeeper as "death on auto rides." She had a passion for cars and never missed an opportunity to ride in one. She took the bus each morning from her parents' home on Webster Street in Lynn to the Dudley Leather Company. Each evening after work the same bus brought her back, and Frances walked the few blocks from the bus stop to her door.

Unless she got a lift along the way.

At 6:00 P.M. on Thursday, July 17, 1941, Frances Cochran disembarked from her bus at the corner of Chatham and Marianna Streets. She dropped a letter in the corner mailbox and began to walk down Marianna toward her home on Webster. Coming from the opposite direction was a square-backed car, described in press reports as "ancient," black with yellow trim and wooden spokes. The driver noticed Cochran, tapped his brake, made a U-turn in the middle of the street, and pulled up beside her. Bystanders saw her smile, approach the car, climb in, and close the door. The car turned onto Chatham Street, away from Webster and her home. The girl was never seen alive again.

Descriptions of the driver were inconsistent, and no one got a clear look at his face, but there was general agreement that he was a "dark" or "swarthy" man with "slicked-back hair." His age was anybody's guess.

Cochran's parents were worried by 7:00 P.M. and frantic by 9:30 when police arrived at the house. Frances Marie, a 1940 graduate of Lynn English High School, was a person of regular hours and habits. Her reputation was "beyond even the whisper of reproach." A fraction over five feet tall, she tipped the scales at a petite 100 pounds. Most men, detectives knew, would have no difficulty overpowering a girl her size.

Harold Cochran was still sitting up, waiting for his daughter at 3:00 A.M. on Friday when a car pulled up outside the house. He went to have a closer look and found two men in the vehicle, one behind the wheel, the other seated in the rear. As Harold approached the car, the driver told him, "She's in back." The second man replied, "No, Frances is in front." With that, the car sped off, and while police rolled out to mount a guard on Webster Street, the strangers were content to play their eerie little joke and slip away unrecognized. If Harold described the car or visitors in any detail, the descriptions have been lost with time.

At 1:00 P.M. on Sunday, July 20, local radio stations broadcast an appeal from Cochran's parents to their missing daughter: "If you hear this broadcast, Frances, come home or telephone at once. If there are any explanations, do not hesitate."

Forty minutes later, an unknown man telephoned the radio station. "If you want the body," he declared, "it's off the Danvers road, off Highland Avenue, at the Swampscott line." The caller left no name, and all police could say about the man was that he spoke in "better than passable English."

Two Swampscott patrolmen drove out to the site, a kind of lovers' lane almost directly opposite the Moose Lodge at the corner of Highland Avenue and Swampscott Road. They found a woman's shoe beside the road and spent the best part of an hour searching the adjacent field before they found what they were looking for.

The body was concealed within a thicket, lying on its back, a stone beneath the battered skull. The woman's face was beaten to a pulp, bone showing through a pair of gashes in her forehead just above the eyes. A number of her teeth were broken, and an inch-thick swamp alder stick was protruding from her mouth, shoved deep into her throat. Her open jacket was pulled up beneath her armpits, and her blouse was torn, exposing bruised and lacerated flesh. Her skirt and slip were bunched up around her hips. Grass and twigs had been stuffed into her vagina. Scorch marks on the victim's shoulders, neck, and chin suggested that an attempt had been made to burn her body. Every inch of skin the officers could see bore witness to "a furious assault." A quantity of sand, identified as foreign to the dump site, had been sprinkled over Cochran's face and breasts. Police identified the body from the initials inside her high school ring.

The coroner initially said Cochran had been suffocated, possibly by choking on the stick, but later he agreed she could have died from the ferocious beating she'd received. In fact, she had been dead a day or two when found. The precise time of death could not be determined, but the slow rate of decomposition told authorities her body had been stored in a cool place, perhaps a refrigerator, while the killer thought his next move through.

Police Chief Edward Callahan predicted an early arrest. "No stone must be unturned," he told the press, "to bring the perpetrators of this foul deed to justice." The first of many suspects in the case, described in media reports as a Lynn resident in his thirties, was found sleeping in his car, a hundred yards from the old field artillery stables on Highland Avenue, at 8:30 A.M. on Monday, July 21. Under questioning, he told police that he had spent the weekend with a couple in New Hampshire and had parked along the road when he became too tired to drive. Authorities reviewed his story and released him. Neither he nor his New Hampshire friends were ever publicly identified.

Another suspect was a young married man who had given Cochran a ride home from her bus stop several days before she disappeared. Police were fishing, however, and he did not match the vague description of the driver seen with Frances on the seventeenth. In fact, detectives never came close to finding the killer despite several arrests, some 1,900 interviews, and more than twenty false confessions in the case.

The Frances Cochran murder bears such a strong resemblance to the Dahlia case, five years and six months later, that it might be called a dress rehearsal for the main event. Both victims were attractive young brunettes, three years apart in age. Both suffered lethal head wounds and extensive mutilation of their bodies. Both were found with vegetation stuffed inside their genitals. Both corpses were kept in cold storage for days before being discarded. In each case the killer was moved to communicate with local media, "assisting" the authorities.

And each crime had a living witness who remained unknown to the police for many years.

It was two weeks short of half a century before Jan Knowlton started to recover memories of Frances Cochran's murder. The circumstances of that breakthrough are recounted elsewhere in these pages, but the substance of her memory is pertinent to our examination of the Cochran case.

In January 1993, Jan recalled a house almost devoid of furniture, lace curtains covering a front-door window. In her memory the living room is absolutely vacant, but a bed remains in the adjacent sleeping room. Jan's father lies atop a dark-haired girl or woman, having intercourse. The object of his lust is fully dressed, her clothing rumpled, disarranged. Jan stares, her very presence in the open doorway a rebuke. Perhaps she speaks.

"I can do as I damn well please," Georgie snarls at his daughter. "Keep your damn mouth shut if you know what's good for you."

Jan at four and a half years old, had already learned the lesson of silence, driven home by the years of abuse.

When George is finished, he dismounts and drags the woman off the bed. The sheet and bedspread come off with her, pooling at his feet. He stands above her prostrate body chewing on a toothpick. Still unsatisfied, he comes for Jan and rapes her on the cold linoleum floor.

Another memory fragment: While driving, Georgie stops along the roadside and surveys a meadow bright with butterflies. It seems to please him, and he drags his silent victim out the driver's side of the car. Jan trails them from the roadster down a gentle slope into the field. There is no traffic on the highway. The blue sky darkens as they work their way into the shadows of a thicket. Georgie takes his time hoisting up the woman's skirt and opening his fly.

"Janice, bring me a stick!"

She hurries to obey and drags a long branch, taller than she is, back to the thicket. Georgie curses Janice for her industry, but he makes do. He snaps off a length of six or seven inches and turns his back on Janice. Long moments after he is finished, he remains beside the body, seated on the grass, palms pressed against his ears. He bears a vague resemblance to the hear-no-evil monkey.

Janice listens carefully, but she cannot detect the sound her father seems so desperate to avoid hearing.

A nagging inner voice perhaps.

A young girl's dying screams.

Frances Cochran's death was not the only local mystery in that July of 1941. Irene O'Brien vanished from her Salem home at 30 Butler Street on Independence Day, but husband John let ten days pass before he notified police. The twenty-nine-year-old bleached blonde had slipped away before, John told investigators, but she always came home in a day or two.

This time was different.

The ex-waitress was petite, like Frances Cochran: five feet four, 114 pounds, with light complexion. She was last seen dressed in black from head to foot and carrying a multicolored purse. Her wristwatch was engraved with the initials A.M.B.

And that was all.

Irene O'Brien had evaporated. Salem officers decline to comment on her case today, perhaps because the ancient files have been misplaced, and there was precious little evidence to start with. There is nothing in the local press to indicate that she was ever found or seen again.

It was a coincidence, no doubt, that Georgie Knowlton and his brood would move to Butler Street in 1943 and settle less than two blocks from Irene O'Brien's home, at number 49.

Irene's family was fortunate, at that. They could pretend Irene was still alive and happy somewhere, living out a private fantasy.

Across the county line in Reading, eight miles west of Salem, relatives of Constance Shipp were not allowed that luxury.

The fifteen-year-old Reading High School junior vanished on July 15, 1941, two days before the Cochran murder, but her fate remained unknown until the night of Saturday, July 19, when a phone call led investigators to a Baptist church one block from where the missing teen resided with her family. The church and parsonage were locked, the pastor was on vacation, and police were forced to kick the door in. They found Constance lying naked in the kitchen, bludgeoned, hacked, and mutilated with a knife. An unnamed teenage "problem child" was fingered as a suspect by the neighbors, briefly held for questioning, and finally released.

No suspects.

No apparent motive, other than demented sadism.

Again, the case remains unsolved.

Police in Lynn were looking for an older square-backed car with yellow trim and wooden spokes, and Georgie Knowlton had one for a while. We know about the car from relatives who have described it and because it shows up in a snapshot of the Knowlton children taken in New Hampshire. In the photo, Janice, Evelyn, and David stand before a fence, with shrubs and what appears to be a horse behind them. Farther back, half hidden at the bottom of a grassy slope, a square-backed car waits.

That photograph was taken in September 1941, a few days after David was belatedly enrolled in school. What happened to the car beyond that point is anybody's guess. In later years it would become an article of faith that Georgie had no car while living in New Hampshire. David still recalls a trip he made to Salem with his father in a horse-drawn wagon, further indicating that the Knowltons were no longer mechanized.

But photographs don't lie—not without a sizable investment in technology. The square-backed car existed two months after Frances Cochran's death, Irene O'Brien's disappearance, and the butchery of Constance Shipp. It disappeared sometime that fall, after which George Junior did his best to rewrite history, pretending there had never been a car at all.

For all intents and purposes, he pulled it off.

The Knowlton clan moved back to Massachusetts in the latter part of 1942 or early 1943. They settled first on Tremont Street in Salem, later moving to Butler Street in the vicinity of Gallows Hill. George started working at the Leonard Iron Foundry, but it was the same old story. He would take off on a whim, usually for hunting trips, and he was tough to get along with when he did show up for work—loud arguments and scuffles on the line, George hassling his supervisor, chasing him around the plant with murder in his heart.

He lost one job, then another. Finally, no ironworks in the neighborhood would take him on. They knew his temper and his tricks. He might be skillful at his trade, a specialist of sorts, but he was too much trouble.

It was much the same at home. He still had trouble keeping up with debts, and he was none too thrilled with Marge's latest pregnancy. Another daughter, Marjorie, was born at Beverly Hospital on September 20, 1943. She came into the world with a defective heart and would be nicknamed Midgie—as in "midget"—because of her diminutive size. Hospital records note her mother's history of ten-day menstrual periods, with barely two weeks in between the bouts of heavy bleeding. A physician's note describes Marge Knowlton as a "not too intelligent woman worn out from frequent menstruation and childbearing." There was also a passing mention of chronic anemia.

The price of loving Georgie.

On the home front, Georgie had refined mistreatment of his children to a minor art form. "I brought you into this world," he would tell them, quoting Mother Gladys, "and I can send you back where you came from." It became a sport for him to wait, catch one of them in a happy moment, and then reach out to slap the smile away. If they enjoyed a pet, he killed it. Periodically he collected their special toys in the yard and burned them. One item that infuriated Georgie was a Bible Janice had received at Sunday school, with the inscription: "For Janice. Sin will keep you from this Bible, or this Bible will keep you from sin."

She scorched her fingers trying to retrieve it from the fire.

Phil Knowlton, a paternal uncle, came to Georgie's rescue, wangling him a job at the McAdams dairy. Georgie drove a horse and wagon, making door-to-door deliveries. The family moved into the crowded second floor of a three-story house on Hollingsworth Street in Lynn, where they had free access to storage in the basement. School records indicate that they moved on January 18, 1944.

The milk delivery job could easily have been an ego-buster, but it had fringe benefits. George serviced randy housewives on his route and made some lasting friends besides. The Radison* and Cardran clans, in particular, opened up new vistas for a man of Georgie's wit and bogus charm.

Attractive Nancy Radison respected George and viewed him with affection, noting that she was the only housewife on his route he never tried to "put the make on." As it happened, Georgie was more interested in Nancy's sister-in-law, Kathleen Harlow Cardran, known to everyone as Kay. A busty blue-eyed redhead with a fiery temper and an endless thirst for alcohol, Kay had married a Lynn police-man and borne his daughter, but the marriage failed. She was on the rebound when she met Pete Cardran and they tied the knot. It was a shaky marriage, and Georgie took advantage of the situation to establish Kay as one of several mistresses. Pete's brother Bob, a harelipped alcoholic, fell in step with Georgie as a new best friend and sycophant who would not shrink from helping with a bit of dirty work from time to time.

The new affair with Kay would last for years and ultimately destroy his marriage, but Georgie never limited his options. He would drive as far as Troy, New York, to gamble and consort with prostitutes, and he was always on the make for young girls in his own backyard. One afternoon in 1944, Jan caught him in the sack with a young woman with alabaster skin and raven hair. He drove her from the room with curses, and Jan found the incident easy to forget, as she forgot so many other dreadful things.

She would recall the young brunette years later.

A familiar face.

In Medford, Beth Short had come to the end of her rope. Massachusetts was killing her. Her asthma had become so severe that she was hospitalized in 1940 for empyema surgery to drain pus from her lungs. Worse than any illness, though, her family and home were stifling. Beth's sisters recall her erratic mood swings—"gay and carefree one moment, in the depths of despair another."

The classic symptoms of manic depression—or child abuse.

We have no proof that Beth Short was molested as a child, but she had all the classic symptoms of a victim: she was angry and rebellious at home; prone to screaming tantrums and mood swings; asthmatic; anxious for the day when she could flee and put miles between herself and what she saw as an oppressive home environment; dwelling in a realm of fantasy. The more conclusive symptoms—codependent bonding with abusive males and sexual abuse of others younger than herself—would only be revealed in later years, when she was on her own in California.

Polite society did not discuss such problems in those days, but there were definitely child-molesters in the neighborhood. George Knowlton, an active pedophile throughout his life, lived no more than six or seven miles removed from

Beth in Salem by the time she entered Medford High School. Georgie's closest friend and fellow baby-raper, Freddie Denno, had been living just across the state line in Melrose since early 1934, and Medford's foundries would have lured Knowlton in his constant trek from one job to another.

Is it too much to suggest that Georgie might somehow have found Beth in those early days? She already fit his classic victim profile: slender, pale, brunette, developing a voluptuous body in her teens. And later, when they openly dated around Los Angeles, Beth would refer to Georgie's Massachusetts roots in conversations with her friends.

Could Beth have been the dark-haired woman-child whom Janice found in bed with Daddy late one afternoon in Lynn? We know that Georgie took his pleasure when and where he could, without regard to sex, race, or age. His partner on that steamy afternoon could well have been some other adolescent girl. It hardly matters in the long run.

Her subsequent behavior in Los Angeles suggests that *someone* was abusing Beth. There is no solid proof that Georgie Knowlton was to blame. We only know that he was ready, willing, and available.

Beth should have been a senior in high school by the end of 1941, but illness had held her back, and she was still a sophomore when she said farewell to Medford High. She headed south, to give her lungs a rest in Florida. There was a war on, and Miami had a bustling army air corps base nearby. No shortage of employment for a bright, attractive girl. Beth fell in love with pilots, as a group and individually, but it was difficult to pin one down when they were always shipping out to Europe or the vast Pacific theater.

Frustration and a longing for the West moved Beth to reach out to her father in the spring of 1942. He was working in a shipyard in Richmond, California, and he sent her bus fare for the trip. They "set up housekeeping," in Cleo's words, but Beth was not cut out to be a maid. She ran around with men, refused to keep the house as clean as Cleo would have liked, and pestered him for spending money.

Sometime in the last part of December or the early days of January 1943, Cleo kicked her out.

She made her way to Lompoc, west of Santa Barbara, where the Sixth Armored Division was training at Camp Cooke. No pilots there, but Beth had reached the point where almost any uniform would fit the bill. The press would later speak of her "hysterical" determination to become a military bride while the war was still in progress, and her actions seem to bear that judgment out, but she could also wear a different face at times.

In January 1943, Beth introduced herself to Inez Keeling at the Camp Cooke post exchange. "I was won over all at once by her almost childlike charm and beauty," Keeling later said. "She was one of the loveliest girls I had ever seen, and the most shy." Inez put Beth in touch with PX manager Ralph Aylesworth, who immediately hired her as a clerk. According to Inez, Beth shied away from dating soldiers, would not flirt at work, and "never went out nights." Instead, she came off sounding almost paranoid about her health, convinced by eastern doctors that she was a candidate for terminal tuberculosis.

Still, despite her maidenly behavior, Beth was not entirely unavailable to men in uniform. That summer she was voted Cutie of the Week, an item in the camp newspaper citing Beth as "a main reason for the steady increase of business at PX 1." There were reports of threats and violence from a sergeant "she was living with." Beth filed complaints with the commanding officer, and the problem was solved when the sergeant went overseas. Reports of her abrupt departure from the army base are vague and contradictory, but rumors spread that she fled for her life after being beaten by a soldier. Beth kept in touch with Inez Keeling for a while, then disappeared.

Another friend of Beth's from camp was Mary Strader, then a member of the Women's Army Corps. Beth lived with Mary and her husband, Carl, in Santa Barbara for a short time after leaving the PX. The Straders later added their votes to the list of those who claimed Beth stayed at home most nights, avoiding dates with men.

It must have been another Beth Short, then, who lived with Vera Green in West Cabrillo Beach, a Santa Barbara suburb, in September 1943. The "new" Beth had more in common with Cleo Short's view of his boy-crazy daughter than with the straitlaced virgin from Camp Cooke. She loved a night out with the boys, especially if there was liquor on the table.

On September 23, Beth was arrested in Santa Barbara, along with a girlfriend and two soldiers, and charged with drinking under age. As a juvenile, she got off with probation and a strong judicial warning to go home. Before she caught the eastbound train, Beth spent some time with Mary Unkefer, a Santa Barbara policewoman who had been present when she was arrested. As Unkefer recalled her houseguest, "She was very good looking, with beautiful dark hair and fair skin. She dressed nicely and was a long way from being a barfly."

And yet, Beth could strut her stuff when she felt the urge. Unkefer noted the tattoo, a stylish rose, that graced the girl's left thigh. Looking back on those days in the wake of Beth's murder, Unkefer would say, "She loved to sit so that [the tattoo] would show."

Beth made it back to Medford safe and sound, apparently relieved to be at home. She wrote to Mary Unkefer several times, stating in one letter: "I'll never forget you. Thank God you picked me up when you did."

The feeling may have been sincere, but it was short on staying power. Winter came again, and Beth went looking for the sun in Florida. She waited on tables in Miami, as before, and tried again to snag herself a pilot.

One who caught her eye was Gordon Fickling, a lieutenant in the U.S. Army Air Corps. He and Beth appeared to hit it off, but Hitler wouldn't wait, and Fickling was dispatched to Europe. Beth was faithful to him, in her fashion, but she soon began to shop around.

Lieutenant Stephen Wolak was another likely prospect. When the army shipped him out, Beth put her hopes and dreams on paper, shooting for the moon. The answer she received from Wolak took the wind out of her sails:

> When you mentioned marriage in your letter, Beth, I got to wondering about that myself. Seems like you have to be in love with someone before it's a safe bet. Infatuation is sometimes mistakenly accepted for true love which can never be.
>
> Love lingers on if properly nurtured, while infatuation is soon dispelled through adverse circumstances. I know whereof I speak because my ardent love soon cooled off and left me wondering how I could ever have felt that way.

Paul Rosie was a bit more tactful, but he put the same message across in answer to one of Beth's passionate missives. "Your letter took me completely by surprise," he wrote. "Yes, I've always had the feeling that we had a lot in common and that we could have meant a lot to each other if only we had been together more often. It's nice to receive a warm, friendly letter such as yours."

In 1944 Beth was back in California, following her alternate obsession—movie stardom—to the very heart of Hollywood. The details of her second visit are obscure, a single witness placing Beth in California. Police accept her presence in L.A. at that time as a fact.

Their source was Arthur Curtis James, who told investigators he was sketching women in a Hollywood saloon sometime in August 1944 when Beth showed interest in his work and they struck up a conversation. Thus began a three-month "friendship," during which Beth posed for James on several occasions. He lost track of her in early November, however, when he was arrested in Tucson as "Charles B. Smith" for violating the Mann Act—transporting women across state lines for immoral purposes. The federal law, while sometimes used against individuals, was passed in 1910 as a means of curbing organized prostitution, the infamous white slave racket. James later told the press that his arrest and subsequent conviction had no link to his relationship with Short, but this remains the first known instance of her keeping company with pimps. It would not be the last.

With winter coming on and Arthur James in jail, Beth drifted back to Florida where she found another waitress job and more pilots. Major Matt Gordon was the pick of the litter, just back from duty in China, sporting an Air Medal with fifteen oak-leaf clusters. Beth seemed to think that she and Gordon were engaged when he shipped out to India. Her letters from the early months of 1945, addressed to Gordon overseas, leave no doubt of that.

My Sweetheart,

I love you, I love you, I love you. Sweetheart of all my dreams.

Darling, those are the words of a new song in the States and believe me when I say that it suits me just to a T.

Oh, Matt, honestly, I suppose when two people are in love as we are our letters sound out of this world to a censor. I don't care, though, if the whole wide world knows it. . . .

It is going to be wonderful, darling, when this is all over. You want to slip away and be married. We'll do whatever you wish, darling. Whatever you want, I want. I love you and all I want is you. . . .

Yes, I have dated since I have seen you last. But most of them disgusted me. Naturally there are exceptions, but you are the only one that interests me. Now that you have asked me to be your wife I do not date. I want you to believe me because I'd never tell you anything that wasn't true. I have faith and trust in you, and always want you to have it that way with me. . . .

No other man could take your place, so please keep loving me. I want you so. God bless you, darling. I love you. All the love in the world.

Beth

A month later the relationship was still on track, at least in Beth's imagination.

My Darling Matt,

I have just received your most recent letter and clippings. And, darling, I can't begin to tell you how happy and proud I am. Darling, I have been waiting for several days for a letter and had begun to think that you had forgotten me. I know different now and I am pleased. . . .

Now that I know you love me there could never be another man meant for me. Darling, I'll always have faith in you because there isn't another person I know who is as thoughtful, kind and considerate.

Darling, of course I'll be waiting when you come home. I'll wait, no matter how long, because my life can never be complete without you. . . .

Yes, I'm yours if you want me, Matt, and I'm praying that you won't change your mind when you come home. I'm so much in love with you, Matt, that I live for your return, and your beautiful letters, so please write when you can and be careful, Matt, for me. I'm so afraid! I love you with all my heart.

Beth

In Medford, Phoebe Short was told that Major Gordon and her daughter were engaged. Beth spread the story everywhere she went, but it appears that she was reading too much into Gordon's letters. One of the assorted clippings she received, from Gordon's family in Colorado, was a wedding announcement, with another woman listed as the bride. The final item, sent by Gordon's mother, was a War Department telegram reporting his death in India. Beth kept both items, crossing out the name of Matt's wife on the wedding clipping. Instead of his fiancée, she began to call herself his widow.

Waiting. Looking for another prospect, somewhere down the line.

Georgie Knowlton did his share of hunting, too. Not always after deer.

Two days before the birth of his fifth child, on Saturday the eighteenth of September, 1943, thirty-eight-year-old Harriet Anderson disappeared from East Lynn. A widow of seven years, the devoted mother of a ten-year-old son, she failed to return from an outing on Saturday night, and her aunt, Alice Flynn, alerted police. Four days later, Frank Vazza was digging clams in the Oak Island district, below a railroad trestle, when he found the missing woman's corpse washed up on shore. No cause of death was ever published, but investigators viewed the case as a homicide. Unfortunately they had nothing in the way of clues or suspects, and the crime remains unsolved.

It is a coincidence, perhaps, that Harriet Anderson not only shared a given name with Gladys Harriet Knowlton but also ran a beauty parlor in her home.

George Junior lived in Salem at the time, two miles away, but we have no proof that Georgie Knowlton was involved in Anderson's death. Years later, Harriet Anderson's daughter, Prudence, would collect press clippings on the case, noting the resemblance of her own mother to Grandmother Knowlton. And again we have the standard pattern of imploding stress: another mouth to feed, the sickly wife, George Junior's inability to hold a job, the proximity of parents who were hypercritical, at best.

If our information about the events of 1943 is speculative, the facts concerning Georgie's kill for 1944 are not. Jan's memories of the event are clear, preserved like buried fossils, finally unearthed in 1989 and 1990: It is fall or winter, early darkness. Georgie is cruising with his daughter on the seat beside him, tall enough to see across the dashboard. Up ahead, she spies a figure in the roadway, gaping at the car, eyes wide with fear as Georgie stamps on the accelerator. There is a jolting impact, and he leaves the engine running as he hurries out to retrieve his trophy and dumps the body on the floor behind his seat.

The victim may have been a woman. Jan remembers wavy hair, a flannel shirt, and slacks. Back home on Hollingsworth Street, he carts the corpse downstairs. The furnace glows with heat, but Georgie cannot risk cremating his victim; the reek of burning flesh would spread throughout the house. The basement floor is dirt. He grabs a shovel, digs a grave, and rolls the body in, face down.

Jan watches in a daze. Her father does not yet grasp the concept of dissociation. He relies on fear to keep her silent, make her an accomplice to the crime.

He drags her to the furnace, opens up the door to let her see the glowing coals within, and tells her this will be her final resting place if she betrays him.

Janice gives her word, but it is not enough. George draws his knife and holds the razor edge against her tiny wrist. "I'll cut your hand off if you ever write a word about this. Do you hear me, bitch?"

She heard and understood. There was no point in taking chances. Little Janice willed herself to be left-handed, just in case. That seemed to do the trick.

George Junior dug at least two other unmarked graves in 1944, but they were not for murder victims. He was planting his children.

Marjorie's sixth pregnancy in ten years was too much for her body to bear, and she miscarried at home on Hollingsworth Street. George couldn't see the sense in shelling out good money to an undertaker when the baby wasn't even born, for pity's sake. He had a shovel in the basement and a spacious backyard with flower beds. He did the job himself.

The other funeral that season took place in a marsh outside of Beverly—another infant, Jan recalls, but not her mother's. She believes the child was Georgie's, from a mistress on his route. Another premature delivery, no records to incriminate the busy milkman. It was better that way, all around. No costly child support or extra tension in the family.

By that time, George was getting restless, yearning to be on the road. The Radisons and Cardrans, eight or nine of them in all, had pulled up stakes and moved to southern California, settling in Long Beach and Artesia. Georgie missed his friends, and he could feel the lure of the West Coast—a dream of adolescence unfulfilled.

And by early 1945, Marge was pregnant yet again, the morning sickness dragging on through afternoon and evening, never letting up. Another mouth to feed, if this one managed to survive.

George Junior needed room to breathe. In March he started driving west alone, to find them all a brand-new lease on life.

Route 66. The name had magic even then, before the ballad and the TV show. A highway stretching out from coast to coast. A man could lose himself out there—or find himself, if he was so inclined.

A picture postcard made its way to Lynn from Desert Center in Riverside County, forty miles west of the Arizona line. Postmarked on March 16, the card displayed a donkey standing in the middle of an arid wasteland, with the caption "Greetings from a Lonesome Jassack." On the flip side, Georgie wrote: "Dear Marge, This card just about tells with a glance how I feel right now. Wish you were already on your way."

George Junior kept on driving, reached Los Angeles at last, and knew that he had found his happy hunting ground. The Radisons and Cardrans were delighted to see him. Kay made Georgie welcome in a very special way.

He set a record driving back to Massachusetts. In North Salem, Shirley Durkee—age fifteen, five feet seven, blond, 127 pounds—went missing from her home on April Fool's Day. Her parents waited two days to alert police.

Another cipher in the limbo of the lost.

School records indicate that Janice Knowlton and her family left Lynn on April 27, 1945. They drove straight through to California, Georgie serving as their tour guide all the way. In Oklahoma there were mountains where, he told them, redskins still came home to die. A little farther west, he "accidentally" forgot the dog and then refused to turn the car around and pick him up. So much for Boo-Boo. The dog was getting old, and they could always find another one in California.

They were headed for the land of golden opportunity.

5

Open Season

> *Murderers, in general, are people who are consistent,*
> *people who are obsessed with one idea and nothing else.*
>
> —Ugo Betti, *Struggle Till Dawn*

ORANGE COUNTY IS THE SIAMESE TWIN OF LOS ANGELES, IRREVO-
cably joined at the hip and subject to most of L.A.'s passing
fancies, yet still as different as night from day. Orange
County is conservative, while L.A. is usually described as
liberal. For over thirty years the quality of politics in Orange
has been a standing joke, the province of John Birchers and
Ku Klux Klansmen. Even Disneyland's creator has been
lately branded as a closet Nazi with a strong right-handed ax
to grind.

There was no Disneyland in May of 1945 when Georgie
Knowlton brought his family to Westminster, four miles
southwest of Anaheim and equidistant from the coast. They
moved into a house on the 7000 block of Texas Street,
paying $50 a month against a purchase price of $2,530. The
place came furnished, more or less, and had two bedrooms,
a knotty pine interior, a detached garage with double doors,
a loft, and yet another tiny sleeping room. They had no
telephone, and any mail went to a post office box, but that
was fine. The smallish yard out back included several trees.
George Junior charmed his way into a local banker's pocket,
and the place was theirs.

Jan's first two friends in Westminster were neighbors Lupe and Johnny Zapata. They made her feel at home, and Jan was puzzled when the other Anglo kids on Texas Street warned her not to play with Mexicans. She had no way of knowing, at the time, how race preyed on the southern California mind. A short two years before her family moved from Lynn, Los Angeles had been the scene of bloody "zoot suit" riots in which Anglo servicemen assaulted innocent Hispanics in the streets. LAPD had jailed the battered victims on fabricated charges. Hoover School, where Jan attended classes briefly in the fall of 1945, had been reserved exclusively for "spics" until the year before, when it was grudgingly desegregated by the county. As it was, the taunts and insults of her Anglo neighbors only made Jan more determined to associate with the Zapatas. They had much in common, she decided: Jan felt like an outcast, too.

George Junior got himself another foundry job and used his free time at the plant to turn out cast-iron pieces of erotica. Marge tried to hide them from the children and her neighbors, but she wasn't always successful. One of her husband's most elaborate creations was an ashtray sculpted to depict a naked man and woman having oral sex, their privates painted crimson.

To a casual observer, life might have seemed to be getting better for the Knowltons, but the same old Georgie lurked behind a smiling mask. He was, in Marge's words, "a house bastard and a street angel," spending freely to impress his friends, deliberately ignoring such necessities as clothing and vaccinations. He always seemed to have enough cash for hunting trips or nights out on the town, but there was no heat in the house come winter, and his children's only new clothes were gifts from relatives on birthdays or at Christmas. David slept in the garage, when it was safe; some nights, when Georgie was in a rage, he was reduced to hiding in a neighbor's shed or sleeping in an open field.

George had his list of rules, and one of them was bedtime silence. "Not a peep," he often warned the girls, inspiring them to huddle underneath their blankets, peeping like a brood of chicks. If Georgie had to silence them twice, his threat was more explicit: "Shut up and go to sleep, or I'll blister your asses."

Prudence's sketchy memories of Westminster include the night she woke to fearful growling from her parents' bedroom. Moving through the dark on tiptoe, she was greeted by her mother at the doorway and hustled back to bed. "It's just your father snoring," Marge explained. "Go back to bed." And Prudence heard the implicit threat: *before he catches you.*

And there was the yard work. One day, on a whim, George handed Jan a pair of scissors and instructed her to cut the grass. She spent all day on hands and knees fastidiously trimming until well past dusk. Her hands were blistered when she finished, but she did her best to make her daddy proud.

Two great-aunts lived nearby and visited the house from time to time. They frightened Prudence, who, at four years old, already feared that her mother would escape from Georgie one day soon and leave her kids behind. Suppose the great-aunts with their scowling faces took her place? It was a terrifying prospect. Prudence often hid and sulked while they were visiting. Sometimes she crept beneath the table where they sat and pinched them, yanking hairs out of their legs.

Around this same time, George—or someone—started digging holes in the backyard. The pits seemed huge to four-year-old Prudence, "like big trenches an adult could fit into." Eight-year-old Janice retained no memory of them at all. One morning, Prudence says, she woke up and the holes were there, outside her bedroom window. Sometime later they were gone, filled in. Whatever Georgie had in mind, it's safe to say he was not seeking buried treasure in the yard behind the house. God's little acre never came within a thousand miles of Westminster.

Another of Prudence's memories is perhaps related to the trenches in the yard: She woke in darkness to behold "a figure" standing in the bedroom, peering out the window toward the back of the property. She did not recognize the prowler, and she dared not make a sound. Suppose it was a stranger? Worse, suppose her daddy found out she was not asleep?

The next morning everything seemed normal—for the Knowlton house, at any rate. She locked the incident away and kept it secret, out of fear.

You never knew what George was up to.

Sometimes ignorance could save your life.

Okinawa, the largest and most populous of the Ryuku Islands, lies half a world away from California, but the spring of 1945 found most Americans intently studying that final pit stop on the long road to imperial Japan. Marines had gone ashore on April Fool's Day—Easter Sunday— supported by the largest naval bombardment force in history. The military planners called it L-Day, for "landing," but marines who found the beaches undefended had another name in mind: they called it Love Day. Smiling as they started inland unopposed, they came up with a brand-new motto: "Home alive in '45."

The love ran out on April 2, though, and some 12,520 American fighting men never made it home alive from Okinawa. The grueling battle dragged on for twelve weeks, until Lieutenant General Mitsuru Ushijima committed suicide at sunset on June 22. In between Love Day and that finale lay some of the Pacific war's toughest action.

Babe Knowlton was a navy medic assigned to the First Marine Division when those war-weary veterans of Guadalcanal, New Britain, and Peleliu assaulted Wana Draw, at the heart of the Japanese defensive line, on May 14. The eight-day battle was primitive war at its worst, often fought hand-to-hand, and it produced four posthumous Medals of Honor. One of those who fell, cut down by machine-gun fire as he tried to rescue a mortally wounded marine, was Corpsman Babe Knowlton. It was June 9, with the fight for Okinawa winding down, before his parents got the word.

That afternoon, Gladys sat down to write a letter her youngest son would never read.

O My Dear Babe,

It's a beautiful sunny morning. The berrys are getting red on Hanson's tree and the humming birds are all around the Wigelia bush. I wish I could send you some but the Gov. says you are dead and I can't even write to you any more.

In fact, she could and did, compiling a diarylike collection of notes over the next nine months. On January 25, 1946, Gladys wrote:

It's been a long time since I have written to you. How I wish I had written all the loving things I wanted to say to you while you could read it but I was afraid of making you lonesome and unhappy. We loved you so much it seems to grow harder to bear, each day. . . . O, if there was only some mistake and you could be found alive I would be so happy. I miss you so.

Mom

But there was no mistake, and final confirmation of Babe's death arrived on March 6, 1946. The next morning, Gladys penned one final message to her absent son.

My darling it happened. We have heard from you and it does relieve our minds a lot to know that you did not have to suffer long. As you planned, Larry Curtis came to see us last night. His first day home and it was very kind of him to come so soon. It set our minds to rest on many things but makes it oh so definite that we will never have you with us again. It is a beautiful morning and reminds me so of you. We are hoping to have you brought home soon.

Mom

In Westminster, George Junior seemed to take the news of Clifton's death in stride, but unexpected bitterness accompanied the word from home. His perfect fair-haired brother had upstaged Georgie one last time by pulling off a hero's death. No matter that Georgie had the best excuses in the world for dodging military service—two bum ankles, a wife, five children, and a sixth one on the way. He *could* have been a hero, given half a chance. Hell, yes. Killing Japs couldn't be that different from killing anybody else.

Except that the Japs fought back.

The newest Knowlton, Sandra Elizabeth, was born at Saint Joseph's Hospital in Santa Ana on September 6, 1945. It was another difficult delivery, and Marge remained in the hospital for several days. "Uncle" Billy Sexton, a hairdresser cousin of Nancy Radison, came to help with the children while Georgie was working.

Uncle Billy was nice, even sweet, to the kids. Eight-year-old Janice had no concept of homosexuality. She failed to grasp it even after she walked in on Billy and her father having sex, but she remembers how he used to dance around the house on tiptoe like a gawky ballerina, four young children imitating him and laughing, orbiting like satellites and mimicking his pirouettes.

The day after Sandra was born, George drove his brood and Billy Sexton to the hospital. He left the lot of them outside, as children were forbidden to enter the premises, and Uncle Billy sent the kids into a nearby orange grove to steal fruit. It was, and is, a crime to help yourself in California citrus groves, but no one caught them at it. Georgie laughed when he came out and found the back seat of his car piled high with oranges, filling up the car with their fragrance.

A few days later Marge and baby Sandra were at home. George introduced the children to their baby sister. Prudence remembers standing in the bedroom doorway, staring from a distance, frightened to approach the bed without permission, terrified that Daddy George would slap her if she made a move.

Janice was enrolled at Westminster Elementary School on September 10, 1945. Quickly recognized for her fine soprano voice, she did well enough to get by in her classes. In fact, considering her home life, any progress whatsoever was phenomenal. Attendance was another problem, though she only missed three days during her first four months of school. In January 1946, Jan missed six days, one-third of the total. She was absent 10 percent of the time in February, but March and April found her back on track, missing only a fraction of one day in two months' time.

The pains were one of the reasons for her absences. At nine years old, Jan frequently complained of stomachaches and abdominal discomfort. Margie took her to the doctor, but he found nothing wrong, and Jan repressed her father's sexual assaults as they occurred.

Back on Texas Street, Daddy's twisted "love" was interspersed with "discipline." When something went awry, George liked to line his children up and grill them. Whose fault was it? He threatened to whip them all unless the culprit made a full confession. Prudence whimpered in fear, and Georgie crouched in front of her, his right hand poised to strike. "Smile, damn you, or I'll give you something to cry about!"

The beatings were routine, and Margie got her share if she attempted to protect the children. Sometimes George beat her for no reason at all.

Looking back at those years from adulthood, prior to the emergence of her graphic memories, Janice compared the Westminster home to a henhouse, with Georgie the rooster pecking at his chicks, keeping them constantly agitated.

Prudence leans toward darker imagery. "He was the gestapo," she writes, "our home was the death camp, we kids were the inmates, and our mother was the inmate trusty—in charge of trying to keep us alive against the odds."

But of course, Margie didn't always succeed in protecting her children.

Aside from sexual abuse and beatings, George took time out from his busy days to make sure that his children always felt like losers. Constantly, by word and deed, he taught them not to strive or to anticipate success in life. The brass ring was forever out of reach. Don't hope. Get used to second best. Life is hard, and then you die.

He was a handsome devil, though. One afternoon, while paging through a magazine, young Prudence spotted a familiar face. She called her mother, pointing to the glossy photograph. "Is that a picture of Daddy?" she asked.

Marge shook her head in weary disbelief. "No," she said, "that's Gregory Peck. Your father is Gregory Peck of shit." The acid tongue, in spite of everything.

If Georgie's kids were doomed to failure, however, he seemed to reckon nothing was beyond his own grasp. The family needed beef, so he went out and bought a bull calf, let the children feed and play with it for a while and begin to regard it as a pet before he killed it, strung the carcass up in the garage, and butchered it before a weeping audience.

Another time he felt like playing veterinarian. If some egghead could neuter animals, why couldn't Georgie? All you really needed was a knife and nerve. He captured a raccoon and went to work, sans anesthetic. It was disappointing when the patient died in agony, but what the hell.

You live and learn.

On rare occasions, Jan struck back. She knew her father's weakness for Mexican food, and the Zapatas always had something on the stove. One afternoon she bought a taco for Daddy, loaded up with jalapeno peppers. Watched him choke on it and race for the water faucet.

Sweet revenge.

Of course, they weren't *all* bad times. Prudence recalls a visit to Tijuana, driving south in the La Salle with Jan and David, Georgie at the wheel. The other kids stayed home with Marge because of some kind of illness. In Baja, Georgie purchased rag dolls for the girls. They had a high old time.

112

But Georgie spent most of his time with his friends. Bob Cardran was a spineless lackey, but he had his uses. He introduced Georgie to his fellow Moose lodge members, who met at the American Legion hall in Culver City. And he watched Georgie's back from time to time, when there was dirty work afoot.

When Georgie felt a certain itch, he went to Billy Sexton.

And of course he still had Kay for straight sex, when he wasn't cruising the saloons in Long Beach, Hollywood, Seal Beach, or Los Angeles.

So many bars, so little time.

Come spring he had a new fixation.

Georgie had Elizabeth.

In April 1946, Beth Short was on the move again. Lieutenant Gordon Fickling was just back from Europe, stationed at Long Beach, California, and Beth resumed her correspondence with the army pilot. Whatever the terms of their parting, Fickling seemed eager to start over, inviting Beth out to the coast. "No one will be any happier to see you," he wrote, "than a certain lieutenant in Long Beach." The invitation was enough to give Beth hope, despite a certain cautionary tone in his letter.

You say in your letter you want us to be good friends, but from your wire you seem to want more than that. Are you really sure just what you want? Why not pause and consider what your coming out here would amount to.

I have been trying to convince myself that you really want to hear from me again after all this time in which I have apparently been ignoring you completely. I have always remembered you. I can't deny that.

Your letter gave me the impression that you didn't want to consider that you had a particular claim on my heart and I started letting things drift along on their own. You really should have gotten me.

I get awfully lonesome sometimes and wonder if we

really haven't been very childish and foolish about the whole affair. Have we?

Do you let your fingernails grow long now?

May I love you?

Gordon

Beth's reunion with Fickling in Long Beach was a disappointing anticlimax. The pilot was certainly happy to see her, and while subsequent letters suggest an intimate relationship, it clearly was not heading toward the altar.

Beth rented an apartment at the Hawthorn Hotel, 1611 North Orange Drive, and started checking out the neighborhood for other prospects, searching for a lover who could satisfy her heart's desire.

Whatever happened in her private life, Beth knew that she was destined to become a star.

It is unclear where Georgie Knowlton got the money he was seen to spend on liquor, cars, and prostitutes, but precious little of it ever reached his family. He could afford his hunting trips, of course. They were important. He would take off for the Sierras, drive into Arizona, sometimes travel as far as Utah in his search for things to kill. Too bad if he got fired for absenteeism. George could always find another job. Tough luck if the children needed medicine. They weren't *that* sick. Until the measles came along.

It seems incredible today, with all the vaccinations, wonder drugs, and space-age medical technology, that anyone should fear a simple case of measles. In the spring of 1946, however, it was quite a different story. This was one of the diseases that had decimated tribes of Indians throughout the nineteenth century, and it was still a killer in the wake of World War II for those who went without the proper treatment.

All of Georgie's children were infected by the second week of May. Jan disappeared from school on May 9 and never really made it back, attending only two more days that year. Weak-hearted Midgie was the first to die, on May 16.

Years later a relative told Jan that Midgie died of anaphylactic shock following a penicillin injection, but the official cause of death is listed as measles with complications leading to pneumonia.

George and Margie laid their child to rest on May 22 at Westminster Memorial Park. Three days later it was Sandra's turn to go. She died on Saturday night at Orange County Hospital.

The double death was front-page news in Westminster. Janice emerged from her delirium long enough to attend Sandra's memorial service. She recalls her mother stooped above the tiny coffin, reaching in for Sandra, crying out, "George, she looks like she's just asleep! Let me take her home!" George pried her clutching hands away and led her from the chapel.

Back at home, while David showed the first signs of recovery, four-year-old Prudence was battling double pneumonia and was expected to die. The Reverend W. A. Havermale, of the local Episcopal church, came by to baptize Prudence, just in case. Salvation Army representatives showed up with a floor heater for the frigid house.

Too late.

The other children would survive, but it was touch-and-go for several weeks. Marge told the four survivors that their sisters were alive in heaven with a loving God. Janice took the message to heart, understanding the importance of a proper funeral. For Prudence, though, "They were just gone, and that was it."

Much later Prudence would hear her mother say that Georgie killed the girls. He spent the money earmarked for their medication on another hunting trip.

In fact, George Junior *did* show symptoms of remorse that spring. He couldn't sleep, and he took to gardening at night beneath a floodlight. He was plagued by stomach cramps and vomiting. The night he saw blood in the toilet bowl, an ambulance was summoned to the house. The doctors diagnosed an ulcer, watched him for a day or so, and sent him home.

And he was still the same old Georgie, muttering to Janice that *she* should have died and let her sisters live. He exploded into rage when David lost some food stamps on an errand to the grocery store, then sent him out in the dark with orders not to come back empty-handed. Janice tagged along, and while they never found the stamps, she finally persuaded David that he did not have to run away from home.

The death of Marjorie and Sandra left their mother stunned. She withdrew from the other children in a kind of wounded daze. Sometimes she stepped outside the house to weep so that none of them would hear her, but they knew exactly how she felt. For Janice, barely nine, it seemed that she was twice abandoned—by the sisters who had managed to escape their living hell and by the mother who had been her chief defender.

There was only Georgie now, and he had plans.

On the evening of Wednesday, July 10, 1946, Gertrude Landon drove away from her home on South Hoover Street, Los Angeles, after telling her husband she needed to mail some letters. It should have been a simple errand—the post office was not far away—but something went horribly wrong. An hour passed, and then another. Kenneth Landon began to worry, and as the night wore on, he telephoned LAPD.

The search, if such it may be called, was casual at best. It took eight days for officers to find the missing woman's car, a thirteen-year-old Plymouth, parked on Menlo Avenue just a few short blocks from home. By that time, Gertrude Landon had become another homicide statistic in Los Angeles.

Detectives almost missed her body, even so. They owed their find to Theodore P. Walther, a shipyard worker out of Wilmington. He had been scavenging a Palos Verdes dump site, due south of Lomita, when he found more than he bargained for: a human arm protruding from a mound of sand.

He verified that he was looking at a corpse, then hurried home to tell his wife. But then the couple drove off to Long Beach and waited six full hours to alert authorities. Whatever the reason for their strange delay, it hardly mattered. Gertrude Landon wasn't going anywhere.

The case fell under county jurisdiction, Captain Gordon Bowers in command. (Six months and one day later, he would be assigned to help coordinate the investigation of the Dahlia case with L.A.'s finest.) At the start, investigators didn't have a clue to the corpse's identity. The woman's body was nude except for panties and high-heeled shoes; her bra was unfastened and dangling from one arm. They guessed that she was in her twenties, years away from Landon's thirty-six, but with advanced decomposition, it was difficult to tell. Detectives staked their hopes for an I.D. on fingerprints and some distinctive jewelry that remained on the corpse—a diamond ring and a necklace made of shells—but even prints would have to wait while Dr. Newbarr put the corpse on ice for several days.

Exactly one week from the day she disappeared, investigators knew that Gertrude Landon had been found. The prints matched up, and jeweler Edward Cottine made a positive I.D. on the engagement ring. The cause of death was strangulation, with no discernible evidence of rape. The sheriff's office had no suspects, but they ruled out robbery, considering the flashy ring that had been left behind. An L.A. newspaper dated July 5 was found beneath the body, but it yielded nothing in the way of clues. A spokesman for the Chandler Sand and Gravel Company, which owned the dump site, told authorities that no fresh sand had been deposited in that location since July 2.

On Thursday, July 18, LAPD discovered Landon's car on Menlo Avenue. The tank was empty, indicating an excursion well beyond the drive from nearby Hoover Street, and on the seat detectives found a pack of cigarettes that were not the Landons' favorite brand. Already hoping for a scandal, the *Examiner* announced that Gertrude's husband "could think of no reason why she should drive to a

rendezvous on Menlo Avenue." In fact, Ken Landon speculated that his wife had been abducted from the post office,
but L.A. journalists preferred to think that she was lying
when she said she left the house to mail a letter.

Anything is possible, of course. And yet . . .

South Hoover Street is nineteen miles from Westminster,
as the buzzard flies. It borders on Gardena, yet another L.A.
suburb where the Knowltons would reside in years to come.
The Palos Verdes dump site lay within five miles of
Georgie's Long Beach haunts. A photograph of Georgie,
taken on July 11, hours after Gertrude Landon disappeared,
reveals peculiar scratches on his forearms.

Circumstantial evidence of murder . . . or coincidence?

In 1991, before she ever heard of Gertrude Landon, Jan
reported having flashbacks that were clearly unrelated to the
Dahlia case. She saw a woman clad in bra and panties,
standing in the headlight beams of Georgie's car. Behind her
was a pit, and heaps of sand. It seemed to Jan that she had
been awakened from a nap in the La Salle's back seat. She
glimpsed her father striding toward the woman—and the
rest is lost, for now.

Forty-seven years after the fact, the Gertrude Landon
homicide remains unsolved. When I requested Landon's
autopsy report in 1992, the L.A. County coroner could find
no record of the case on file.

Two days after Gertrude Landon's murder, before the
body was found, Beth Short moved from the Hawthorn
Hotel to the Atwater (later the Washington Hotel) at 53
Linden Avenue in Long Beach. If she chose to stroll a few
blocks farther east, she could have visited the Radisons,
where Georgie Knowlton was a frequent guest from 1945
through most of 1947. She was known to spend her evenings
—some of them, at least—around the Pike, a neighborhood
amusement park of sorts, off Ocean Boulevard.

Short's famous nickname got its start in Long Beach, but
its origins remain elusive to the present day. It has been said
by more than one reporter that newsman Bevo Means made

up the Dahlia handle as a hook for selling papers, but the journalists may be wrong. Witnesses from the IF Club, a gay bar at Seventh and Vermont, recall Short calling herself the Black Dahlia in 1946. We also have apparent confirmation from the press. On January 17, 1947, the *Hollywood Citizen News* quoted Long Beach Detective Inspector E. C. Boynton as stating that Short "was known to police as the Black Dahlia for her custom of wearing sheer black clothing."

We can only speculate on Short's involvement with police in Long Beach, as no records have emerged, but it seems unlikely that overworked detectives in an L.A. suburb would waste time collecting sobriquets for honest would-be actresses.

Whatever Short was doing during her three weeks at the Atwater before she left on August 3, she never lacked for male companionship. Fred Smelser, manager of the hotel, recalled a "very jealous" army officer who called on Beth from time to time, and she was also seen with sailors on the premises. She dated actor Paul MacWilliams off and on for some four months in 1946, but he was always vague about dates. MacWilliams would remember Beth as starstruck, thrilled when he arranged an introduction to Errol Flynn.

And then there was Marilyn Monroe. She was called Norma Jean in those days, with the surname shifting— Monroe or Baker, sometimes Dougherty in deference to an early marriage that had broken up in 1945. In early 1946 she had a few months left to go before she cut a deal with Howard Hughes at RKO and started up the ladder of success. Years later, in a private conversation with her famous acting coach, Lee Strasberg, Marilyn admitted that her early days in Hollywood included prostitution. Strasberg recalled that "She told me she was the one summoned if anyone needed a beautiful girl for a convention."

Sometimes, when she went out on a call, the future Marilyn Monroe had company.

Milo Speriglio, a well-known private eye in southern California who has tirelessly investigated Marilyn's suspicious death and every other aspect of her life, reports that Norma Jean not only knew Beth Short in 1946 but went out drinking with her when Beth was rooming at the Hawthorn, close to Marilyn's apartment at the Roosevelt Hotel. Friends at the IF Club openly regarded Short as "a high-class call girl," but class is a matter of perspective. Joe Jasgur, long an L.A. newsman, has referred to "several sources" placing Short and Norma Jean at the Ambassador Hotel and sundry bars on Wilshire Boulevard. Actor Ted Jordan, a friend of Monroe from her teens, reports that Marilyn's price for sex in those days, with male or female tricks, was five dollars. As for the future star's relationship with Short, tabloid reports quote Jordan as saying, "They were both bisexual, and they definitely had sex together." He also reported that the stunning duo worked together on an average of once a week, while Beth gave the impression she was hooking constantly. When she was murdered, Jordan says, her famous friend was grief-stricken for days.

On August 3, Beth left the Atwater for Carlos Avenue. A friend and would-be actress, twenty-two-year-old Anne Toth, introduced Beth to theater owner Mark Hansen, and he added Short to his collection of live-in wanna-bes, all waiting for the big break. Before she left a few weeks later, Beth stole one of Hansen's address books and filled it with the names of boyfriends or acquaintances. It was the book her killer mailed to the *Examiner,* with crucial entries missing, ten days after she was found at Thirty-ninth and Norton.

From Mark Hansen, newsmen and detectives learned of Beth's alleged propensity for dating hoodlums. Hansen did not offer names, but one or two have filtered down. Girlfriend Phyllis Cyr informed police in January 1947 that Beth used to "run around a lot" with one racketeer— referred to as "Lee" in press reports—who sold black-market nylons in the neighborhood of Sunset Boulevard and Gower. Lee was strictly small potatoes, though, compared to Mickey Cohen who, according to some reports, once admitted making Beth's acquaintance in a Hollywood saloon. Anne Toth recalled that Beth was dating several men on Carlos Avenue, but she avoided introducing them to the other girls.

From active prostitution to her choice of friends, Beth clearly had connections to the L.A. syndicate. She was determined to remain in the vicinity of Hollywood at any cost, until she saw her name in lights. When roommate Marjorie Graham gave up and went home to Boston, Beth told Anne Toth that "she would rather die than bear the cold back east."

In time she got her choice.

Between her stint on Carlos Avenue and her return to North Orange Drive, she spent some time on Argyle Avenue just north of Sunset, two blocks west of Gower, where her hoodlum boyfriend Lee hawked nylons. She had reached the very heart of Hollywood, within a mile of Paramount Studios, and the Argyle address, ironically, has yielded one of the strongest links between Beth and George Knowlton.

One of her roomies at the Argyle Avenue flat was Della, yet another would-be starlet whose last name is sadly lost to history. A friend and sometime date of Della's was character actor John "Tex" Driscoll, pushing sixty at the time, with some five hundred movie credits to his name in a career that spanned four decades. After Beth was murdered, it was Driscoll who recalled her dates with Georgie while she lived on Argyle.

"It was always 'Georgie this' and 'Georgie that,'" Tex told his neighbors in the late 1950s, thirty years before Jan Knowlton's memories returned to change her life. Tex never learned the boyfriend's surname, though they met on more than one occasion. Georgie was "a rugged type" who hailed from Massachusetts, and he worked "in some kind of foundry." He was also an avid deer hunter who "loved to butcher animals" and "shoot anything on four legs." It was a common ritual for Beth to be stood up while Georgie took his gun in search of game, but she appeared no less infatuated with him. Tex, for his part, didn't trust Short's swarthy boyfriend, sizing him up at a glance as "a guy that loves 'em and leaves 'em."

If they were lucky, he left them alive. Mid-September 1946 found Beth back at the Hawthorn, rooming with teenage Lynn Martin and at least one other girl. Together they would prowl the Hollywood cafés, perhaps in search of tricks to help them pay the rent. Sometimes, the Hawthorn's clerk recalled, Beth's bills were paid by a man described as "short, dark, and about thirty-five."

George Knowlton, we should note, turned thirty-four in 1946.

Lynn Martin moved out in late September, leaving Short to make her way alone, but Beth was not without resources. She could still trade on her looks, and there was always Georgie and his elusive promise of marriage which was probably a figment of the Dahlia's imagination.

Georgie seldom felt the need to promise anything.

Lynn Martin's exit from the Hawthorn posed a golden opportunity for Beth. She did not have to sneak around for dates with Georgie any more, and if she had some free time on her hands, well, there were always other lonely men with cash to spare.

And there was always Georgie's sideline in pornography.

It is known that Beth, for all her efforts, never even made a screen test for a major Hollywood studio. Occasional reports of "frequent walk-on parts" are fabricated out of wishful thinking, sometimes fueled by fantasy as desperate as the Dahlia's. A persistent rumor links Short to at least one porno reel, perhaps also featuring young Lynn Martin, but the film has never surfaced.

Jan knew none of this when she began to glimpse the Hawthorn love nest in a string of flashbacks starting in 1990. She saw Beth Short and noted her different faces, alternately kind and cruel—a woman who could sit down with a nine-year-old and chat on equal terms, or turn around and sell that child to sweaty strangers for the money in their pockets. She could be solicitous, then brutal and perverse, her moods shifting with the fluency of a bizarre kaleidoscope.

It is impossible to fix the date when Jan first visited "Aunt Betty" at the Hawthorn, but her memories of spending several weekdays at the flat are buttressed—circumstantially, at least—by school attendance records. Jan missed class for three days running in the first part of October 1946, from Tuesday the eighth through Thursday the tenth, with no known illness in the family to explain her absence. Georgie never took his girls on hunting trips, and there is no clear explanation for her missing school—unless we listen to her memories.

By autumn 1946, her parents' marriage had begun the last, long spiral toward divorce. It was a miracle that Marge had managed to survive twelve years of Georgie's abuse, but she was barred from seeking shelter with her parents if she brought the kids along. Ken Hatch suggested foster homes, but Marge had already lost two children, and she refused to give the others up.

There was a problem when it came to Janice, though.

We can but speculate on the extent of Marge's knowledge when it comes to Georgie's sexual abuse. The beatings were a daily fact of life, and we have reason to believe that she caught George molesting Janice as an infant, but the rest of it is shrouded in the mists of time and in memories discarded in the interest of survival. There was clearly tension between the mother and her oldest girl. Jan instantly repressed each violation by her father, working overtime to earn his love, and Marjorie may well have viewed her daughter as a traitor in the family, perhaps a rival for the husband Marge both loved and hated. Jan recalls a raging argument that seems to coincide with memories of Beth Short at the Hawthorn. Georgie marched toward the door, with Marge right behind him, exercising her sharp tongue.

"Go on, then," she sneered at him. "Take your precious daughter with you."

Georgie did as he was told. He took her to Aunt Betty's little flat on North Orange Drive.

Most of Jan's recollections of the Hawthorn are a waking nightmare. Short seemed happy to begin with, when the three of them were all together, but she fumed at being stuck with baby-sitting chores when George stepped out alone. She took her anger out on Jan in a variety of ways, including sexual abuse that, one is tempted to suggest, most likely mirrored incidents from Beth's own childhood. There were also insults, scathing tirades, flailing fists and feet. Sometimes, when Georgie was away and Beth expected other men to call, she relegated Janice to the closet, leaving her to curl up on an old moth-eaten blanket like a dog.

Jan watched her through a crack in the sliding doors while Beth was entertaining guests. She favored men in uniform, as always, but the servicemen who stopped were not potential husbands. They were in and out, cash on the barrelhead. Sometimes there was a threesome for variety.

Jan sat and stared. She "went away."

On one occasion, Beth retrieved her "doggie" from the closet, forcing Jan to bark and crawl around the room on hands and knees. Two soldiers watched, laughing fit to bust. Jan crawled back into the closet when Beth adjourned with her heroes to the double bed.

Turning tricks was risky, with a madman in the neighborhood, and Short took pains to hide the evidence. Jan has remembered her bustling around the flat, her white robe flapping, naked underneath, intent on cleaning up the place before her man came home.

George might not kill her if he knew, but she could never be sure.

It was a different story, of course, when bringing in the visitors was *his* idea. He wasn't pimping for Beth, though. Georgie had a better plan in mind.

One evening, "a movie producer" came to stage a "screen test" at the Hawthorn. Beth had taken time to braid Jan's hair and pay the child a compliment. "You look like

Margaret O'Brien," she declared. She poured a brimming glass of wine for Jan, to keep her placid while the fat man raped her and the cameras rolled.

He was not Jan's only caller at the Hawthorn flat. Next time around, her father had a movie camera mounted on a tripod in the bedroom. Georgie Knowlton served as director, cameraman, and producer, all rolled up in one.

Across the street, Jan caught glimpses of a school, with children trooping in and out. She missed school, her mother, and the other kids in Westminster. She challenged Aunt Betty, reaping fury for her efforts. Short informed her, "I could get rid of you like that." She snapped her fingers for emphasis. "You'd better keep your mouth shut and do as you're told or you'll never see your mom again."

Jan stood her ground, tears streaming down her face. "I hate you!" she blurted out before Aunt Betty reached her. "I wish you were dead!"

There was another argument, this time with Georgie in the room, when Jan called Beth a bitch. Her father went berserk, as if the word had never crossed his mind or lips. He tackled Janice, tried to stop her sobbing by pressing a pillow against her face. Beth dragged him off in time to save the child, but for a moment Georgie feared that she was dead.

"Jesus Christ!" he wailed, remorseful in his sudden panic. "Margie's gonna kill me!"

Janice had a secret weapon, though. She told her father about the soldiers stopping by in his absence. Ego dominates all psychopaths, and he was no exception. He banished Short from the flat without appeals. Her lover was the court of last resort. Jan watched while Aunt Betty packed her suitcase, flicking hateful glances at the child who "sold her out."

In the Los Angeles of 1946, there was no homeless problem as we understand the term today. A drifter with a dollar in his pocket could find lodging for the night, and Beth Short did exactly that, at 1842 North Cherokee, apartment 501. The flat was filled with other would-be actresses, but that was fine with Short. It was a pit stop, nothing more.

Until the roof fell in.

Within a few days of her move to the apartment on North Cherokee, Beth knew that she was pregnant. Apparently believing that Georgie was the father, she decided to let him know. They met for lunch in late November on neutral ground. George brought his live-in alibi along, and Janice got to watch it all.

There was no easy way for Beth to break the news. She stalled a bit, and finally had to blurt it out, inquiring what he planned to do about their situation. Georgie went ballistic, slamming back his chair and storming out of the café. If Janice didn't feel like walking home to Westminster, she had to catch him before he reached his car.

Beth watched her last best hope drive away. There would be other conversations—Georgie would send Janice up to the apartment on North Cherokee to call Beth out—but he had never been a great one for responsibility.

Suppose he lost it altogether and decided he was better off without a living witness to his infidelity?

Beth needed time to think, concoct a plan to salvage something from the ruins of her adolescent dream.

She started looking for a place to hide.

The seeming rupture of his love affair-cum–business partnership with Beth did not slow Georgie down where pimping Janice was concerned. He had developed contacts of his own, and while he was never a big-time operator, Georgie got around. He kept his eyes wide open, one ear to the ground. He had a bloodhound's skill for sniffing out corruption, anywhere he went.

One hot spot was the Culver City Moose lodge, which shared quarters with American Legion Post No. 46 on Hughes Avenue between Venice and Washington, a half-dozen blocks from Columbia Studios. The brothers of the Moose met there after their own headquarters, in the

Benson Hotel, burned down and before their new lodge was built on Washington Boulevard in 1950. They enjoyed the Legion's slot machines, and sometimes there was other entertainment on the premises.

One evening, Jan recalls, her father forced her to go up on stage and sing for the assembled Moose herd. Her selection was ironic: "I Want a Pardon for Daddy." The unintentional humor was wasted on the crowd, though, because none of them were listening. They were preoccupied with their cigars and beer mugs, slot machines and raucous laughter.

Never mind. The main event was waiting after Janice came off stage. George steered her toward the men's room and into a smelly toilet stall. She was forced to perform oral sex on a man while Georgie stood watch in the doorway, puffing on a cigarette.

He found another opportunity to peddle his daughter's flesh in a bizarre religious cult. Jan's first fragmented memories of ritual abuse appear to center on the period immediately prior to Halloween in 1946, when she was nine years old. The holiday has terrified her ever since.

Between emerging memories and personal detective work, Jan now believes the public building where her first cult ritual took place was in the part of Pasadena bounded by Marengo Avenue, Green Street, and Colorado. She suspects it was a church. Bob Cardran tagged along, a second pair of eyes, but he was obviously nervous. "Jesus, Georgie," he complained, "I don't think we should be here."

Jesus has no part in what comes next. Jan's father leads her to a basement room, where men in hooded robes form a circle, chanting in a language Janice does not understand. The one man who disdains a hood is shiny bald, his scalp shaved clean. The strangers watch as George guides Janice into oral sex, the strange chant droning in her ears.

Jan's memories of ritual abuse are still emerging day by day. There may have been more rituals and other meeting places. Georgie may have paid his dues and sworn allegiance to the cult's pet demon, or he may have simply grasped the opportunity to take a little pleasure with his business.

He had been molesting Jan for almost ten years by now. The novelty was wearing off. But this was money in the bank.

At first glance, Jan's description of a devil-worship cult molesting children in Los Angeles seems fantastic. It evokes weird echoes of the latter-day McMartin Preschool case, wherein adults were charged with ritual abuse of several dozen children, kinky sex combined with prayers to Satan, butchery of animals designed to terrify, impressing tiny victims with their own mortality. McMartin wound up as the longest-running trial in L.A. history, with five defendants discharged in preliminary hearings, one acquitted, and the seventh grudgingly released when two successive juries failed to reach a verdict. In the wake of those proceedings, it is fashionable to reject the very thought of ritual abuse as something conjured up by crazy fundamentalists to launch another Salem witch-hunt.

As it happens, though, there *was* an active cult devoted to pursuit of "sex magic" in Los Angeles during the period that Jan describes. Its leadership, location, and activities are documented in sources ranging from J. Gordon Melton's prestigious *Encyclopedia of American Religions* to the popular nonfiction works of authors Bent Corydon and Arthur Lyons. It is not a matter of opinion or belief. The facts are plain for all to see.

The mystic Ordo Templi Orientis—Order of the Eastern Templars—founded by German occultist Karl Kellner in 1902, claimed a spiritual link to the crusading Knights Templar, with all of that order's magical trappings intact. Never one for understatement, Kellner told his followers that "Our Order possesses the key which opens up all Masonic and Hermetic secrets, namely, the teaching of sexual magic, and this teaching explains, without exception, all the secrets of Freemasonry and all systems of religion."

Be that as it may, the secret of longevity eluded Kellner. At his death in 1905, he was replaced as leader of the OTO by disciple Theodore Reuss. The order expanded under new management, planting chapters in Denmark, France, and England. Sexual magic was especially appealing to Aleister Crowley—demonologist, drug addict, and self-styled Great Beast 666—who took over leadership of the British OTO in 1912, soon adding a homosexual "eleventh degree" to his branch of the order. Doctrinal differences led to a rift with the German home office in 1916, but Crowley later patched up the relationship, succeeding Reuss as international chief of the OTO in 1924.

Meanwhile, sex magic had bridged the Atlantic, with OTO disciple C. S. Jones—a.k.a. Frater Achad—planting chapters in Los Angeles, Washington, D.C., and Vancouver, British Columbia. Crowley himself visited the Vancouver lodge in 1915, there meeting Winifred Smith—Frater 132 —and giving him permission to start a new lodge of his own. Fired up with evangelical zeal, Smith lit out for Hollywood, where he set in motion a chain of events that were bizarre even by OTO standards.

Newly appointed by Crowley as Frater Achad's replacement to head the North American OTO, Smith got things rolling in Hollywood by luring celebrities to special invitation-only "gnostic masses," typically featuring Smith's coupling with as many women as possible. No one seemed to mind that Smith's Agape Lodge practiced group sex; if anything, that may have been the Hollywood OTO's main selling point. One of the women Smith seduced was the wife of disciple John Parsons, an explosives expert at the California Institute of Technology and Smith's successor, in 1942, as head of the lodge.

Apparently untroubled by his wife's infidelity, Parsons took up with his sister-in-law, moved the lodge headquarters to his Pasadena home, and renamed it the Church of Thelema. In the autumn of 1945, Parsons joined forces with a friend named L. Ron Hubbard to attempt an "incarnation of Babalon." Dark rituals were crafted in an attempt to produce an infant devoid of human spirit and therefore open to possession by "Babalon," who was apparently regarded as "the mother of the universe." (The OTO denies

Hubbard was technically a member, but freely admits his participation in rituals with Crowley.) Francis King described the preparations in *The Rites of Modern Occult Magic.*

In order to obtain a woman prepared to bear this magical child, Parsons and Hubbard engaged themselves for eleven days of rituals. These do not seem to have produced any marked result until January 14th when, so Parsons said, Hubbard had a candle knocked out of his hand. Parsons went on to record that Hubbard called him, "and we observed a brownish yellow light about seven feet high. I brandished a magical sword and it disappeared. Ron's right arm was paralyzed the rest of the night."

On the following night, so Parsons said, Hubbard had a vision of an enemy of the O.T.O. and "attacked the figure and pinned it to the door with four throwing knives with which he is an expert."

All this seemed to achieve its desired result and, on January 18th, Parsons found the girl who was prepared to become the mother of Babalon and to go through the required incantation rituals. During these rituals, which took place on the first three days of March 1946, Parsons was High Priest and had sexual intercourse with the girl, while Hubbard who was present acted as skryer, seer, or clairvoyant and described what was supposed to be happening on the astral plane.

Parsons described the chosen mother of Babalon in a letter to Crowley, soon after the ritual was completed.

She turned up one night after the conclusion of the operation, and has been with me since, although she may go back to New York next week. She has red hair and slant green eyes as specified. If she returns she will be dedicated as I am dedicated! All or Nothing—I have no other terms. She is an artist, strong minded and determined, with strong masculine characteristics and a fanatical independence. . . .

I am under command of extreme secrecy. I have had the most important—devastating experience of my life between February second and March fourth. I believe it was the result of the ninth degree working with the girl. . . . I have been in direct touch with the One who is most Holy and Beautiful as mentioned in the Book of the Law. I cannot write the name at present. First instructions were received through Ron, the Seer. I have followed them to the letter. There was a desire for incarnation. I do not yet know the vehicle, but it will come to me, bringing a secret sign. I am to act as instructor guardian guide for nine months; then it will be loosed upon the world. That's all I can say now.

"You have me completely puzzled by your remarks," Crowley wrote back to Parsons. "I thought I had a most morbid imagination, as good as any man's, but it seems I have not. I cannot form the slightest idea of what you can possibly mean."

Days later, writing to occultist Karl Germer, Crowley explained, "Apparently Parsons and Hubbard or somebody is producing a moonchild. I get fairly frantic when I contemplate the idiocy of these louts." A second letter from the Beast to Germer clarified the situation slightly.

It seems to me on the information of our brethren in California that—if we may assume them to be accurate —Frater 210 [Parsons] has committed . . . errors. He has got a miraculous illumination which rhymes with nothing, and he has apparently lost all his personal independence. From our brother's account he has given away both his girl and his money—apparently it's the ordinary confidence trick.

The "confidence man," in Crowley's opinion, was Hubbard, accused by Jack Parsons of skipping town with

Parsons' mistress and a cool $10,000 from OTO's treasury, rolling on to found his own Church of Scientology a few years later. Hubbard, for his part, denied any theft, and no charges were filed. In 1947, Crowley's years of drug addiction and debauchery caught up with him, and Karl Germer replaced his late friend as chief of the OTO. Jack Parsons, meanwhile, embarked on a "black pilgrimage," changing his name to Belarian Armiluss Al Dajjaj Antichrist. As he wrote in his private journal: "I am pledged that the work of the Beast 666 shall be fulfilled, and the way for the coming of BABALON be made open and I shall not cease until these things are accomplished." In fact, Parsons ceased four years later, vaporized at age thirty-seven in the explosion of his basement laboratory, where he bootlegged nitroglycerine for private sale.

At this point it should come as no surprise to learn that rumors of cult-related child pornography were current among Los Angeles social service workers in the 1940s, four decades before the witch-hunt hysteria of McMartin and similar cases began.

The OTO lives on. As recently as 1988, the order claimed forty-eight chapters in the United States, nine in Canada, two each in Australia, Norway, and Germany, one each in England, France, Guadeloupe, New Zealand, and Yugoslavia.

The order's guiding principle, today as in the 1940s, is drawn from Crowley's *Book of the Law,* supposedly dictated by the Egyptian demon Aiwass in 1903: "There is no law beyond 'Do what thou wilt.'" That principle, adopted by various satanic cults since 1966, is a blank check for the faithful to amuse themselves in any way they please—with sex in all its varied forms, with drugs and alcohol, perchance with death.

What psychopath could ask for more?

* * *

Before she left the Hawthorn, Beth made one more try at landing Gordon Fickling. He was stationed on the East Coast by that time, counting the days until his discharge and return to civilian life. We can surmise the content of Beth's letter from the tone of his reply, mailed on the second of November.

You've got to be just a little bit more practical these days. I am glad you have ambition to become a cover girl. You deserve to be a success. After all, you have a lot to work with.

My plans are very indefinite and uncertain. There's nothing more for me in the army and there doesn't seem to be much outside. Don't think I think any less of you by acting this way because it won't be true.

On November 13, Beth moved into apartment 501 at 1842 North Cherokee. Six or seven other women shared the flat at any given time, paying a dollar a night for the privilege of sleeping like sardines. If Beth was worried by her pregnancy, she kept it to herself. She went out two nights running, on the first and second of December, with Jimmy Harrison, a civilian mechanic at the San Bernardino Army Air Base, and while Beth seemed to enjoy herself in the various nightclubs, Harrison never saw her again. On December 5, with manager Juanita Ringo nagging her about the rent, Beth vanished out the back door with her bags. Before she left Los Angeles, Beth told Anne Toth that she was heading north to spend some time in Berkeley with her sister.

Either Beth was lying to confuse pursuers, or she had a sudden change of heart, perhaps occasioned by another note from Gordon Fickling in the first week of December. "Time and time again," he wrote, "I've suggested that you forget me as I believed it is the only thing for you to do to be happy."

On the evening of December 8 she surfaced at the Aztec

Theater in San Diego, where she struck up a conversation with cashier Dorothy French. Beth let it slip that she was hungry, broke, and homeless; she also said she'd been widowed when her husband Matt was killed in action. Dorothy invited her to spend the night. Elvera French made no objection when her daughter brought a total stranger to the Bayview Terrace Housing Project on Camino Pradero in suburban Pacific Beach. It was the least that she could do for such a pretty girl in need.

One night with the Frenches became a month as Beth stayed on, rent-free. On Sunday, December 15, she met Robert Manley—at the bus depot, he later said—and took him "home" to Camino Pradero. Beth introduced him as Red, a business associate, and they spent every evening together for the next six days. On the twenty-second, Dorothy recalled, Red seemed to vanish from the picture, and Beth was out with a different man every night until New Year's.

The nightlife served as a distraction, but she knew that time was slipping through her fingers. She saw marriage as a solution to her problem with the baby. She did not intend to be an unwed mother living from hand to mouth. If she decided that the baby had to go, Beth knew that she would need a "scrape," and soon.

Beth still cherished her dream of marriage to a serviceman, and Fickling seemed to fit the bill despite his obvious objections, but she was running out of time and hope. Beth wrote to Gordon several times from San Diego, but she did not always mail the letters; she sealed some of them and tucked them away inside her luggage.

"Your devotion is my most precious possession," she wrote to Fickling, in one letter that she never sent. "How many lips have joined with yours since ours last met? Sometimes I go crazy when I think of such things." On December 13 she penned another note that never made it to the mailbox: "I do hope you find a nice young lady to kiss at midnight on New Year's Eve. It would have been wonderful if we belonged to each other now. I'll never regret coming west to see you. You didn't take me in your arms and keep me there. However, it was nice while it lasted." A few days later, knowing she would never send the letter, Beth proclaimed: "If everyone waited to have everything all smooth before they married, none of them would ever be together. I have no right to preach to you, Gordon darling, but you are missing so much of life. I know, though, that you'll be happy some day soon, darling." By that time she had started saving up for an abortion.

Elvera French recalled that "While she was with us, she apparently needed a great deal of money for something. Just before Christmas she sent a telegram to Mr. Fickling, who was then in North Carolina. Two days later Betty received a Western Union money order from him for one hundred dollars." Beth also tapped Anne Toth for twenty a couple of days before Christmas, but she always seemed to need more.

In Charlotte, Fickling rejected at least two other pleas for cash. His first wire read: "Darling, your request impossible at this time. Other obligations have me against a wall. Try to make other arrangements. I'm concerned and sorry, believe me." And again, some days later, he wrote, "Honey, I'm terribly sorry about that wire you sent. Couldn't raise the money on that short notice. Glad you managed O.K. I want that picture of you very much."

Money and the secret pregnancy were not Beth's only worries in the final weeks of 1946. Elvera French recalled, "She also told me that a woman chased her and a friend of hers on Hollywood Boulevard just before I met her in early December. Betty seemed constantly in fear of something. Whenever anyone came to the door she would act frightened."

Enough was enough for the long-suffering Frenches, however, and they gave Beth Short her walking papers shortly after New Year's. "She was only going to stay a night," Elvera later told reporters, "and she stayed a month. We had to ask her to move because our home was so crowded."

On January 7, Beth received a wire from Red, instructing her to wait for him to come and pick her up. That same night, while the Frenches were asleep, a tan coupe pulled up outside the housing project on Camino Pradero. Two men and a woman walked up to the door, knocked and waited, departing when no one responded. Elvera French slept through the visit, but a neighbor filled her in next morning. "When I heard of the visitors," Elvera later said, "I asked Betty about them. She admitted hearing them knock and said she peeked at them through the window. She was terribly frightened, though, and refused to talk about them. She was evasive when I asked other questions, so I gave up."

French's neighbors were unable to provide descriptions of the visitors beyond their sex, but one recalled seeing a transfer sticker on the car that read either Huntington Park or Huntington Beach. She also thought the license plate contained the letter *V*.

On January 8, while waiting for her ride, Beth wrote a final nine-page letter to Gordon Fickling. "Do not write to me here," she instructed in parting. "I am planning to go to Chicago to work for Jack." Weeks later, questioned by police in North Carolina, ex-Lieutenant Fickling guessed that "Jack" had some connection to the world of fashion modeling.

Or maybe not.

At 6:00 P.M. on January 8, Beth took her leave of Bayview Terrace carrying two suitcases and a hatbox. Elvera French recalled her leaving on foot, but a neighbor spied Red pulling up to the curb in his black Studebaker, looking dapper in a pin-striped suit.

And Beth was gone, leaving behind a hat, some convoluted lies about her marriage to Matt Gordon . . . and a mystery. Who was she frightened of each time someone came knocking on Elvera French's door? Who drove the tan coupe and knew where she was staying in Pacific Beach? If she had given out her address to the visitors of January 7, why was she afraid to greet them at the door?

If the driver of the coupe was Georgie Knowlton in his tan La Salle, come to threaten Beth or fetch her back against her will, who were his two companions on the trip? Bob

Cardran seems a likely prospect, weak enough to tag along on any errand, even when it worried him.

And there was always Kay. Her own adulterous relationship with George was strong enough by this time that she would not have hesitated to help him deal with any minor hitches as they came along. A pregnant tramp? No problem. Barely three weeks later, Kay would even help her lover beat the rap on L.A.'s most sensational and grisly murder. She was useful that way, in a pinch.

But at the moment, rolling out of San Diego in the early-evening darkness, Beth was still alive, and still carrying her married lover's child. If no one else would help her, there was always Georgie. She was not about to give him any choice.

6

Paper Doll

There is something in corruption which, like a jaundiced eye, transfers the color of itself to the object it looks upon, and sees everything stained and impure.

—Thomas Paine

WHEN ROBERT MANLEY PICKED BETH UP, HE FOUND HER IN AN agitated state. He couldn't tell if it was anger, nerves, or fear. One of the first things he noticed was the scratches on her arms. The marks were not fresh, exactly, but they were new since he had seen her last, on December 21.

Beth blamed the scratches on a spat with an "intensely jealous" boyfriend two days earlier. She gave no name, but she described him vaguely as "Italian, with black hair."

Red let the subject go.

Beth told him she was bound for Berkeley, going Greyhound from Los Angeles, to see her married sister. If she had a plan beyond that point, she kept it to herself.

Red's brain was working overtime. It is a quick two-hour drive from San Diego to Los Angeles, but he was on a business trip, of sorts. Some of it was monkey business, granted, but he still had calls to make on Thursday morning. Someone might be checking up, and Manley had to make it look good for his boss, his wife, the world at large. But staying over meant a night alone with Beth.

Perhaps it was another "test"—Red trying to decide if he

still loved his bride of fifteen months, a question that clearly preyed on Manley's mind—or maybe it was simple lust.

They checked into the patriotic-sounding U. S. Grant Hotel and gobbled take-out burgers, Manley looking forward to dessert. Beth disappointed him, complaining of a stomachache with chills and nausea before the food was fairly out of sight. Red blamed the meal; Beth's illness could just as easily have been the early warning signs of a miscarriage.

Manley was a stranger to the finer points of chivalry. He slept alone in the bed and left Beth huddled in a chair all night. A workingman needed his rest. She seemed to feel a little better in the morning. Manley bolted breakfast, made his calls, and came back to retrieve his passenger. They hit the road at half past twelve, stopped for lunch en route, and reached Los Angeles, by Manley's estimate, around four-thirty in the afternoon.

He drove Beth Short to the Greyhound depot, where she checked a hatbox and two bags. They drove on to the Biltmore, where Beth said her sister would be waiting in the lobby, but Virginia didn't show up. Red stuck it out until six-thirty, fidgeting, afraid of being seen, and finally left for home.

Beth hung around the Biltmore lobby for the next three hours, more or less, as if expecting to be met. Whoever she was really waiting for, we know her sister did not have a clue about her travel plans. Around nine-thirty, Beth made change at the cigar stand, used the public telephone, and spoke for several minutes to a party on the other end. The phone booth door was closed, and no one overheard her final public conversation. Perhaps she was making deals, demanding help.

She left the phone booth, crossed directly to the exit, and was gone by ten o'clock. The clerk at the cigar stand later told police that Beth wore a beige coat with a black dress underneath. Her blouse was white and frilly, her matching gloves spotless. Descriptions of her shoes and purse are contradictory, but black appears to be a safer bet than red.

The next time Beth showed up in public she was naked, dead, and sliced in half.

What follows is extracted from the memory of Janice Knowlton, pieced together during four and a half years of therapy and supported by the independent evidence she dug up on her own (recounted in the final chapter). LAPD flatly rejects her memories on every point, without explaining why they think she's wrong. With no coherent theory of their own, department spokesmen shrug, refer to evidence allegedly contained within their super-secret files, and turn away.

A choice between the false assurances of LAPD and a victim's raw, soul-wrenching memory is no real choice at all.

We may assume the Biltmore call was relayed to Georgie by Nancy Radison or the Cardrans, since the Knowlton household had no telephone. Years later, Nancy Radison told Janice that on numerous occasions "Your father would get a message from someone while he was visiting us and take off." In any case, Beth reached the house in Westminster that Thursday night.

George put her up in the detached garage out back. By this point in his life, it was routine for him to flaunt his infidelity. Marge would not make his floozy welcome in their home, but neither would she actively protest. She had observed her husband in a rage too many times. Arousing the "house bastard" could be tantamount to suicide, and anything that kept him away from her and her children came as a relief.

The Knowlton house was nothing but a brief stopover for a would-be actress on her way to fame and fortune. Marilyn was making it, and so could Beth, once the baby had been "taken care of."

Janice, of course, had repressed the incidents of physical and sexual abuse as they occurred, and she was glad to see "Aunt Betty." Jan's mother had been living in a kind of private world since May, so Beth's attention sparked memories of the maternal love Jan had experienced in bygone days. That feeling had been reinforced when Short herself, that first day at the Hawthorn, had told Jan, "Your daddy and I are getting married." In the child's mind, any woman who was married to her father automatically became a mother figure.

But motherhood was nowhere on the Dahlia's list of things to do. She had mapped out a new campaign, albeit vague and based on wishful thinking. She despised the growing life within her that would, if given half a chance, derail her dreams a second time. As soon as she got rid of it, she would be on her way.

Abortions were illegal at the time, but George could arrange one. He knew things, knew people. Getting him to foot the bill was something else, but Beth had managed to collect some money while she hid in San Diego. If she couldn't pay the whole tab on her own, then George would have to split it with her. Fair was fair.

That, however, was an argument she never had to face.

By Friday afternoon Beth's fever had returned, accompanied by nausea, cramps, and spotting. She was losing the baby. There was no toilet in the back garage, so she used a chamber pot. The fetus—eight weeks, give or take—was more reptilian than human in appearance.

Janice didn't know the difference. It was still a baby to the child, just ten years old herself, who had raised baby chicks and stray kittens. She ran to fetch her mother. "Mama, come quick! Aunt Betty's sick."

Marge shook her head in weary disbelief as she followed Jan back to the garage. "She's not your Aunt Betty," Marge said. "You *have* an aunt Betty back east." Marge found Beth resting under blankets on the bunk bed. There was nothing she could do, assuming she had been inclined to help. Defeated, she stood over the younger woman, muttering, "She's just another one of your father's whores." Finally she turned away, but Janice caught her by the skirt and showed her the bloody chamber pot.

"What about the baby, Mama?" It was the wrong thing to ask.

"She's not the only one with a dead baby," Marge replied, and went back to the house.

Beth came around in time and seemed to feel a little better—almost manic, really, now that her worst fear had been laid to rest. A little pain and blood were nothing, in the scheme of things. There was a whole wide world in front of her, all neon and applause. "I really need a bath," she said.

Elizabeth hastily donned a housecoat and slippers and followed Jan into the house and to the bathroom. Marge was in the master bedroom, seated on the bed she shared with Georgie, watching while her daughter ran the bath. It was too much for Marge to bear, Jan falling under the spell of Georgie's latest trollop, and she made her way out to the side yard, turning her back on another betrayal. Another child lost.

While Beth was in the tub, Jan dropped the toilet lid and sat to keep her company, absorbing Beth's hollow fantasies as if they were the most sensible and logical ideas on earth. Cruel Aunt Betty from the Hawthorn had evaporated, leaving in her place a magical beauty whom Janice longed to emulate.

One problem nagged at Janice, though: Beth's hyper fantasies did not include a funeral for her fetus. "What about the baby?" she asked.

Beth glared back at Jan with murder in her eyes, the "mean Elizabeth" returning in a flash, but then the anger passed. The little girl was ignorant. Dead babies were no obstacle at all.

When she was finished bathing, Short rose from the tub like Botticelli's Venus rising from the sea, stepped out, and dried herself with the towel Jan eagerly provided. She was moving toward the mirror when her one-girl fan club stopped her with a question.

"Mama says I have an aunt named Betty," Janice told her, dead serious. "What should I call you, then?"

"Elizabeth," she said, as if bestowing an inestimable gift on the child. "You can call me Elizabeth. That's the name I'll be using in the movies."

Janice watched Elizabeth go through the motions of preparing to meet her public—combing her hair, applying face cream. The ten-year-old made note of every movement. This was not Jan's enemy, her tormentor. This was a star. It was an honor just to fetch her robe and slippers when she finished putting on her face. Her smile was Jan's reward.

Emerging from the bathroom, Short expressed a strong desire for coffee. Jan heated some left over from the morning, careful not to let it boil, since twice-boiled coffee was a criminal offense in Georgie's house, enough to make him fling the coffee pot across the room. When it was ready, Janice served the coffee in her mother's finest cup and saucer, going back for seconds when her guest consumed it rapidly.

The coffee seemed to galvanize Elizabeth. She shook her hair back and surveyed the kitchen, then rose from her chair and moved toward the living room. Marge was ironing near the sofa, trying to distract herself with drudgery, when Beth entered. It might have put another woman off, this walking tour of her married lover's home and family, but Short was on a manic high, pacing the floor and spilling her dreams like a ritual chant, noticing everything, from the furniture to the framed photographs on the wall. Little Midgie, strad-dling a pony. You would never guess that she was nine months dead.

Marge soaked in the scene, her anger building. This intruder was no star in her eyes. Short was just another whore, and when would she get the hell out of the house?

Jan sensed a change in the atmosphere. Her mother's anger was stirring, approaching critical mass. "Come on, Elizabeth," Jan urged. "We'd better pack your things for the trip to L.A."

Feverish with anticipation now, Elizabeth followed her only fan back to the garage.

Marge saved her pent-up bile for Georgie, who breezed in from work, or from somewhere else. Jan was killing time with Beth in the garage and was not privy to their conversation, but it would not be difficult to draft the script.

"I don't want that tramp coming in the house."

"What do you mean?" All wide-eyed innocence from Georgie as he tried to determine what the hell was going on.

Marge told him, maybe threatened to tell Gladys—lit the fuse.

Out in back, Beth Short was getting ready for the road. She chatted on to Janice as she packed: "Your daddy's taking me to stay with friends. You'll see me in the pictures one day. I'll be famous. Wait and see."

"And I'll come see you?" Janice sounded hopeful.

"Sure." Beth drifted back to the bed, sat down, still talking.

Georgie cleared the threshold like a fighter answering the bell, his voice thick with anger. "Where the hell do you think you're going?"

"Back to L.A." Beth was confused. "I was just telling Janice—"

"Telling her what? That you just dropped your brat in my garage? That my wife saw it? Now you think you can just take off and leave me with this mess?"

He moved before she had a chance to answer, his strong hands reaching for Beth's throat. Jan stood paralyzed at the familiar sight of her father venting his rage through violence. He lifted Beth by the neck and shook her, like a wildcat with a captive rabbit.

"Daddy!" Janice is barely whispering, her voice just loud enough to register with Georgie.

"Janice, get my rope!"

The child was helpless to refuse. She knew from experience that Georgie's rages came and went. One moment he was pounding her; the next, he drifted away. Sometimes he seems contrite. On rare occasions, there is even an apology of sorts.

When she brought him the rope, she found Georgie choking Beth as if he meant to wring her head off. Beth, in bra and panties, was pale and terrified, panic in her eyes, dark hair half covering her face.

George took the rope and let Beth drop back on the mattress. Then he straddled her body and leaned forward, taking time to snap at Janice, "Get your ass out of here!"

Jan backed away, retreating, and the door slammed in her face.

George kept his hostage tied up Friday night and all day Saturday, her wrists and ankles tethered to the bedposts, a running loop around her neck to choke her if she tried to rise. The ropes left marks that Dr. Frederick Newbarr, the pathologist, would describe at Beth's postmortem. If she had been hoisted by her ankles, as the press and some detectives still insist, there would have been no reason for a noose around her neck.

Jan crept in once and tried to set Beth free, but Georgie had a way with knots. When he tied someone up, the person *stayed* that way, by God, until he changed his mind.

By Saturday, well after sundown, it appeared that George had done exactly that. His rage seemed spent. A kind of apathy enveloped him. Marge hadn't kicked him out; she never would. The little bitch out back was so much excess baggage. He could simply send her on her way, whereas killing her—a woman he had dated openly around Los Angeles—had built-in risks.

Jan trailed him to the makeshift sleeping room. He stood beside the bed at Beth's left side and drew his hunting knife. He leaned across Beth, reaching for the rope securing her right arm to the bed.

Beth gasped and pulled away, recoiling from the knife—a stinging insult to her captor's undeserved generosity.

George drew the gleaming blade across her face.

Dr. Newbarr's autopsy report leaves no room for speculation: Beth's right cheek received a three-inch slash, her left a cut of only two and one-half inches. This was puzzling at the time, but now we know the right-hand slit was longer and deeper because George slashed her face from right to left as she lay facing him. His blade was sliding up and out, retreating from her left cheek as he pulled the knife away. When a person gasps, the mouth drops open and the tongue locks automatically behind the lower teeth in front. A finger—or a hunting knife—passed through that open mouth will miss the teeth and gums entirely and will only graze the tongue if it is forced back nearly to the hinges of the jaw. Beth's teeth, gums, and tongue were untouched by the knife that ripped her lower face apart—a simple explanation, as the truth so often is.

But she is choking on the blood now, writhing on her bed of pain, the loose skin on her cheeks sagging like a rubber fright mask. Georgie can't believe what she has "made" him do. The selfish little bitch! How can he let her go now, in this condition? She might run to the nearest hospital and spill the whole story to the police. Revenge alone would be enough to make her tell.

The only roles that she can hope for now will be in horror films.

Disgusted with the whole damned mess, he cuts her free and helps her upright. Janice brings a towel to stanch the crimson waterfall. George wraps the ruined face in the towel, concealing most of it while leaving Beth a space to breathe. His voice sounds reasonable, even kind. "It's not that bad," he lies. "I'll take you to a doctor, but you'll have to walk to the car."

Beth seems to be in shock, but Georgie gets her moving and guides her out to the main garage. His tan La Salle is parked nose-in. The fridge—where he stashed Beth's fetus on Friday night—and the workbench are on his right as he enters the garage. Beyond the car, tucked into a corner on his left, there is a straight-backed chair. "Just sit here a minute," he says. "Hold that towel against your face. I have to open the garage doors."

Beth sits and waits. She does not have the strength or the clarity of mind to run away. George leaves her in the chair with Janice gaping at the bloody ruin of her "friend." In the garage, he dawdles by the workbench, picking up a hammer, switching on the radio. Beth and Janice hear the *William Tell* Overture heralding yet another adventure with the Lone Ranger and Tonto. It is 8:30 P.M.

George ducks back into the bedroom and returns with the rope. Elizabeth is taken by surprise and has no power to resist him as he ties her hands behind the chair. A naked bulb suspended from the rafters gives him light to work by as he fastens his knots.

No longer able to conceal her ravaged face, Beth looks up to her right. Toward George. Barely human now, she is no longer pretty. She is watching Georgie as the hammer falls, gashing her forehead. She slumps against the ropes, and Janice, standing in front of the chair with its slack burden, freezes.

Incredibly, Beth lifts her head a second time, her eyes swimming out of focus, crimson everywhere.

George rages at her, "Die, goddammit! I didn't want to do this! You *made* me!"

His voice releases Janice from her trance. Still staring at Elizabeth, she crumples to the floor and scuttles backward, wriggling under the La Salle to hide, but taking one last look upward as the hammer strikes again. Then Jan "goes away."

She comes back sometime later, uncertain what has roused her, not knowing how much time has passed. George stands above Elizabeth, his arm cocked for yet another blow—the coup de grâce—if she shows any sign of life. But then something distracts him.

The outside door swings open: little Prudence has heard the Lone Ranger theme song from the house. George gapes at her and drops his hammer. Skating on the very edge of sanity, he has seen a ghost. "Midgie!"

George then leads Prudence off into the night while Jan stands before the trussed-up body of her "friend," in shock.

Returning moments later, George ignores her, making one last grab at rationality. This thing is getting out of hand. He hoists Beth in a fireman's carry, chair and all, returns her to the bedroom, and deposits her directly opposite the open door. Jan follows, like a junior zombie.

In the back room, he releases Beth and lays her on the bed again, then lights a cigarette. Jan steps up to the bed and crosses Beth's hands on her chest. She plants a kiss on the bloody forehead, then settles in a chair beside the bed.

George sneers at her around his cigarette. "What are you doing, havin' a wake?"

The second blow felt lethal, but he takes no chances. Rope again, securing her wrists. In the garage, he wipes blood off the walls with another towel and scuffs the dirt floor with his precious cowboy boots to cover all traces of the kill. He almost seems amused. There isn't that much cleaning up to do.

Fatigue is setting in, though, and Georgie needs his beauty sleep. He leads Jan out of the garage and locks the double doors behind him.

Beth Short isn't going anywhere.

She will be waiting for him any time he feels like picking up the game.

Next morning. Sunday, January 12.

George is about to take the next step in disposing of his problem. Janice stands at the head of the bunk bed, staring down at Elizabeth's body, noting that her arms are drawn up, bent at the elbows, as if fending off an attack. Rigor mortis has stiffened her muscles, transforming her into a mannequin.

Disgusted by the latest complication, George falls back on a solution he has used before, with deer. He checks the outer door of the garage, makes sure that no one can surprise him, then stops at his workbench on his way back to the bedroom. He takes down his Skil saw from its wall mount and plugs in the long extension cord.

Janice watches, wide-eyed, even as she "goes away." The saw's round blade is too small to bisect a human torso on a single pass. He starts on Beth's left side, the sudden pressure forcing her head and shoulders upward, off the mattress, her rigid fingers clutching empty air.

Georgie turns to face her, seems to see her mother staring back at him. "Cheer up, Margie," he tells her. "Everything's gonna be all right." He moves toward Janice, takes her in his arms as if prepared to lead her in a dance. She stiffens. Georgie's grin becomes an angry snarl. He flings her bodily against the bedroom wall.

Returning to the Skil saw, he half turns Beth Short and works on her back until the blade snags in the fabric of her housecoat. Deer hide never gets in Georgie's way like this.

He pulls the blade free, pushes back the tattered fabric of her housecoat, rolls the carcass partway over, and starts with the saw again, working toward her spine. His left knee pins the lower portion of her body to the bed as Georgie guides the Skil saw, probing with his fingers for the space between her vertebrae.

Jan hears the spinal column separate, a sound she will recall years later. *Bonk!* The top half of Beth's body wobbles off the bed and lands on its elbows, face down. To Jan, it looks as if Beth is climbing out of a hole in the wooden floor.

For nearly half a century, the self-styled Dahlia experts have insisted Short was killed with running water close at hand to help the butcher drain her corpse of blood. From that assumption, they spin Gothic tales of secret labs and mortuaries commandeered at midnight.

They are wrong.

An old cloth mattress filled with cotton batting makes a perfect sponge, and you can always burn it later.

Georgie puts the saw down and walks around the bunk bed, staring at his fallen trophy. Grudgingly he lifts the upper torso, drops it back onto the mattress, and tosses a blanket over the severed remains. More concerned about the Skil saw now, he inspects the blade, then returns to his workbench, wipes the saw with a rag, and hangs it back on the wall. Another job well done. Distracted, he begins to wipe at something on the bench itself, taking his time.

Survivors have all the time in the world.

On Sunday afternoon George makes his first attempt to dump the body. He wraps Beth in a heavy blanket, bundling her remains, and puts her in the trunk of the La Salle. He takes Jan with him as a cover. How suspicious can a man look to the world, out riding with his daughter on the Sabbath?

Jan is carrying Beth's mutilated fetus in a child's shoebox. A tiny casket. When George promised Beth a proper funeral, he was mocking Janice, but she means to see it through. And she must stage a service for the baby. Child and mother, reunited in the presence of God.

Alive and well again, just like her sisters.

Georgie drives west to the ocean, parks his La Salle on Ocean Avenue, adjacent to the Seal Beach fishing pier. Inclement weather means they will have the pier all to themselves. He doesn't need much time.

The Seal Beach pier is noted for deadly riptides that make it treacherous for swimmers. Diving in the water there, a swimmer runs a major risk of being sucked beneath the pier and flayed by barnacles encrusted on the pilings.

Dead or alive.

Jan follows Georgie to the water's edge, the towel-wrapped fetus tucked beneath her arm. She watches as her father flings the bisected corpse into the ocean and waits for the tide to dispose of it.

Beth foils him at the last. Her body doesn't sink. The lower half falls into shallow water at Georgie's feet and bobs in the surf. Some trick of buoyancy propels the body's top half to the surface. Georgie has to wade in armpit-deep, lunge to grab her hair, then retreat awkwardly toward shore.

Defeated! Mad frustration mounts in him and is vented in a string of curses as he pulls the corpse from the surf and dumps its two halves back onto the sodden blanket. "Get your ass up that beach," he demands of Janice, "and keep your eyes open!"

Georgie looks around and has a sudden inspiration. Bundling up the severed corpse, he lifts it and moves toward a nearby picnic area. There is a shed for cleaning fish, and Georgie carries Beth inside. A reeking drum of offal makes the unfurnished enclosure smell of death. A sink is mounted on one wall.

He stations Janice at the door to serve as his lookout. She cannot help weeping for her friend, and that makes Georgie angry. "Stop that goddamn whining, you little bitch."

Jan sits on the discarded blanket, cradling the shoebox-casket in her arms. She hears the ocean, and her father humming a tune to himself. It sounds like "Ten Little Indians."

One little . . .

Georgie's knife scrapes across the concrete floor, grating on Jan's nerves like fingernails across a blackboard. He is trimming something from the midsection of the corpse.

Two little . . .

The intruding blade releases some dark fluid. George dabs some of it across his lower face and turns to Janice with a ghastly smile.

Three little . . .

He is chewing something as he pokes his fingers into Beth Short's lower body. "Here," he offers, "wanna try some?"

Janice turns away.

Four little . . .

Water running in the sink, now. Georgie cleaning up. He carries something to the trash can, drops it in, and stirs it into the fish guts to disguise his contribution. Beth lies white and bloodless on the concrete floor. George smiles. "Clean as a whistle."

No little Indian boys.

Janice brings the blanket on command. He spreads it on the floor and makes the bundle fast again. Beth's arms and legs are limp now, having shed the rigor mortis. Georgie lights a cigarette and looks around the cleaning room to see if he's missed anything. Outside, the sun has set, but there is still light in the sky.

Suddenly a man appears out of nowhere. Khaki shirt and slacks. Perhaps the pier's custodian. The heavy bundle rests at Georgie's feet. "Hi, there."

Georgie smiles back at the stranger. "How ya doin'?"

"All right. Good catch?" He does not seem to notice that they have no fishing gear.

"I did okay," says Georgie. "Better go, before it gets too dark."

The stranger takes his leave, and Georgie hoists the blanket-wrapped remains. They hike back to the car, and Beth's corpse is shut up in the trunk. He leans against the La Salle, lights another smoke. "This is our little secret," he says. "You can never tell your mother any of this or I'll kill you, you little bitch, do you hear me?"

Tell her what?

He still has no real grasp of Jan's ability to come and go inside her mind. George pictures her recounting details to her mother, Marge perhaps informing the authorities. She wouldn't dare, of course . . . unless he happens to push her a little bit too far. The hassle with Elizabeth was bad enough, for Christ's sake. All he needs is Margie going on a tear about some worthless bitch who's dead and gone.

Well, not *quite* gone.

They drive back to the little house on Texas Street, Georgie Knowlton threatening his daughter all the way.

Beth spends the next two days with Georgie, in and out of the refrigerator at his whim. His private sex toy. Oral, anal, vaginal. Jan hears him singing "Paper Doll" while he is handling Beth's remains. At one point, crouched beside the bed, he starts to slash her right breast with his knife as he coaches little Janice in the joys of puberty.

"When you grow up," he tells her, "you'll have titties just like these."

Jan wishes she were dead like Beth. Out of her misery.

When he is finished carving, George devises yet another game. Beth always wanted to perform, and now she has the chance. There is no speaking part for her, of course, but she is still a central character. George brings a chair for Janice, orders her to sit and watch.

George puts his leading lady back together, more or less. He places her lower body at the foot of the bed, knees flexed and splayed, sheet-draped. Jan does not recognize the props of a delivery room, but there is something familiar in her father's face as he begins to smile and wag his eyebrows, up and down.

She has it! Groucho Marx!

George parodies the story of *A Day at the Races*—leaning in between Beth's legs, doing a fair impersonation of the wacky Dr. Hackenbush. "Mrs. Knowlton," he declares, "you have a fine new son!"

And he answers himself in a woman's voice, not unlike that of Mother Gladys. "I don't want him. Send him back where he came from."

Then Georgie loses his composure. Tears roll down his face as he begins to paw at Beth's vagina, whimpering in his own voice now. "I want to go home. I want to go home."

The moment passes. He regains control, throws back the sheet, and studies Beth. The sight of her arouses him. He pulls another chair up to the bed, sits down, and brings himself to climax with his hand.

When he is tired of playing with his toy, George empties the refrigerator, wedges Beth's remains inside, and shuts the door. One item of unfinished business still remains.

The baby.

Georgie is prepared. He has a hand-crank food grinder bolted to his workbench, normally reserved for venison. He takes the tiny fetus out of the refrigerator, dangles it above the grinder's open maw.

The sight is more than Jan can tolerate. "No, Daddy! Don't! *Please* don't!"

Her father smiles. "What will you pay me?"

"Wait!" She races for the house and retrieves her piggybank. No time to break it. *He* can do that. She runs back to the garage with the jangling treasure in her hands.

Too late.

As Jan arrives, the final piece of mutilated gristle is slithering from the grinder. Georgie gives the crank another twist to clear the blades, and stares down at a job well done. The baby? She would never know for sure.

Jan chooses the alternative to total madness.

She shuts down.

But even in the depths of a psychotic episode, George knows that the corpse has to be disposed of. If it is dangerous for him to dump the body, keeping it is certain death. A one-way ticket to the green room at San Quentin. Sucking gas for breakfast one fine morning, with the cops and lawyers smirking at him through a pane of glass.

No, thank you.

Well before dawn on Wednesday, the fifteenth, George puts his final plan into action. Marge is worried. "Janice has to be in school," she tells George.

"I'll get her back in time."

Marge bundles Jan up in her coat against the early-morning chill. Jan takes the little shoebox with her, praying that today, at last, Elizabeth and her unhappy child will get the funeral they deserve.

George drives the thirty miles to Culver City, parks on Hughes, outside the combination Moose and Legion hall. Post No. 46. He lets himself in through the back door. People know him here. They trust him with a key.

Inside the rec room, George unwraps his playmate and sets her on the billiard table. A dusty-looking moose head stares at him glassy eyed. Beth stirs him, even in her present state. More so, perhaps, than when she was alive. He pulls her legs and pelvis to the table's edge and penetrates her.

Janice tries to slip away unnoticed, but a scuffling sound distracts George from his pleasure and he suddenly remembers his daughter after several strokes.

He grabs Jan, bends her over, pushes up her skirt, and

yanks down her underpants. He tries to sodomize her, jabbing painfully, but his erection fails.

No matter. There is time.

He leaves Jan huddled on the floor and carries Beth into the men's room shower stall. As he scrubs the corpse Jan hears him singing a show tune, "Singin' in the Rain."

Jan follows the sound of his voice and peers into the shower stall. The lower half of Beth's body is propped up or suspended on something, held upright, while Georgie masturbates above it. He turns toward his daughter with a ghastly smile.

Jan bolts from the men's room, away to the left. A flight of stairs leads to the basement and the swimming pool. George catches her a few feet from the bottom of the stairs and grabs her by the throat, strong fingers choking her. She welcomes the encroaching darkness as the room begins to spin.

And wakes to find George coming back downstairs. He brings the top half of Elizabeth's body, his hands cupped beneath her armpits, his knees bowed to accommodate his burden. Beth's dark hair dangles in her face, obscuring her mutilated cheeks. Jan struggles to her feet, but there is nowhere she can hide.

George drops the body, catches Jan, and throws her down at poolside, one hand locked around her throat, the other fumbling beneath her skirt. He tries to rape her, but he cannot get it up. He has to use his mouth on her instead. That does the trick, and Georgie finishes himself by hand.

He stands up, hauling Janice to her feet. She should be catatonic, but she starts in on the same old theme, as Georgie lifts the bloodless torso: "Daddy, don't! She needs a funeral."

You want a funeral, bitch? Let's try a burial at sea.

He flings Beth's torso out into the deep end of the pool. As Jan gasps in shock, he shoves her into the water. A second splash. Jan surfaces and starts dog-paddling awkwardly. Can't even swim, the little bitch. She *should* be able to, as many times as George has tried to drown her.

Sadly, this is not the time or place to finish off the job.

George looks around and spies a long pole with a hook at one end, not unlike a shepherd's crook. He picks it up and pokes at Janice, prods her toward the bobbing torso, which is floating head-down, buoyed by lung-trapped air.

"You wanna rescue her?" he bellows. "Go ahead! Rescue her!"

Jan ducks beneath the floater, glimpsing naked, mutilated breasts. Somehow she thrashes her way to the shallow end and grabs the concrete lip of the pool. She is hysterical, enough noise pouring out of her to wake the dead.

George grabs her skinny arms, hoists her from the water, and drags her upstairs, Short's torso clutched beneath his free arm.

He deposits Beth's pale upper body on a counter near the sink in the men's room and orders Jan to fix Beth's hair. He wants it pulled back from her face, he says, to show the "ugly, mean bitch that she was." He tosses Jan his black plastic pocket comb. When she hesitates, he plays upon her weakness, telling her that Beth will need a hairdo for her funeral.

Jan does her best to fix Beth's hair. She does so well, in fact, that Georgie is inspired to take his plaything on a final spin around the rec room, waltzing as he sings "Paper Doll."

The moment passes. Georgie comes back to a semblance of reality and sets his dancing partner down, deciding it is time to pack. His duffel bag is waiting for him in the rec room. Janice watches as he begins the grisly chore. The lower half is easy to pack, folding at the knees to fit inside the duffel. It inspires another song from George: "Pack Up Your Troubles in Your Old Kit Bag."

And smile, boys, smile.

The upper torso is more stubborn, flopping arms resisting Georgie as he tries to pack the bag. His bitter curses drag Jan back to something like reality. She flees the rec room, running aimlessly, with darkness on her heels. She finds a heavy trunk or chest, opens it, and crawls in. It feels like a coffin. Safe at last, she goes away.

George glances up and finds his daughter gone. The little bitch! As if she had a chance, against the greatest hunter of them all. Following the pathetic trail of water droplets from her dress, he traces her directly to the chest, throws back the lid, and drags her out.

The sudden rush of light and panic brings her halfway back to reality.

George recognizes shock, knows Jan will be no help to him if she is in a daze. He drags her to the shower cubicle and turns on the warm water, letting it drum on her head and shoulders, bringing her around. Her dress is sopping wet, but it no longer smells of chlorine from the swimming pool. George blots it with a towel and helps Jan slip into her woolen coat.

The sound of someone entering the Legion hall distracts him. Georgie shoves the duffel bag behind a tall screen that sections off one corner of the room. When Jan is slow to move, he orders, "Get your ass behind that screen!" George is alone, to all appearances, when the new arrival enters the men's room.

Peering through a small gap in the hand-carved screen, Jan catches glimpses of a man in uniform. Some kind of watchman on his rounds? The stranger knows her father and does not appear surprised to find him in the Legion hall at that peculiar hour. "Oh," he says, "it's you, Georgie."

"Yeah. Just finished cleaning up in here."

The man in uniform is satisfied. He nods. Says, "Don't forget the lights." The door clicks shut behind him.

We may never know if Georgie meant to leave Beth's corpse at the Culver City Legion hall, but now he had been seen on the premises. Whatever plans he had in mind, they needed swift revision. Time was running out.

George can't afford to leave a trace of evidence behind. He scans the men's room, still not satisfied. Jan has to scrub the shower stall on hands and knees until it shines.

He lifts the heavy duffel, steers Jan toward the parking lot, and locks the door. Nearby, the early shift is clocking in at

Culver City Hospital, but there is nothing they can do for Beth.

George stows the duffel on the floor of the La Salle, in front of the passenger seat, on Jan's side. His daughter folds her legs beneath her, yoga-style, avoiding contact with the lumpy bag.

They drive off into darkness, racing with the sun.

The tan La Salle rolls east on Washington toward Normandie. Rosedale Cemetery draws George like a magnet. He feels at home with so much death around him, monuments and headstones spreading out for acres in the predawn darkness. Janice wants a funeral for the scheming bitch. This ought to do the trick. A proper bone yard.

Parking on a slope, he sets the brake, walks around to Jan's side of the car, reaches past her for the duffel bag. She watches him retreat into the shadows.

The night has been replete with horrors, but it is not over yet. Before Jan's very eyes, the cemetery comes alive. One scarecrow figure, then another, rises on shaky legs among the gravestones and lurches toward the car.

Jan screams in terror, and the piercing sound brings Georgie running back, the heavy duffel nearly throwing him off balance. Hobos! Jesus Christ, the place is full of bums!

He elbows his way past them, cursing, driving them away from the La Salle with threats and with the sheer strength of his anger. Opening the trunk, he dumps the corpse inside and slams the lid. Climbs in behind the wheel and starts the car, cursing nonstop as he jams it into gear and roars off, searching.

George finds a neighborhood that makes him feel at home, below Koreatown. He cruises past New England Street, New Hampshire, and Vermont. It would be fun to dump the body here, a slap at Mother Gladys that she would never even recognize, but there are far too many houses.

He keeps on driving. East on Washington, then south on Hoover, twelve blocks down. The road dead-ends at Jefferson, bordering the University of Southern California.

"Shit! Son of a bitch!"

He blunders onto the campus proper, mistaking it for another residential neighborhood. Narrow winding roads with dorms and classroom buildings close on every side. In no time, George is lost. Whichever way he turns, he gets nowhere. He is traveling in circles.

Then the La Salle stalls.

He climbs out, stalks around the car, and slams his fist against the hood.

"Son of a *bitch!*"

A young man approaches on foot, calling out, "Need some help?"

George leans into the car, grabs Jan, and jerks her toward him. "One peep out of you," he said, "and you'll get what *she* got. You hear me?"

He lets go, and Jan slumps back into her seat. All phony smiles from Georgie as the Good Samaritan draws closer, asking what the problem is. George tells him, and the new arrival helps him push the car until the engine catches. Georgie thanks him from the driver's seat and pulls away.

The near-miss momentarily improves his mood. He jokes about the silly bastard, not suspecting anything. And if he had, so what? Beth's body could be passed off as a specimen for the dissection theater, the workshop for young doctors in the making.

Still lost, Georgie cruises slowly through the campus. Ogling. Scoping out directions. Moments later, he is rolling west on Exposition Boulevard, past Catalina, Raymond, Normandie, and Western. Veering left onto Rodeo, and again, in half a dozen blocks, on Coliseum. En route to Crenshaw, Georgie spots his last best opportunity, and makes a hasty left on Norton, headed south.

His mood has turned again, and he is cursing Janice, snarling that he should have killed her, too. He could be dumping two sluts now instead of one. Tramps! Whores!

He cruises past the weed-choked lot, spots houses up ahead, passes Thirty-ninth, then throws the La Salle into reverse. Jan feels her stomach lurch, safety slipping through her fingers, as he backs up, away from the encroaching houses.

Georgie pulls over to the curb and sets the parking brake, gets out and opens the trunk. Jan climbs out on the passenger's side and watches him lift the heavy bag.

George takes a few steps off the pavement, drops the duffel in the grass. The zipper makes a whirring sound. Removing the two halves of the corpse, he deposits them beside the duffel bag, letting the slack limbs flop in the weeds. He leaves a space of several inches between the severed halves and steps back to admire his handiwork.

Not yet.

George stands between Beth's feet and kicks at each in turn to spread her legs into a yawning inverted *V*. Jan holds the shoebox, waiting for the funeral service to begin. Her father kneels between Beth's legs, but not in prayer. Jan sees him pluck a fistful of grass and weeds and stuff it, as he is fond of saying, "where the sun don't shine."

Jan kneels beside the body, crossing Beth's arms on her chest, funeral-style. She leans forward, squinting against the horror, to plant another kiss on the lacerated forehead.

Georgie is incredulous. "What the hell are you doing?"

"I have to get her ready for the funeral," Jan replies.

He explodes. "Goddammit, I'm gonna kill you, you little bitch!"

Lurching to his feet, George grabs the shoebox. He reaches out for Janice, but something in her eyes stops him cold. She is staring past him, south toward Thirty-ninth Street, where a young boy on a bicycle is pedaling their way. "We gotta get the hell out of here!" George snaps. "Get in the goddamn car!"

Jan hesitates. "I have to pick some flowers."

"Get your ass in the car *now!*"

He shoves her in and slams the door. Tires screech as Georgie makes a U-turn in the middle of the street and retreats to the north. Jan is grateful, looking back, to find that Beth is hidden by the weeds.

"I don't want to hear any more of your whining," Georgie

says. "Remember, if you *ever* tell your mother, it'll kill her. Do you understand me?"

Winding toward the coastline, George suddenly becomes paranoid, imagining suspicious stares from other motorists. "What the hell are you looking at?" he snaps, glaring at them. And to Janice: "Keep your head down! If that kid describes this car and you, you whining little bitch, my ass is in a sling."

As they roll through Redondo Beach, his anger reaches fever pitch. "I'll throw you off the pier," he snarls. "You'll *never* get a funeral. The fish will eat your goddamn face. They'll chew your eyes out, you whining little bitch. Your mother will never know what I did with you."

Jan does not argue with him. He is capable of anything. Her very silence seems to bleed his anger by degrees.

At some point, near the ocean, Georgie stops for coffee and doughnuts, giving Jan a sip from his cup. "Here," he says, "drink this and stop your whining."

Janice has no appetite. "Where are we going, Daddy?"

"Home."

In the garage on Texas Street, George leads Janice to his workbench, giving her another close-up of the Skil saw. "Keep your mouth shut," he reminds her. "If I hear you say *anything* to *anybody* about this . . ."

Jan nods acquiescence. She will soon forget the threat, as she has already repressed the nightmare scene at Thirty-ninth and Norton. The survival mechanism is kicking in.

George seems satisfied. He checks his watch. "Go to your room and change your clothes, then get to school."

Jan does as she is told. As she changes, she hears her parents talking, but their voices sound remote and muffled, barely audible. She does not miss the shoebox or its contents that she risked her life to salvage.

It is just another morning in the henhouse, Georgie pecking at his chicks. And life goes on.

For some.

7

Manhunt

A little inaccuracy saves a world of explanation.

—C. E. Ayres

THE LOS ANGELES POLICE DEPARTMENT NEVER HAD A BETTER friend in civilian life than Jack Webb. For most of a quarter-century, from 1952 to 1974, the Hollywood actor-writer-director-producer of programs like *Dragnet* and *Adam-12* preached weekly sermons on the courage, skill, and incorruptibility of L.A.'s finest. Webb adored Chief William Parker, his successors, and the men who held a thin blue line against disorder in the City of Angels. In 1958, Webb wrote *The Badge,* an LAPD history of sorts, which elevated Parker to the company of saints and showed off the department as a fine-tuned, infallible machine. His introductory remarks about the Dahlia case are typical: "Right from the first erroneous report to the police at 10:35 A.M. that gray mid-January day in 1947, the investigation was askew through no fault of the police. In the days, months, years of sleuthing that followed, it never quite got back into balance, again through no fault of the detectives. More than any other crime, murder is sometimes like that."

In other words, Webb threw the blame for LAPD's failure to identify Short's killer back on Betty Bersinger and unnamed others who confused the issue "through no fault of the police." He fails to note the *second* call, from Bill Nash, that described a butchered woman in the weeds, but there is reason to believe that Webb, for all his posturing as an insider, was denied admission to the LAPD's secret Dahlia files.

If nothing else, at least he got the timing right.

Five decades have done nothing to diffuse the aura of confusion that surrounds Short's murder, but it seems peculiar that the time of Betty Bersinger's report should vary by a full three hours in assorted published chronicles. Authors John Austin *(Hollywood's Unsolved Mysteries)* and Kenneth Anger *(Hollywood Babylon II)* are farthest off the mark, placing the discovery of Short's body at 7:30 A.M. Ex-newsman Will Fowler, allegedly first at the scene, claims that the first report of "a naked drunk dame passed out in a vacant lot" was broadcast at 9:05. In fact, the call from Bersinger described a drunken *man,* and Fowler has admitted that the times recorded in his book, *Reporters,* are "not accurate," having been plucked from thin air "for dramatic effect." Another reporter, Craig Rice, logs the call into LAPD at 10:45, but his Dahlia chapter in *Ten Perfect Crimes* is riddled with errors.

Today we know that Betty Bersinger's call was received by police at 10:35 A.M. Webb's published estimate of a ten-minute response time for Patrolmen Perkins and Fitzgerald seems reasonable, but Craig Rice gives them credit for a speedy three-minute response. Unfortunately, as with every other aspect of the Dahlia case, LAPD's refusal to release even the most innocuous of documents ensures that speculation will continue breeding errors. As it is, when all the different versions of that morning's action are compared, we have no way of knowing whether Perkins and Fitzgerald found Norton Avenue deserted or whether several witnesses were standing by to greet them at the scene.

Will Fowler claims that he and Felix Paegel, a photographer for James Richardson's *Examiner,* reached the scene well ahead of police. In *Reporters,* Fowler has time to pose for photographs, examine Short, and probe her viscera before the cops arrive with pistols drawn and order him to raise his hands. And it was Fowler, we are told, who notified his editor about the crime.

James Richardson, writing six years after the fact—compared to Fowler's forty-three-year lag—presents a rather different sequence of events. In *For the Life of Me,* Richardson credits the first vague report of Short's murder to newsman Bill Zelinsky, who was working the police beat. Richardson instantly sent "every reporter and photographer in the office out" on the call, and Sid Hughes is named as the first to call back with details of Short's mutilations. Will Fowler, for all of his self-proclaimed "firsts," is totally absent from Richardson's view of the case.

And then there is the problem of the not-so-solitary cyclist.

Several published sources mention the appearance of a young boy on a bicycle who reached the field on Norton Avenue before, or shortly after, Perkins and Fitzgerald. Fowler calls him Bobby Jones and says he pointed him out to the patrolmen, then fingered the boy as a potential witness when detectives reached the scene. Twenty years before Fowler's report, a retrospective in the *L.A. Times* identified the boy as Bobby Smith, eleven years of age in 1947, married with children of his own by 1971.

Whoever the youngster was, his observations have not been recorded for posterity. If he—or they—saw anything of value to detectives, it remains a secret, locked up in the LAPD's Dahlia file. Whatever clues lay waiting in the vacant lot at Thirty-ninth and Norton, they would have to be unraveled by detectives working on the case.

If we believe Will Fowler, media manipulation of the Dahlia case was under way before police arrived at Thirty-ninth and Norton. By his own admission, in *Reporters,* Fowler tampered with the evidence by closing Beth Short's eyelids, kneeling at her side for photographs, and poking around in her exposed viscera, which he found "palpable and soft to the touch." Nor was contamination of the scene confined to Fowler's efforts as an amateur pathologist. Detectives Finis Brown and Harry Hansen were surrounded by reporters as they viewed Short's body, cameras snapping, pencils scribbling pithy quotes from this or that detective on the fringes of the crowd. It is impossible to say what evidence was lost or trampled by the mob, but members of the press, including the *Examiner's* Jim Richardson, have gleefully admitted meddling in the case from beginning to end.

It was the staff of the *Examiner,* as we have seen, that helped police identify Beth Short when storms disrupted LAPD's contact with the FBI. If Richardson had stopped at that, he might deserve our commendation for a public service, but the news game, then as now, was a cutthroat business, with rival papers sparing no expense to scoop the competition. Short's I.D. provides a case in point: while the *Examiner* dispatched Short's fingerprints to Washington, the rival *L.A. Times* took credit for the coup on January 17, with the announcement on page one that "Capt. Jack A. Donahoe, given the identification by The Times, launched an immediate investigation to trace the movements of the girl before she fell prey to the perverted sadism of a person who apparently tortured her before she died."

It was heady stuff, albeit fabricated nonsense. Richardson fought back with an assemblage of talent praised by Fowler as "the finest crew of newspaper reporters and editors ever grouped to cover a murder case of this proportion." In fact, we are told, "Richardson's crews worked so effectively with the clues we were digging up on our own that we were able to start making deals with LAPD homicide. This made Donahoe furious, but he had to go along." Richardson, in his memoirs, recalled that upon publication of Short's name, his office was swamped with telephone calls from the public, feeding his newspaper "dozens of leads to run down."

And in the finest journalistic tradition, no lead was shared with the authorities until reporters had milked it dry.

One of the first tips came from Santa Barbara, where police remembered Beth from her arrest in 1943. Her place of birth was named as Medford, Massachusetts, on the booking sheet, and Richardson assigned Wain Sutton, rewrite man at the *Examiner,* to track Beth's family down. Directory assistance put him onto Phoebe Short, and Richardson instructed him to call Beth's mother, seeking background information for the next edition. Fearing Mrs. Short might hang up when she heard about her daughter's murder, Richardson provided Sutton with a grotesque twist. He was to say that Beth had won a beauty contest in Los Angeles, and the *Examiner* required some biographical material before the story ran.

Wain Sutton followed orders, scribbling notes and holding back the news of Beth's demise until he got the cue from Richardson. Incredibly, despite the cruel deception, Phoebe Short stayed on the line once she was told the truth. Her consolation prize, approved by Richardson, would be a round-trip airline ticket to L.A., courtesy of the *Examiner.* "This way," writes Fowler, "the *Examiner* would be able to keep Mrs. Short away from the police long enough to explore any new leads she might have to offer." Chief among them was the tip that Beth had spent her last month with a family in San Diego. Mrs. Short produced a letter Beth had sent to her from Pacific Beach, providing Sutton with the name and address of Elvera French.

The San Diego lead turned out to be a gold mine for the press. Elvera French and daughter Dorothy spilled everything they knew to newsman Tommy Devlin. He recorded their description of a man called Red, who drove away with Short on January 8. He also learned that Beth had spoken of a trunk stored at the American Railway Express office in Los Angeles. A January 18 phone call indicated that the trunk had been moved to a local warehouse, where it was being held for nonpayment of storage. James Richardson describes what happened next.

We got the trunk but I had to call in police to get it. The company wouldn't turn it over to the reporter. I called Jack Donahue [*sic*], chief of the homicide squad.

"If I tell you where you can find the Dahlia's trunk will you agree to bring it to the *Examiner* and open it here?" I asked.

"Look, Jim," he said. "If I do that every other paper in town will be after my scalp. Don't put me on the spot like that. You've caused me enough goddam trouble the way it is with all those stories you've been breaking."

"You want the trunk, don't you?" I said. "No deal, no trunk."

Jack actually moaned. I could hear it.

"All right," he said, "it's a deal. I'll send a couple of the boys to you. But if you were a friend of mine you'd give me a break."

"If you're a friend of mine you'll give me a break," I said. "Let's be friends somehow, Jack."

"All right, but I'm sure going to catch hell," he said.

So much for the "all-powerful" and "incorruptible" Jack Donahoe.

The trunk was brought to Richardson, as promised. It contained "a lot of clothes," some photographs of Beth with different men, and "dozens" of letters from various boyfriends, dating back several years. Each name and face provided the *Examiner* with leads to follow. "And the letters," Richardson allowed, "made good reading when we printed them."

From the moment Red's nickname was mentioned to Tommy Devlin in San Diego, finding him became job one for Richardson and the *Examiner*. Determined to nab the elusive suspect before he was bagged by police, reporters laid siege to Pacific Coast Highway, checking motel registers, displaying photographs of Beth's male friends to clerks and maids. It did not take them long to find the registration card with Robert Manley's name and license number. From there they traced him back to his home address in Huntington Park.

Jim Richardson immediately sent a four-man team to Huntington Park to find the suspect. "If he's there," the editor commanded, "grab him. Try to get him to come down here to the office. If he won't, grab him. And I mean grab him. Throw him down and sit on him if it's necessary. Just don't let him get away from you. I'll do the rest."

Will Fowler takes credit for confronting Harriet Manley at home. "A strikingly beautiful red-haired young woman answered the front door," Fowler writes, "and I flashed my Los Angeles County Sheriff's badge without saying I was an officer of the law."

Harriet clearly mistook Fowler for a detective, as Fowler intended. She told him that her husband was in San Francisco on a business trip with Harry Palmer, scheduled to return on Sunday night. According to Fowler, Manley phoned home while the newsmen were there, but Harriet obeyed his order not to tip her husband off. In parting, Fowler asked if there were any family photographs around the house, and Harriet produced a set of portraits. "She didn't seem to object," Fowler writes, "when I asked for them all, and instructed her—a bride of only fifteen months —not to talk to anyone, especially if newspaper reporters started coming around the house."

From that point on, through Sunday night's arrest of Manley at the Palmer home in Eagle Park, a team of Richardson's commandos camped outside Red's house, prepared to grab him if he showed his face. Will Fowler was on hand with a photographer when Manley was arrested by Detectives Sam Flowers and J. W. Wass—and again police played second fiddle to the press. "I was surprised," Fowler recalls, "when Flowers allowed me to get away with shouting questions at Manley before he was interrogated downtown by homicide." Jim Richardson goes even further, reporting that Manley was first debriefed by newsmen, after which "Jack Donahue's [*sic*] men took charge the next day" and cleared Manley as a suspect.

One useful tip from Manley was a lead that sent reporters to the Greyhound depot, where they found two suitcases and a hatbox checked by Beth Short. As before, the newsmen were denied access to Short's luggage without a police escort, and Richardson got on the phone to his good friend Jack Donahoe. Will Fowler described the scene in *Reporters:* "The day our new information hit the street, Richardson called Donahoe and said, 'You're welcome to the luggage, but I want it understood that story is ours exclusively.' What could Donahoe say? If he didn't agree, Richardson said he could damned well read about the case's progress in the *Examiner.*"

In fact, according to Richardson's memoir, Donahoe had finally worked up the nerve to deliver a frail ultimatum. "This is the last deal I make with you, Jim," the tough chief of detectives insisted. "Absolutely the last. Understand that. I can't take the heat from the other papers any longer. I'll resign first."

Worried more about his public image than about finding a solution to the mystery, Jack Donahoe caved in—again. By that time, though, it hardly mattered, for the case had effectively slipped beyond his grasp.

As with every other aspect of the Dahlia murder case, confusion reigns in the reports of Beth Short's injuries and about the cause and time of death. Fred Newbarr's autopsy report, published in these pages for the first time, is still considered off-limits to the public by LAPD homicide investigators. They profess to believe the case may yet be tried in court or resolved "by other legal means." In the absence of official documents, reporters have been free to speculate at will.

The time of death is clearly relevant to any understanding of a murder, but in Beth Short's case, authorities were never able to decide upon the day, much less the hour, when the crime occurred. At Thirty-ninth and Norton, two anonymous detectives told the *Long Beach Independent* that the victim had been killed five to nine hours earlier, based on their observation that "the upper half of the body was still warm." As late as January 20, police were still telling the press that Beth Short was killed "sometime after midnight" —that is, early Wednesday morning, the fifteenth. And seven years after the fact, Hank Sterling reported that LAPD believed Short had been murdered eight to fourteen hours before her body was found.

In fact, the closest public guess was off by some three days.

The barest whiff of truth was aired on February 4, when the *Daily News* reported that "a veteran officer" assigned to the investigation from the start had indicated there were "some evidences that the remains had been refrigerated for a period of hours." By that time, the manhunt was hopelessly bogged down in nonsense, LAPD spokesmen hinting that Beth had been carved up in a funeral home.

If time and date of death eluded the authorities, Short's injuries, at least, should have been obvious. Unfortunately, Harry Hansen's trick of holding back "key elements" to weed out false confessions, while entirely sound in theory, left the door wide open for erratic speculation by the press. Police chemist Ray Pinker, for example, had remarked on lifting "a few bristles" from Short's body, identified in the press as fibers from the floor mat of a car. By February 1, Jim Richardson's *Examiner* had twisted that slim bit of evidence into a flat assertion that "a thick-bristled brush of coconut fiber" had been used to scrub the corpse.

Nor was that all.

On the day Short was found, the *Hollywood Citizen News* falsely reported that her right leg was broken below the knee. Ten days later, the *Daily News* announced that Beth's eyebrows were bleached with peroxide, while henna was used to lighten her "jet black hair." Neither fact was confirmed by the autopsy. The *Long Beach Independent* found Beth's eyebrows "colorless," reporting in the wake of her postmortem that her torso had been severed "by at least three instruments, one believed to be a butcher's knife." The *Orange County Community News* and *Culver City*

Evening Star both quoted medical examiners as saying Short was "cut or sawed in two."

The newsies came closer to the truth than they would ever know. The *Daily News,* in fact, hit closest to the mark with this report on January 25: "Detectives now are convinced that the body was divided not as torture but for means of disposal, so that it could be placed easily in a gladstone bag, or military duffel bag or sea chest. They feel that only a woman . . . would think of this. A man would force the body into a trunk or wrap it in canvas, not worrying about how neat his job might be." Gender aside, the anonymous gumshoes were right on the money . . . but was their report based solely on speculation?

Given the confusion over Beth Short's injuries and time of death, it is only natural that the killer's motive and background should remain obscure. As late as 1971, reporter Bevo Means insisted that the Dahlia autopsy had revealed some unspecified "evidence of lesbian pathology" on the killer's part. Harry Hansen, interviewed the same year, had "no idea" what Means was talking about. He recalled that unnamed "medical authorities" had fingered the killer as someone with "medical finesse." Lieutenant Freestone, Hansen's nominal superior, with access to the same authorities and files, meanwhile described Short's body as having been carved up "as a hunter would dress a deer."

With such dissension in the ranks, could Hansen and his cohorts possibly have solved the case?

Before the Hillside Strangler panic of the 1970s, the search for Beth Short's killer was described by all concerned as L.A.'s "biggest manhunt ever." There is no good reason to dispute that claim, considering the scores of LAPD officers and reinforcements from the county sheriff's office who were active in the search. How, we are tempted to ask, could such an army of investigators have failed to get their man?

For openers, they had a dearth of clues to work with at the

site where Short was found: the body, mutilated elsewhere, washed before the killer dropped it off; some "hairs" or "bristles" found on the corpse, apparently belonging to the floor mat of a car—or to a scrub brush, if the daily papers are to be believed; a "small amount" or "single tiny drop" of blood; some skid marks in the street; a partial footprint that could never be identified. And that was all.

No fingerprints. No semen or saliva. Nothing.

There were at least two witnesses, however, or so it seemed, before investigators analyzed their statements. Walter Johnson, a resident of Welland Avenue, seven blocks west of Norton, had burned some rubbish on Tuesday night, January 14, in a vacant lot across the street from where Short's body was discovered on Wednesday morning. He recalled seeing an "old battered four-door sedan" parked across the street. Admitting for the record that he "didn't pay much attention," Johnson estimated that the car was ten or twelve years old, its color cream or tan. "There was a man near the car," Johnson said. "He walked a little way up the street, then he came back. I didn't pay much attention until he walked over and looked in my car. After that, he got into his own car and drove off."

It was a tantalizing lead, but ultimately worthless. The cream-colored car rang a bell, evoking memories of Beth's unwelcome visitors on January 7, in Pacific Beach, but her remains had not been dumped on Tuesday evening, and Johnson's vague description of the meandering motorist fit half the men in L.A.

A second witness, unidentified in press reports, resided closer to the scene, on Norton Avenue itself. Around 6:45 A.M. on Wednesday, he saw a black sedan, a 1936 or 1937 model, pull up to the curb not far from where Short's body was discovered. It remained in place for some three minutes, but "the weeds cut off my view. I couldn't see what happened." Once again, the timing was unfortunate, since passersby had seen no body in the lot as late as half past eight.

Once Beth had been identified, of course, the police had no end of leads to follow. Short's former roommates were debriefed, on the assumption one of them might know who had a killing grudge against the victim. One, "blond and shapely Lynn Martin," gave police the slip for several days, but she was picked up at a motel in the San Fernando Valley after LAPD issued statewide bulletins for her arrest as a material witness.

Born Norma Lee Myer, Ms. Martin had passed for twenty-three when she shared digs with Short at the Hawthorn Hotel. In fact, she was still three days shy of sixteen when police reeled her in on January 21, but reporters described her as "sophisticated and hardened beyond her years." A certified delinquent, Martin had been locked up for a year at El Retiro School for Girls and then had hit the streets to make her own way at fourteen, in 1945. Six hours of grilling verified that she had shared many friends and acquaintances with Short, but none—at least, according to official statements—seemed likely to be a killer. She had parted company with Short, said Martin, on September 20, 1946, and she had no idea what Beth had been involved in since that time.

There was at least one puzzling statement in her testimony, though. At some point in the long interrogation, she remarked, "I didn't think I could get away with it." She allegedly clammed up tight when detectives pressed her for an explanation. Five decades after the fact, author James Ellroy says, on the basis of personal research, that Martin admitted performing with Short in pornographic films. The man in charge, according to Ellroy, was named by Martin as local hoodlum Edward "Duke" Ellington, but again, the strict "no comment" policy of LAPD makes this lead impossible for independent hunters to pursue.

On January 27 homicide detectives heard from Gerson Abrams, a dealer in secondhand clothing on Santa Monica Boulevard. Abrams had received a phone call on the morning of January 14, he recalled, from a man who said, "I have women's coats, dresses, shoes, et cetera. I want you to pick them up at eleven o'clock tomorrow morning. Make sure you don't come before or after 11:00 A.M. Come to 1842

North Cherokee, apartment 501." Abrams wrote down the address but never kept the date, as he was "always leery of a deal in which a man is attempting to sell women's clothing or vice versa." He thought no more about the call for several days, until the newspapers informed him that the caller had provided him with Beth Short's address.

Once again, police were interested, but there was nothing they could do with Abrams's information. There was no man living in the Cherokee apartment, and the caller had not given his name.

Joe Grill, the operator of an ice cream shop in Farmers Market, handed police another lead on February 6. Some information had come to Grill thirdhand, from his maid, whom he had overheard discussing the Dahlia case. One of her friends, employed pumping gas for guests at the Beverly Hills Hotel, had reported a strange incident between 2:30 and 3:00 A.M. on January 11 or 12. A tan Chrysler coupe, vintage 1941 or 1942, had pulled in at the pump. A sandy-haired man sat at the wheel, and two women shared the front seat of the car with him. The witness, who was reported to be "in fear of his life should his identity be disclosed," identified one of the women as Elizabeth Short. Aside from her description, she had been addressed as Betty by the driver. Her female companion, seated in the middle, was described as an American, several inches shorter than Betty, with darker hair and pallid skin. The witness sold his customers a dollar's worth of gas, but he did not record the license number of their car . . . and there, unless the suspects walked in and identified themselves, the matter would inevitably rest.

There was no shortage of red herrings as the case dragged on, days running into weeks and months. A dancer at the Gay Way nightclub on South Main Street reported seeing Short on January 9 and again three days later, sitting alone at the bar. Another sighting from January 9 was reported by a female acquaintance of Short's, who placed Beth in the lobby of the Chancellor Apartments, embracing a young man "dressed like a gas station attendant." On January 10, a bartender at the 4-Star Grill on Hollywood Boulevard allegedly saw Short between 9:00 and 10:00 P.M., accompanied by two women "of dubious reputation." Beth, he recalled, had looked "seedy," as if she had slept in her clothes. Late the following afternoon, a bartender at a cocktail lounge below the Cecil Hotel on South Main said he'd spotted Short and an unidentified blond woman, arguing with a pair of sailors. That evening, an L.A. taxi driver claimed to have picked up Short and "a bossy blond" companion as fares. He saw them again two days later, parked in a 1937 Ford sedan at Hollywood and Highland, and he struck up a conversation with them. "The blonde kept insisting they drive off," he reported, "and finally they did. She seemed jealous of Beth talking to me."

Between those last two sightings, on the morning of January 12, Beth allegedly checked into a hotel on East Washington Boulevard. She was accompanied, said the proprietor, by one of the anonymous young men who appeared in a photograph reprinted by the press. The couple registered as husband and wife. "I'll swear it was Elizabeth Short," the hotel man declared, "and I'm almost sure that was the man. They went to their room and we did not see the girl again. The man was absent for a few days and then returned, saying he expected his wife to join him. I think it was Wednesday. I said to him, 'We thought you might be dead.' Then he got very excited and left."

Unknown to the amateur Sherlocks, Beth Short *was* already dead on January 12, and the same objection holds true for a flurry of sightings on the fourteenth, when Beth was reported to have spread herself thin to an almost supernatural degree. A Greyhound driver remembered Short boarding his bus at 1:00 A.M. that Sunday morning, disembarking at 4:15 in Los Angeles. Jack Fleming, a cashier at an L.A. market, had Beth buying change for the pay phone and making several calls on January 14, but he wasn't sure about the time. Nearby, a man who tried to hide his face from Fleming "studied the customers in the market and then hurried away." Fleming "wasn't quite sure," but he thought the furtive stranger might have been Red, who had not yet been identified as Robert Manley when the cashier gave his statement to detectives. Yet another witness, William Sullivan, a clerk at the Railway Express Agency, identified Short as the woman who dropped in on Tuesday afternoon to inquire about a shipment of luggage to Ketchikan, Alaska. Short allegedly identified herself to Sullivan by name. A black-haired man had paced the floor nearby, impatient to be gone, but Sullivan could not describe him further. Down in San Diego, meanwhile, drive-in waitresses Jadell Gray and Adelene McSwain placed Short in the neighborhood of Balboa Street between 5:00 and 5:30 P.M. Their sighting was confirmed by a gas station attendant "who knew her slightly." Beth was traveling, they said, with a red-haired man who wore "either a green suit or a marine uniform."

Even police officers, trained as observers of detail, were not above contributing to the rash of impossible sightings. Policewoman Meryl McBride, working the bus depot at Sixth and Los Angeles Streets, recalled that a tearful young woman matching Short's description had approached her on Tuesday night, "four hours before the murder." The woman begged for protection from "a jealous marine" who had threatened her life, but there was no such man in evidence, and Officer McBride did not obtain the would-be killer's name before she sent Short's doppelgänger off with warnings to be careful.

If there was any hope of capturing Beth's killer, it appeared to lie somewhere in the chaotic snarl of her frenetic social life. Newspapers cited an "amazing array of night spots" patronized by Short in her final months, and a list published on January 21 included fourteen taverns, with the heaviest concentration around Hollywood and Vine. The press did say, however, that "Although she spent long hours in the night spots, barmen recalled that she usually ordered soft drinks."

One angle of attack that surfaced early on, was an attempt to learn if Beth Short had been "queer." The L.A. cabbie's chronologically impossible report of Beth out cruising with a "jealous blonde" on January 12 was echoed by one John Jiroudek, former jockey, interviewed by the *Examiner* on January 21. Jiroudek claimed that he and Short had known each other at Camp Cooke "in 1945," when she was also chummy with "a domineering blonde."

Thad Stefan, a detective with the L.A. County sheriff's office, Hollywood Division, put in days and nights of legwork on the rumored lesbian connection, coming up with inconsistent information. One Bill Magee told Stefan that he "knew [Short] well and spoke to her on many occasions" but had never dated her. Magee said Short preferred the company of "masculine" lesbians or female impersonators.

Magee accompanied Stefan to a gay bar, the Flamingo Club, and fingered a female impersonator, Hector "Bobby" Walden,* who was said to match the vague description of "a person seen with the victim a number of times." Employee records showed that Walden had been off the nights of January 9 and 12. Magee confided to Stefan that Walden "knew Beth Short and purchased dope for her." Investigators grudgingly described Walden as "a pretty good looking fellow," but dismissed him as "queer for both men and women." His name disappears from the case at that point, and no charges were filed in connection with drugs or the death of Beth Short.

Another female impersonator, referred to in Stefan's notes as "Jane," recalled that a young woman matching Short's description had arrived at the Flamingo Club on January 10 "accompanied by two persons dressed in men's clothes." Jane remembered the trio "because they were not in his opinion drunk, but appeared to be under the influence of some narcotic. They sat at a table and the blonde made over the woman, possibly Miss Short, and [Short] seemed to become bored and called a young fellow at the bar over to their table and made a play for him." The trio soon got rowdy, with the blonde so furiously loud that they were asked to leave the club.

And so it went, in the pursuit of lesbians, female impersonators, and the like. The manager of the Flamingo Club also remembered Beth, but he could not recall the dates when she dropped by or whether she had come alone. He gave authorities a list of drag queens to investigate, and while a number of them claimed to recognize the Dahlia as a frequent customer at L.A. gay bars, none of them had any information that would speed up the desperate manhunt.

Once drugs were mentioned, the investigation took a whole new turn. Thad Stefan reports that Bill Magee saw Short alone outside the Owl drugstore between 5:00 and 7:00 P.M. on January 9 or 10. Magee "observed her taking orally a dope-pill which she was known to be using. . . . On previous occasions, he stated, he had observed her taking these pills at the fountain, either with a glass of water or placing the pill in a stick of gum, folding this gum over the pill, then proceeding to chew it. In another interview, on January 31, Magee declared, "Victim has been known to be an opium user; that a druggist on the boulevard had been furnishing her and her friends narcotics free of charge. Recently she and several lesbians have been purchasing narcotics from a syndicate operating in Hollywood. The person selling to victim is a Mexican who is known to informant by appearance only, that he is the last person selling narcotics to victim, that since her death, being in fear of becoming implicated in the murder case, [he] is reportedly hiding out in Tijuana."

Beth's pusher apparently slipped through the net and was never detained. In the absence of proof, no drug-trafficking charges were filed, and Dr. Lloyd Tainter, at West Hollywood Emergency Hospital, provided an alternative explanation for Short's alleged habit, advising Thad Stefan that severe asthma victims often took morphine or adrenaline for relief of their symptoms.

Overall, detectives assigned to the case were arriving at generally negative views of the victim. Cleo Short set the tone for Thad Stefan on January 21 by dismissing his daughter as "lazy" and "boy-crazy," often writing letters to as many as twelve men in a single night. When Beth traveled west to join him, back in 1942, Short said, her bus had rolled on through Vallejo without stopping. Beth showed up the next day in a taxi from San Francisco, sporting a new fur coat. Her story—that another woman on the bus had spilled a drink on Beth's cheap coat and had given her the fur to make it right—was patently absurd. As Stefan noted in his field report to Captain J. G. Bowers, "Mr. Short later learned she became acquainted with a man on the bus, continued to San Francisco with him, and spent the night with him in a hotel." According to Beth's father, "Victim was lazy, would not keep the home clean, just demanded money and wanted to run around downtown."

In time, it seems the men assigned to catch Beth's killer somehow came to feel that she deserved her fate or, at the very least, that she was somehow less entitled to respect than "decent folk." Detective Hansen, speaking from retirement in Palm Desert, described Beth Short as "a bum and a tease." The basis for that judgment has remained a secret, but he had clearly come to terms with his failure to catch her murderer.

The lady's dark side made it easier to look the other way.

Jack Webb reports that LAPD's sleuths were on the job from day one of the Dahlia murder case, intent on finding a solution to the crime. "Efficiently," Webb wrote in 1958, "detectives fanned out through the neighborhood" in search of Betty Bersinger until they tracked her down, obtained her statement, and presumably rebuked her for the false report that had caused the case to go "askew through no fault of the police."

Webb makes no mention of Captain Nash, who would surely have been a more reliable observer than the frightened housewife who had lied to the police in her anonymous report. To date, LAPD has not acknowledged Nash's sighting of the corpse, a fact that may or may not be explained by the fact that police departments did not tape incoming phone calls from the public in the 1940s. If there is a written memo of the Nash report, it has been lost or sealed forever in the LAPD's secret Dahlia files.

Technology aside, it is difficult to understand why Nash was twice more overlooked when he attempted to report his finding of the corpse. Detectives brushed him off Thirty-ninth and Norton, and they never followed up on the report of a patrolman who came knocking at his door, routinely canvassing the neighborhood for witnesses and clues. L.A.'s finest beat the bushes, taking eight days to identify a woman who had lied to them in the beginning and had nothing more to tell, but Bill Nash was filed away, ignored, forgotten.

At that, the loss of a potential witness ranks as small potatoes in comparison to some of the reports from journalists and former homicide detectives who claim that LAPD and certain members of the county sheriff's office deliberately subverted the investigation. Veteran newsman Bill Welsh recalls persistent rumors on the city desk that "someone powerful" had "fixed" the Dahlia case, but he could never dig up the specifics needed for an exposé. Niesen Himmel of the *L.A. Times* is more emphatic. He insists that the Short investigation was "a cover-up by the police department of that day." It was, in Himmel's view, "exactly like" the novel *True Confessions,* wherein LAPD homicide detectives solve a case identical to Short's and then deliberately destroy the evidence.

Such musings from the press are easily dismissed as fantasy, but Welsh and Himmel aren't the only sources pointing to a whitewash in the Dahlia case. Six separate homicide detectives blew the whistle on a cover-up at different times, but their reports have been suppressed through fear, official orders, and the standing LAPD policy of secrecy where the Dahlia is concerned.

Homicide Detective William Ernest Harmon was one of numerous plainclothesmen assigned to investigate Short's murder and, if possible, arrest her killer. Late in January 1947, Harmon told his family the case was "virtually solved." He seemed excited by the prospect and was "almost ready to go to the district attorney" with his evidence, but that evidence never saw light. Instead, Harmon was called on the carpet by his superior officer, ordered to turn in his personal notes and "never discuss the case again." Relatives reported that Harmon was "greatly disturbed" by that twist in what he called "the most significant case he ever worked on." Harmon never named the killer to his family, but he did say that the case was buried when it came "too close to some important people" in Los Angeles. Harmon's family understood him to mean that the cover-up involved "an interface between city government and the underworld."

Joe Jasgur was a photographer for the *Hollywood Citizen News* at the time of Short's murder. He covered the scene for his paper, recording grim images of the killer's handiwork, and kept in touch with detectives as the manhunt dragged on. One cop in particular, his name forgotten after almost fifty years, seemed bitter at the lack of progress. "Every time we get a good clue," he told Jasgur privately, "we get called off."

Two other LAPD homicide investigators waited fifteen years before they spilled their aggravation to a colleague on the job. Detective Vincent Carter was assigned to a narcotics detail in the early 1960s, teamed with longtime partners James Ahern and Archie Case. While killing time on stakeout duty, Case and Ahern reminisced about the old days, and in time their conversation came around to the Black Dahlia. They had found the place where Short was murdered, Case and Ahern said, but they were ordered by superiors to keep the information under wraps. Even today Carter speaks in guarded tones about the Dahlia case. One of his sources is deceased; the other is still afraid to speak out publicly, for fear of repercussions from the ancient murder case. Carter himself has a pension to protect, and LAPD takes a dim view of alumni with loose lips.

Thad Stefan, the L.A. County detective, was scouring gay bars and various dives in a search for some motive or clue in Short's death when he too was ordered to cease and desist.

According to Stefan, the strange directive came from Lieutenant Pete Sutton, who dropped by the Hollywood sheriff's station with a personal order for Thad to "back off." Stefan was so surprised that he went over Sutton's head, telephoning Captain Bowers to confirm the stand-down order. Bowers promptly countermanded Sutton's order, and while the lieutenant went away fuming, he need not have worried. None of the gay leads in Short's death paid off.

Two years after the crime, in December 1949, further evidence of a police cover-up in the case was aired before a special grand jury impaneled to discover why the Dahlia homicide was never solved. One officer who testified was LAPD detective L. K. Waggoner, assigned to work the "Long Beach angle" in Short's murder. Waggoner told the grand jury that he and his partner were making "remarkable progress" on the case, when they were abruptly reassigned to other duties without explanation. "The case could have been solved if we had been allowed to carry on our investigation," he declared under oath. "I was suddenly taken off the case, and I never did learn the reason why."

Why *would* a major metropolitan police department shield the killer of a beautiful young woman, knowing that he might repeat the crime?

From the early days of Prohibition onward, gangland payoffs were the rule at LAPD, the sheriff's office, and even City Hall. Graft was pervasive in Mayor Frank Shaw's administration, and successors to the office likewise had their hands out for a little something on the side. New York gangster Ben Siegel and his sidekick Mickey Cohen, working with the likes of William Robertson, had gambling, drugs, and vice sewn up throughout Los Angeles, and they were not above performing favors for the mayor.

In 1949, for instance, the Los Angeles police commissioner phoned Mickey Cohen to ask for some off-the-record help with Alfred Pearson, a hard-nosed radio repairman who had sued one of his customers, elderly widow Elsie Phillips, over an unpaid repair bill of $8.95. Pearson not only won his case but was allowed to attach the widow's home and charge her ten dollars a week in rent. A group of sympathetic cops from Wilshire station paid the tab, but Mayor Fletcher Bowron had a more permanent solution in mind. On March 19 seven thugs from Cohen's gang showed up to picket Pearson's shop, and when he came out to complain, they put him in the hospital. The so-called Seven Dwarfs were charged with battery, but not before the *L.A. Times* reported that patrolmen in the neighborhood had been instructed to ignore reports of any violence outside Pearson's shop on March 19. Reporters stopped short of naming the "responsible citizens" who had ordered the attack, and Cohen came out the loser, paying some $300,000 to spring his goons from jail.

That was peanuts, however, compared to the profits Cohen earned from gambling, prostitution, and affiliated rackets, all of which were protected by the men in blue. "At one time, during the 1940s and 1950s," Cohen recalled in his memoirs, "I had the police commission in Los Angeles going for me. A lot of the commissioners didn't have any choice. Either they would go along with the program, or they would be pushed out of sight, because I had what you would call the main events. It was all the way up to the top of the box at different police stations."

One of the officers whom Cohen counted among his "very, very closest friends" was Captain Jack Donahoe, chief of detectives for LAPD—this despite the fact that Donahoe had busted Cohen more than thirty times, by Mickey's count. "He would come see me sometimes when I was in the county jail," Cohen recalled. "In fact, he often brought me up a steak sandwich."

Even Chief William Parker, hailed by Jack Webb and others as an incorruptible reformer when he started "cleaning up" LAPD in 1950, was fingered by Cohen as one more cop on the take. In May 1957, during a live TV interview with Mike Wallace, Cohen blasted Chief Parker in graphic, profane language, calling him a "sadistic degenerate," among other comments, and Parker responded with a libel suit against Cohen and ABC-TV. The case was ultimately settled out of court, with Parker pocketing a tax-free $45,975 to forget the whole thing, but ten years after Parker's death Cohen had the last laugh, describing the chief in his memoirs as "an absolute bagman for Mayor Frank Shaw's administration."

Granting that municipal corruption was a fact of life in L.A. and environs during the 1940s and beyond, how does the atmosphere of graft relate to Beth Short's murder? At a glance, there seems to be no link between the web of syndicated crime and one young woman's random, brutal death. The link becomes apparent, though, when one notes a convergence of geography and deviant psychology: Beth Short was killed in Westminster. The killer had been seen with Short's remains, although the witness didn't know it, in Seal Beach, the very heart of gambler William Robertson's Orange County bailiwick. Beyond that, Georgie Knowlton was a regular at brothels, bars, and gambling clubs throughout the area. We have no way of knowing if he ever drew a paycheck from the syndicate, but his involvement in pornography, and later in drugs, suggests more than a marginal acquaintance with the local underworld.

It would not be required that Robertson or Mickey Cohen know the killer's name. Such "businessmen" are educated where it counts: they know their history, the immutable physics of cause and effect. When Jack the Ripper started carving up London prostitutes in 1888, the public uproar turned a spotlight on his chosen hunting ground and ruined countless pimps who saw their business wither under scrutiny from Scotland Yard. More recently, the same year Mickey Cohen left Ohio for Los Angeles, police were turning Cleveland upside down in their attempt to catch the wily Torso Killer. They would fail, but in the meantime, the pervasive heat made life unpleasant for the very mobsters who sent Cohen west.

A wise man learns from history, the better to avoid repeating his mistakes.

Bill Robertson and his superiors would not be anxious for the Dahlia manhunt to invade Orange County and disrupt the profitable status quo. A word or two would be enough, if whispered in the proper ear. Forget about that tan La Salle. Ignore that witness; he's a punk, a queer, a hophead. Let it slide. The little tease was asking for it anyway.

Would L.A.'s gung-ho press have permitted a cover-up, assuming that the facts were known? In that regard, it helps if we recall that the *Examiner* and the *Herald-Express,* both edited by Jimmy Richardson for William Randolph Hearst, were running with the Dahlia story in their teeth, outstripping their competitors with story after story, freely tampering with evidence, dictating terms to the police through a compliant Captain Donahoe. And Richardson, as luck would have it, was a bosom friend of Mickey Cohen, described in Cohen's memoirs as "a pretty good drinker" of many years' acquaintance. Richardson let Cohen sleep at the *Examiner* from time to time, when he was on the dodge, "because I kind of took care of him when he was drunk—I helped him sober up and lead [*sic*] him to his desk."

Nor was Richardson alone in his admiration of Cohen. Old man Hearst was fond enough of Mickey that he issued a special order to Richardson in the spring of 1949. "Jim," Hearst declared, "I don't want you to refer to him as a hoodlum any more. You can call him a gambler, but I wish you'd see that he gets a fair shake."

A major cover-up, to pass inspection and survive the test of time, must not be obvious. It calls for subtlety or, at the very least, a credible diversion. In the Dahlia case, as luck would have it, LAPD caught a break.

It was no trick at all to lose track of one man when they had suspects coming out their ears.

The glut of suspects was a problem—or a blessing in disguise—for homicide detectives working on the Dahlia case from the beginning. On the first night of their search, before Beth Short had been identified or autopsied, police reportedly eliminated some 150 suspects. One who rated booking was a transient in his early twenties, Cecil French, picked up on charges of molesting women at a downtown bus depot. Police were briefly interested in French's car—a black 1936 Ford with no back seat. Suspicious stains were found on the floorboards, but the stains were merely rust. He was freed, no charges filed.

The next hot tip came out of San Diego, where a dapper-looking man called Red had been the last one seen with Short while she was still alive. The L.A. papers tracked him down, exposing Robert Manley's clumsy infidelity not only to his bride but to the world at large. It was revealed that Manley had been discharged from the army air force on psychiatric grounds in April 1945. The army shrink's report said Manley was possessed of homicidal tendencies, a trait considered mandatory in most soldiers during wartime but disdained in members of the marching band.

The ink was barely dry on headlines sketching Manley's link to Short when visions of a speedy murder trial went down in flames. Red's alibi was solid from the afternoon of January 10 to his arrest on January 19. The polygraph confirmed his innocence. He walked, and Captain Donahoe looked glum on January 23 when he declared, "We're right back where we started."

Even so, the tale of Red was far too colorful to die. Three San Diego witnesses insisted they had seen Beth Short on January 14 with "a second Red." They looked at Manley's mug shots, shook their heads, unanimously negative. The second Red, they thought, was a marine.

In Hollywood, beautician Alex Constance told police that she had done Beth's hair from time to time. On one occasion she had seen Short with a tall, red-haired marine, but she could not recall the date. Beth had expressed grave fear of the marine, informing Alex that she dated him only because she was afraid to turn him down.

Around the same time, red-haired Jeff DuBois* was picked up in Los Angeles for questioning. DuBois had lately been employed at the Mayfair Hotel, but he failed to report for work on the night of the murder, January 14, and when he did return, he stubbornly refused to talk about the brand-new scratches on his face. The manager dismissed him and reported him to the police, but DuBois was subsequently cleared of all involvement in the case.

When it came down to leads and suspects, LAPD struck a veritable gold mine in the Owl drugstore at Hollywood and Vine. Beth Short had been a frequent customer between October and December 1946, when she took off for San Diego, but employees argued over whether she more often came in with a man or on her own. Three waitresses told homicide detectives "they were under the impression that [Short] was addicted to narcotics as she would occasionally have a glassy stare and appear to be in a daze. On other occasions she would appear to be in a gay mood." And it was also in the drugstore, we recall, that Bill Magee reportedly watched Beth consuming "dope-pills" and chasing them with water or chewing gum.

Barber Carl Feranna, dropping in from his shop on Hollywood Boulevard, recalled seeing Beth several times at the Owl lunch counter. As summarized in one police report, "He [Feranna] further stated that she was the type of girl who would attract the average man's attention due to her figure and the manner in which she dressed, indicating an effort to display every portion of her anatomy, including low-neck dresses."

Casual observations aside, the Owl provided manhunters with at least four suspects in the Dahlia case. First up was a sandy-haired John Doe, described as twenty-five years old, five feet eight, 165 pounds, with a rosy complexion. He was observed on one occasion only, sometime in early December 1946, waiting for Beth while she made a telephone call. On that day he wore an "army pink overcoat" over light-colored slacks and tan shoes. It was too little to go on, and the man remains unidentified to this day.

The second drugstore suspect was more intriguing. Right from the start he had a name: James Edward Walker.* Better yet, he had red hair, and friends were known to call him Red. A thirty-six-year-old former hairdresser reduced to jerking sodas for a living, James Walker had worked at Owl drug from August 12 to September 28, 1946. His attendance was spotty at best, and unauthorized vacations had prompted his dismissal, but co-worker Cyril Judd told police he had seen Walker "watching [Short] many times." Police interviews produced the observation that Walker "appeared to have a low mentality, his attitude ignorant, occasionally replied to questions in a sarcastic manner, vocabulary very limited." As frosting on the cake, Walker's landlady told detectives he had "never been seen associating with any women." In the absence of any solid connection to Short, he was scratched off the list.

A fellow employee of Walker's at the drugstore, waiter Carl Albert Green,* had resigned without notice the day Walker was fired. Was it coincidence, mere friendship, or complicity? Detectives traced Green to his room at the YMCA, where neighbors described him as "queer." Interrogated on January 31, Green denied being gay but admitted consulting a psychiatrist over persistent fears that he *might* be. As noted in a summary of the debriefing: "Suspect stated that he has been accused of being a queer, due to the fact that he had enlarged breasts, which he insisted on exposing to officers as proof." Green knew Beth Short by sight, from visits to the drugstore, but there was no further link, no evidence of any crime, and he was finally released.

Yet another suspect from Owl drug was Juan Luis Morales,* a twenty-three-year-old Angeleno "of Spanish extraction" who worked at the drugstore for four days in November 1946. His brief employment ended on November 18, when he was jailed by LAPD officers for molesting a fourteen-year-old boy. The charge—"arousing passion of a minor child"—was subsequently reduced to one count of contributing to the delinquency of a minor. Investigators noted that Morales also "associates with known homosexuals," and while he made bail on December 26, in plenty of time to murder Beth Short, his preference for boys seemed to rule out a heterosexual sex crime. As with his predecessors from the drugstore, Morales was discounted as a viable suspect.

There were plenty of others to deal with, however.

Leo Jackson,* age thirty, was fingered for detectives by acquaintances who called him "very high-strung, sex pervert, lone-wolf type, who usually followed the women as they left the various spots, so thereby [he was] never seen leaving with them." Jackson was said to frequent "all the gay spots," but the notation "homosexual" is crossed out on one official report to accommodate his apparent interest in females. Jackson was known for his nightly visits to the Continental Café on Santa Monica Boulevard before he suddenly dropped out of sight on January 12, 1947. An informant recalled seeing Jackson chatting with Beth Short at the Continental, but the dates were hazy and left much to be desired. Jackson's brother had filed a missing-person report on January 31, telling police that he "cannot understand where [Leo] is." The words had barely passed his lips when Jackson's brother contradicted himself, stating that "he believes [Leo] may have run off" with a waitress who lived on Highland, north of Hollywood Boulevard. If detectives ever found their man in this case, they did not record the fact.

Another suspect, thirty-five-year-old bartender Frank DuPont* was arrested on February 4 and held for questioning in Hollywood. Authorities described DuPont as "separated from his wife and children, but queer." He had been stationed at Camp Cooke in 1943, while Short was there, but further investigation placed him in San Francisco continuously from November 1946 to January 14, 1947—one more name deleted from the list.

Then came George.

The name cropped up like magic in defiance of official reluctance to see the truth. On January 17, a front-page story in the *Times* referred to five acquaintances of Beth's in Hollywood, described only as "three youths and two young women," who "said she told them of her plans to marry George, an army pilot from Texas." That information should have set alarm bells clamoring, as the report of Red and other suspects would do in days to come, but George immediately disappears from newsprint, his debut and swan song all wrapped up in one.

Not so with the police reports.

On January 26, Thad Stefan at the sheriff's office took an urgent call from Dorothy Perfect, a waitress at the Hub Café on Santa Monica. She was concerned about a man who introduced himself as George—no last name—and professed to be an agent of the FBI assigned to work the Dahlia case. On January 21, George visited the Hub and hung around the bar, where he was "very talkative" with customers and staff alike. The bartender asked to see his G-man's badge, but George "became perturbed" and drifted to the restaurant, where Perfect was on duty. There he once more identified himself as a federal agent, "rambled about being unafraid of guns," and "further told informant he could tell her who killed Elizabeth Short." Digressing for a moment, George told Perfect that "he could obtain an apartment for her on the Sunset Strip without any effort whatsoever," but she declined the offer. George soon lost interest and excused himself. A short time later, while comparing notes with bar employees, she found out that George had come into the Hub twice previously within the past six days. His last appearance, on Saturday, January 25, was cut short when he spotted Perfect in the dining room and beat a swift retreat.

The George described by Hub employees was Caucasian, in his early forties, roughly five feet seven and 150 pounds, with wavy hair and glasses. In regard to his jumpy behavior, Dorothy Perfect suggested that he "didn't appear drunk, but may have been under the influence of a narcotic." As far as we know, he never returned to the Hub, and Stefan never tracked him down.

There is no public record of Los Angeles police investigating the man named George, beyond that passing mention in the *Times*. Still, we know that LAPD interviewed Short's former roommates, when they could be found, placing special emphasis on questions about strange men in the Dahlia's life. We may assume that one or more of those young women mentioned Georgie, his hometown link to Short, his cowboy boots and foundry job, his irritating tendency to cancel dates and run off to the mountains to shoot deer. Detectives may have found Tex Driscoll in the process of unraveling Beth's past, but they would not have needed him. George Knowlton didn't hide from women, and Beth, despite a tendency to make him over as an officer and gentleman in conversations with her friends, had made no secret of their love. As Tex remembered, "it was always 'Georgie this,' and 'Georgie that.'"

All things considered, how could Hansen, Brown, and company have failed to notice George?

The false confessions helped—around five hundred of them through the years, according to the estimate most often published. There were some persistent regulars, like "Confessing Tom" and the hard-driving Mormon described in Chapter 1. Some homeless drunks also made a practice of confessing when they wanted food and lodging for the night, but most of those who voluntarily surrendered were content with one confession. Their motives ranged from the pathetic to the practical. One man confessed in the hope that the publicity would help to reunite him with his missing wife. A woman jailed in Barstow promised to identify Short's murderer "if the reward is large enough." There was even a "fatal attraction" case, involving an L.A. businessman and a relentless female stalker who had met him in a wartime car pool. She had "dogged, threatened, and slightly black-mailed" the businessman, but all in vain. When he continued to reject her, she turned him in to LAPD as the killer of Beth Short.

Some confessors were more convincing than others. Daniel Voorhees telephoned police on January 28 to say he "couldn't stand it any longer." His one-sentence written confession—"I did kill Beth Short"—was a trifle short on details, but Voorhees tried to make up the difference in his dialogue with detectives. "I met Beth two weeks ago at Fourth and Hill," he said. "That's where I first saw her in '41." By that time, of course, police knew that Beth Short had come to L.A. for the first time in 1943, and other details of the Voorhees confession were equally wide of the mark.

Joseph Dumais was different, or so it seemed, for a time. An army corporal stationed at Fort Dix, New Jersey, Dumais was locked up in the brig for embezzlement when he confessed to Short's murder on February 8. In a fifty-page handwritten statement, he said he was bar-hopping with Short on January 9 or 10 when he "blacked out" from drinking too much liquor. He remembered nothing more until he woke up in a taxi days later, outside Manhattan's Pennsylvania Station. "It is possible I could have committed the murder," Dumais wrote, "but to the best of my knowledge I am still not positive." All the same, at his arrest in Jersey, Criminal Investigation Division investigators searched the corporal's wallet and removed a story about Short's murder, clipped from an L.A. paper. Captain William Florence, of the Fort Dix CID, was "definitely convinced" of Dumais's guilt, and even Jack Donahoe placed "some credence" in the suspect, but it all fell apart three days later, with discovery of "unimpeachable evidence" that Dumais was in New Jersey on January 15.

And so it went . . . until the killer lent a hand.

The parcel of Short's belongings, intercepted by police on January 24, remains a controversial topic in the Dahlia case, primarily because of LAPD's long "no comment" policy. There is good reason to believe this package should have solved the case, but after so much time and speculation in the media, with false and contradictory reports permitted—or encouraged—by police, the seeds of speculation fall on barren ground.

It is established that the package had been "soaked" or "washed" with gasoline, in an attempt to wipe out fingerprints. That effort seems to have failed, for the various reports unanimously grant that fingerprints *were* found. The *Daily News,* on January 25, quoted an LAPD lab report to the effect that "exceptionally clear prints had been obtained" from the parcel. The *L.A. Times* describes "two good sets of fingerprints" found on the outside of the package. Jim Richardson's *Examiner,* however, never seemed to get the story straight. On January 25, page one reported "several" clear prints lifted from "a fingerprint-spotted envelope," with still more inside. Two of the prints, in fact, were photographed and printed for subscribers to examine over breakfast. One day later the *Examiner* backed off, reporting that only two fingerprints had been obtained "from the envelope or its contents." The *San Diego Tribune,* on January 25, noted the discovery of "a dozen clear fingerprints on a crude patchwork letter."

What became of those "exceptionally clear" fingerprints is anybody's guess. We find no further mention of them in the press after January 26. They disappeared from news-print with unseemly haste, spent seven years in limbo, then resurfaced with a cagey explanation from Hank Sterling in *Ten Perfect Crimes.* The L.A. prints were rushed to Washington for study by the FBI, writes Sterling, but "too many over-eager employees of the post office had handled the envelope and its contents to make any identification possible." David Rowan, writing in 1957, disagreed. While the prints were "exceptionally clear," he reports, they simply were not found in any state or federal file. Jack Webb, arriving late at the scene of the crime, tries to help L.A.'s finest off the hook by declaring that *no* prints were found.

There was even some doubt, deliberately fostered by detectives, as to whether the package was mailed by Short's killer. In one statement, summarized by the *Examiner* on January 25, "It was pointed out that while fingerprints on the outside of the envelope could have been left by any one of dozens of people who handled the letter, prints on the back of the clipped-headline words could only have been the killer's." That same afternoon, speaking to the *Orange County Register,* Finis Brown declared, "These are effects of Miss Short, but we believe they were mailed by someone who had no connection with the killing, possibly by a former landlord."

Predictably, confusion reigns in any effort to describe the

parcel's contents. All sources mention Mark Hansen's address book, but they can't decide if one page (Sterling) or "about a hundred pages" (Webb) were ripped out prior to mailing. Harry Hansen, looking back across a quarter century, remembered only that the book contained "about seventy-five names." One anonymous detective told the press, "This book is going to be dynamite," but it fizzled in the long run, leading nowhere. All the names belonged to men, apparently, and all had known Beth Short, but their relationships had ranged from casual to intimate, without a killer in the lot.

Other items retrieved from the parcel, or not, as listed in various sometimes contradictory reports, included Short's birth certificate and Social Security card, an unspecified I.D. card, a comb and makeup, a membership card in the Hollywood Wolves Association, a Greyhound luggage claim check dated January 9, "a few" snapshots, a press clipping on Matt Gordon's marriage with the bride's name crossed out, plus "miscellaneous cards and papers, scraps with numbers and names on them." Police had no reason to doubt that the objects belonged to Beth Short, but none of them helped put the killer in jail. In fact, after viewing the items, one spokesman for LAPD told the *Daily News* that investigators were divided between suspecting "a brittle, masculine type" of woman who killed for revenge and sadistic pleasure, and "a weak, frustrated man—an egomaniac who never received the attention or affection he desired."

Hopes were raised when the next note arrived, predicting the killer's surrender on January 29, but the only lesson learned on that Wednesday afternoon was that media had a gift for throwing detectives off the track. Jim Richardson describes the scene.

That was the day the detectives were posted at the *Examiner* doors and reporters from other papers came boldly into the building. We chased the reporters away and I called Jack Donahue [*sic*].

"Get your boys away from here," I said. "Nobody is coming in with them standing there all eagle-eyed. If he comes I promise to call you."

"All right, but understand I'm taking him out of there at once," Jack said. "No deal this time. You can't hide out a murderer without getting yourself into real trouble. You know that, don't you?"

The captain could have saved his breath. As noted in the final message posted to authorities, Short's killer had decided for himself that he was "justified."

On February 1, Jack Donahoe admitted that his men were stymied. Barring a surprise confession from the real assassin or some hot new lead, LAPD's detectives were officially conceding failure. Donahoe's announcement might have closed the case as far as newsmen were concerned, but Jimmy Richardson refused to let go of the story. If there was no new suspect in the Dahlia murder, he would manufacture one—or better yet, a handful. He would publish "profiles" of the killer lifted from the sharp imaginations of the hottest writers in the movie business. Hollywood was right next door.

The first writer to grace the pages of the *Herald-Express* was Ben Hecht, a Chicago crime reporter turned Hollywood screenwriter, producer, and sage. His screenplays included *Wuthering Heights* (1939), *Notorious* (1946), *Scarface* (1932), and *The Front Page* (1931). Hecht was also a good friend of Mickey Cohen. He wrote about Cohen's "good deeds" and, in 1957, proposed a Cohen biography. Mickey liked the notion of a book so much that he sold "stock" in the project to various friends, collecting $25,000 in "loans" that were never repaid.

Hecht opened his review of the Dahlia case with a salute to forensic endocrinology, proclaiming that "The manner in which the 'Black Dahlia' was done to death, befouled and butchered after expiring under divers tortures, bespeaks the looks, sex, height, weight, coloring, and even type of hair of the killer." Proceeding from the false assumption of torture, Hecht assumes the killer must have been female, since "In nearly all torture cases and mutilation after death, homosexuality is the basic motive." Likewise, the killer's presumed sadism convinced Hecht that there was "no element of revenge in the killing." A man may torture for revenge, Hecht theorized, but anger dies with the victim. Meanwhile, "The painstaking and physically arduous trouble the killer went through in dismembering and outraging the dead 'Dahlia' spells paranoia. There is nothing as patient and thorough as lunacy." To summarize Hecht's view:

> It was a crime done by a Lesbian—and not intended as a crime. The killing itself may well have been part of the didoes to which the 'Black Dahlia' had submitted herself. She, too, was an odd one, and because of her physical and glandular and psychic makeup given to humoring the fancies of women as well as men.

At this point, Hecht is flying in the realm of pseudoscience, concluding that posthumous mutilation of Short identifies her killer as "a hyper-thyroidic type of human with over-developed thymus gland at work." The overkill exhibited on Short was produced, Hecht assures his readers, by "the hyper-thyroid, driven into a thyroidal storm by some great shock."

Another indicator of the killer's sex, at least to Hecht, is found in faulty grammar. In one note to the press, Short's killer boasted: "Had my fun at the police." For Hecht, the use of "at" in place of "with" becomes "a female malapropism, and an infantile one (an over developed thymus bespeaks infantilism). Little girls often say, 'Give it at me.' "

From these astute deductions, Hecht proceeds to offer a description of the killer: "She is a woman of forty. She is 5 feet 7 inches tall. She weighs 115 pounds. She is thin, almost gaunt. She has a rudimentary bosom. Her face is long and narrow. She has a receding chin. Her teeth are slightly oversized. She has brown and very wavy hair. Her fingers are long. And she has large eyes—unusually large and arresting eyes.

And she would have a "European" accent, as well.

Despite his confidence, Hecht covered all his bets with "a secondary version of the crime and its perpetrator which I am unable to offer this or any other paper." In the alternate version Hecht claimed to know the name of the [a male] killer, and the psychology of his deed. All things considered, though, Hecht put his money on the woman. "I am awaiting," he wrote, "the arrest of a tall, thin, brown-haired, large eyed, bosomless woman of 40 named 'Miss———.'"

Next up was crime novelist and screenwriter Steve Fisher, whose scripts included *Destination Tokyo* and *Song of the Thin Man.* Schooled in melodrama, he began his profile of the suspect with a statement that "After writing this I am going to leave town, and I won't return until the killer of the 'Black Dahlia' is under lock and key." By following the case in media reports, wrote Fisher, "I think I know who the killer is. I'm sure the police do, too, and that in a very short time they will have his name."

Fisher's anonymous suspect was a male ego-maniac who would challenge police to "a spectacular movie finish" once his identity was known. "He will put up a terrific fight," Fisher predicted, "but he will be taken alive." An insanity plea in court would be foiled by the killer's stubborn refusal to appear demented. Fisher claimed that his man was infuriated by the false confessions registered to date and was driven to assert his claim on Short by writing to the papers and police. In custody, he would be happy to confess. ("Some of the torture he inflicted upon the nude girl," Fisher confides, "is unprintable.") In fact, Fisher suggested that police might force the egocentric killer to reveal himself if they accepted someone else's false confession as legitimate and formally declared the Dahlia murder solved.

It was a thought, but no one took it seriously, and the cavalcade of speculation rolled on toward Act Three.

Novelist Leslie Charteris, creator of "Saint" Simon Templar, opened his column on the Dahlia murder with a promise that "my friends at police headquarters can be sure that what they told me in confidence will be kept that way." Charteris brands his subject as a loner, dismissing Hecht's hypothesis of a lesbian orgy gone wrong as "too fanciful even for me." He specifically denies any link between Beth and organized vice, insisting that she was not "what you might call a party girl." Charteris also notes: "The fact that with surprising unanimity all the male associates who have been questioned insist that in spite of appearance she never delivered what they were after has, I think, an important bearing on the case."

Charteris "deduces" that the killer is between thirty-five and fifty years old, "either underweight or overweight," possessing a full head of hair, prominent eyes, and—"for associated glandular reasons"—a sallow complexion. He is married with children, compulsively neat, soft-spoken and right-handed. His formal education ended with high school, and Charteris had unspecified "reasons for suspecting he is a baseball fan." While appearing normal to most acquaintances, the killer was really a lone wolf and sadist, plagued by sporadic impotence linked to alcoholism. Most of Beth's mutilations were "strictly spontaneous and [were performed] without any idea of inflicting pain." More to the point, the killer was "almost certain" to repeat his crime.

"I can see him," writes Charteris, "saying something like 'So you think you can laugh at me, do you? I'll keep that laugh on your face for good'—and he slashes her cheeks from the corners of her mouth to her ears, in the ghastly grin which is preserved on the morgue photos." Charteris might have been a fly on the wall in the Knowlton household, describing Georgie to a T and echoing one of his famous threats.

Novelist David Goodis (*Dark Passage*) brought up the rear in Richardson's celebrity parade of speculation, approaching the case from "a careful study of all facts thus far brought to light." He deems the crime a sadistic murder wherein the killer "took his time" and "gloated over it," but since the Dahlia was presumably his only victim, the police were dealing with "no ordinary sadistical [*sic*] killer." Goodis also takes a cue from Harry Hansen's personal opinion of the victim, blaming Beth for her own murder: "In the 'Black Dahlia' affair, the killer demonstrates extreme psychotic tendencies—the kind of tendencies that can be brought to the surface only by excessive external stimulation. This, therefore, becomes a case wherein two unusual personalities met each other, had an abnormal effect on each other, lit the fuse of a box of emotional dynamite."

Goodis pronounces the killer "completely insane" at the time of the murder, but "when the fit—and it was probably a schizophrenic fit—had reached its breaking point, the killer was no longer a raving madman, but a cold, calculating murderer." Assuming screams and other noise attendant on a nonexistent torture session, Goodis wrote, "Pure logic points to the fact that the victim was murdered in a deserted shack or remote area, probably on the outskirts of the city."

In the Goodis scenario, Beth met her killer in a bar, and her erotic conversation literally blew his mind. "Suddenly he was insane—completely," Goodis wrote. "But Elizabeth Short did not notice this." To solve the case, the killer "must be baited, rather than hunted," using "another 'Black Dahlia'" whom he would find irresistible, even while fearing a trap. The plucky lass should make a date with Mr. X and keep a wire recorder handy. Homicide detectives would swoop in once he revealed himself in conversation and invited her to "his place."

Once again, the sage advice fell on deaf ears at LAPD Homicide. As far as Finis Brown and Harry Hansen were concerned, the case was winding down, with theory and conjecture taking the place of legwork.

On the afternoon of February 1, while Ben Hecht cautioned Angelenos to beware of tall, flat-chested women with protruding eyes, Jack Donahoe informed the press that he believed the Dahlia kill site was "a remote building or shack in a thinly populated district on the fringes of Los Angeles." Donahoe was forced to that conclusion, he explained, "by the failure of anyone to report a possible place where she was killed within the city limits. If she was slain in a house or a room or motel in the city, it seems impossible that some trace has not been reported or found"—unless, of course, the killer's family lived in daily terror and assisted him in covering his tracks.

Without explaining why, Donahoe further "reasoned that the place would not have cooking facilities." And since LAPD now believed that Short was held for several days before she died, detectives were busily "checking all eating places outside the city in an effort to get a line on any suspicious persons who took out meals from January 9 to 14."

This was the wildest long shot yet, and the results were perfectly predictable. One diner was suspected by a fellow customer because "he had an apprehensive look and ordered only half a cup of coffee," but the damning evidence would not stand up in court.

The rest came down to hot air, educated guesswork, and repeated efforts to explain why LAPD had failed to bag its man—or woman. "In our files of the Beth Short murder case," said Donahoe on January 24, "we have hundreds of names, and I'm sure one of them is the name of the friend who committed this horrible crime." Years later, David Rowan wrote that Donahoe had formed his private theory of a female killer within two weeks of the murder. The lesbian thesis, shared by newsman Bevo Means, Ben Hecht, and others, was based on "a number of reasons," including certain injuries deemed "similar" to wounds observed in other cases rooted in homosexual jealousy.

Reporter Aggie Underwood, Jim Richardson's eventual replacement on the city desk, advanced a different theory. She insisted to her dying day that the police had "very grave suspicions" about one man they had grilled in the case, but Underwood refused to reveal his name when she was interviewed in 1971, claiming that the suspect was deceased. "The evidence at hand was almost conclusive against this particular suspect," whom she described as a man questioned by police but not well known to the public.

Finis Brown, for his part, told James Ellroy that police had been closing in on one likely suspect, an L.A. abortionist, when the man cheated justice by killing himself. If Harry Hansen ever knew about the nameless butcher, he had apparently forgotten by 1971, when he told an interviewer, "I know for certain that I never met the killer face to face. I know he didn't manage to slip through with the other suspects."

Jim Richardson went to his grave expecting the Dahlia's killer to strike again, or at least to call back for a chat. "I am convinced," he wrote, "that his mad ego will cause him to commit another crime in the same manner. Either that or he will come forward again with taunts about the Dahlia murder. He may even furnish a clue that will start the search all over again. Eventually he will make a mistake that will result in his capture. It may be that what is written here will do it. He knows my name and he has talked to me. If he knows about this book he will read it. If he does, the warning about his eventual mistake won't stop him, because he believes himself the superman incapable of making a mistake."

Psychiatrist Paul DeRiver was inclined to agree with Richardson. "This case is symbolic of a man's work," DeRiver told the press in January 1947, "and if he runs true to type, it will be very easy to gain a confession from him." Most likely, thought DeRiver, Beth Short's killer would be prone to boast about his crime.

In fact, the editor and the psychiatrist were both correct. Short's killer *did* repeat his crime. He *did* confess and boast about his grisly acts, but not to the authorities.

He had a captive audience at home.

8

Werewolf at Large

No one keeps a secret as well as a child.

—Victor Hugo, *Les Miserables*

LIFE WAS VEERING TO THE LEFT OF NORMAL AT THE KNOWLTON house in Westminster, that January. George was ill, for one thing, though no records have survived to tell us what his symptoms were or how they were resolved. His ulcers may have flared up, with the stress of killing Short and all that followed, but we simply have no way of knowing. Nine months later, there was a balance of $8.60 outstanding on his bill from Dr. Russell Johnson, mailed to the Westminster house in October 1947 with an urgent plea for payment. The bill indicates that Georgie was treated by Dr. Johnson between January 9 and 17, with the cryptic notation "in__ptn" following the dates.

Among surviving family members, even Georgie's loyal supporters are unclear about the meaning of this bill and its significance. Some think that Dr. Johnson's code means Georgie was an inpatient at some local hospital, thus incapable of having murdered Short, but no one in the family recalls him being hospitalized in 1947. The bill for eight days in a hospital would surely have exceeded Dr. Johnson's modest tab, even in that thrifty era. Lacking guidance from the doctor, long since gone to his reward, it is a fair alternative to suggest that the billing dates may refer to an inclusive treatment period, between the first report of symptoms and their cure, as in the standard week-long regimen of antibiotics prescribed for most minor infections.

Even without Jan's memories, there are repeated pointers to her father. References to "Georgie" from Beth's friends, including Tex Driscoll, which police refused to follow up. Too many witnesses for any man to silence on his own.

And there were fingerprints. The packet mailed to newsmen on the afternoon of January 24 contained at least two prints, and perhaps as many as two dozen. Some of them, at least, were said by the police and press to be "exceptionally clear." It is a relatively simple task to match up fingerprints, but any match requires two sets for physical comparison. A flesh-and-blood defendant is unnecessary; records will suffice.

George Knowlton never made it into military service, he was never fingerprinted for a job in government, and California drivers' licenses did not display a thumbprint in the postwar years. He did have at least four brushes with the law, however—two in Massachusetts, the arrest in Tucumcari, and the lethal incident down south—that could still have repercussions for him, though. No expert on police procedures, he had seen Beth Short identified by federal agents overnight from fingerprints, and who could say the awesome FBI would not reach out from Washington to pluck his teenage records from the files of some remote police department?

Georgie needed help.

He needed Janice.

Ironically, her helping hand had set the latest series of events in motion. While cleaning up the back room after Short was gone, she had retrieved an overnight bag from behind the chest of drawers. Jan opened it, removed several perfumed scarves, and wrapped one of them around her neck. Eau d'Elizabeth. A manila envelope caught Jan's eye, and she worked it open, spilling out shiny snapshots of Elizabeth and sundry private papers. She was sorting through them when she heard a sound and turned to find her mother watching from the doorway.

"Janice, let me see them!" As Marge scanned the contents of the envelope, the color drained from her face. She slumped against the door frame while Janice stared. Neither of them heard Georgie coming, but suddenly he was there, filling the doorway, dark eyes shifting from one pallid face to the other and back again, concentrating on Marge and the items in her hand.

"You did it," Marge accused, throwing one of his lies back in his face. "You didn't just leave her there. You killed her yourself! George, *you* killed her! Oh, my God."

Marge sat down on the bunk bed. Jan felt an urge to warn her off—it was a deathbed, after all—but she could not produce the necessary words.

George sat to Marge's right and put his left arm around her shoulders as he tried to explain. "Margie," he told her, "I did it for you and the kids. She could have gotten us all killed. I know the kind of people she hung around with, and I couldn't risk it. I had to protect you and the kids."

Brave Georgie, standing up for hearth and home against Beth's underworld connections. Never mentioning that he was one of them—perhaps the very one who introduced Beth into whoring and pornography as the route to fame in Tinsel Town.

Marge was not convinced. She wanted Beth's belongings sent to the police. She would be watching for a sign of their delivery. If Georgie failed her, she would do the job herself. "I don't care how you do it, George, but if I find out you're lying to me again . . ."

The unspoken threat intimidated Georgie. He was unable or unwilling to silence the love of his life.

He needed a plan, and he drafted Janice to assist him. It was her fault, anyway, for snooping in the overnight bag, getting Margie all upset about a worthless slut who had gotten what she deserved.

Jan remembers sitting in the living room in Westminster surrounded by her elders. The images are clear: Georgie sits in his favorite chair with his slippers on, red-faced from weeping. Marge is visibly upset but keeps her distance, the emotions locked inside. Kay Cardran stands between them, helping Georgie organize his scrambled thoughts.

Another visit from the other woman.

"You have to help me," Georgie whines. "I didn't mean to do it. They'll put me in the electric chair if you don't help me."

Little Janice knows the words are meant for her. She does not want to see her father sit in the electric chair, whatever that may be. It sounds uncomfortable.

"She tried to kill me," he declares to no one in particular.

Kay seems convinced that Georgie "had to" kill Beth Short in self-defense. He must now attempt to frame a nonexistent "crazy person" for the crime. "Don't worry, Georgie," Kay says. "The little tramp deserved it."

Sitting on the floor with flour paste and scissors, clipping words from the *Examiner* as directed, Jan gets the message loud and clear. If Daddy "has to" kill, his women will protect him from the "goddamn cops."

Next time he is compelled to kill in "self-defense," the victim may be Jan herself. Lord knows that death threats are as common as rapes and beatings under Georgie's roof, and she has seen them acted out on pets, on total strangers, on Elizabeth.

Jan understands that there is no one to protect her or avenge her death if Georgie runs amok. She must defend herself, and that means following the monster's rules.

Jan does as she is told.

George does his best to sanitize the package, swabbing it with gasoline. If he considers fingerprints on the reverse side of the pasted letters, it is nothing to concern himself about. His ten-year-old accomplice has no rap sheet for the FBI to scrutinize.

Another chilly afternoon in the garage. No windows in the back room to admit the pale gray light. George stands beneath a naked light bulb dangling from the rafters and surveys his handiwork.

His daughter is stretched out on the bed, bound hand and foot.

Jan pleads with Georgie not to kill her. There is something dull—no, *dead*—about his eyes. She has a feeling that he isn't seeing her. His eyes are focused on Elizabeth.

"Won't take much to cut *you* in half," he observes. Muttering around his hand-rolled cigarette, he complains about "wasting another mattress."

He leaves for a moment, returns with the Skil saw, and holds it close enough for Jan to see the metal shark's teeth, catch a whiff of machine oil. Georgie snarls at her, inches from her face, "If you ever—do you hear me?—if you *ever* open your big mouth about any of this, I swear to God I'll cut you in half with this saw. Are you gonna make me do that?"

"No, Daddy. I swear."

He thinks it over, lays the saw aside, then sits down in the death chair at the foot of the bed, legs crossed, running a thumb over the stubble on his jaw. Finally he rises, hitches up his dungarees, and draws his belt knife from its sheath. His thumb explores the cutting edge.

"Don't kill me, Daddy!" little Janice pleads tearfully. "I love you. I won't tell, I promise. *Please* don't kill me!"

Georgie leans across the bunk bed—Beth revisited. This time his sharp blade makes it to the rope securing Jan's arms. Another slashing movement frees her skinny legs.

Jan thinks to herself, He must love me, because he didn't kill me. He didn't even cut my face.

George brings a beer back from the fridge and slouches in his chair, sipping while he picks at the sole of one boot with his knife blade. He is complaining. Here he's brought the whole damned family to California for a brand-new start, new house, new everything. So where's the frigging gratitude, for Christ's sake?

Jan apologizes, soaking up the guilt and begging for another chance to make it right.

George straddles her, unzips his fly. Jan takes him in her mouth, a token of her love, repressing the memory even as he shudders into climax.

Sometime later Janice finds him in the driveway, hosing off the tan La Salle. She helps him towel it dry. When they are finished, Georgie leads her to the screened porch, sprawls out on the sofa there, and pulls her face into his lap. He seems to take forever this time, but she barely notices.

Jan's mind goes away.

And comes back to discover they are lying side by side, with one of Georgie's arms around her. He has pinned her left hand to his crotch.

Jan wonders how she ever could have doubted Daddy's love.

The L.A. papers taunt him with their "werewolf" headlines, speculating that the killer must be crazy. That was Georgie's plan, of course, to fool them all, but it is getting out of hand. Some of the goddamn cops profess to think a queer killed Beth. Worse yet, a *female* queer.

George reads their nonsense. Ben Hecht's skinny, pop-eyed woman. Spokesmen for the city spelling out how Beth was strung up by her heels and tortured over several days before she died. Whenever *that* was. Tuesday night, for God's sake.

Using the refrigerator had really helped to throw them off the track.

Beth's letters are the worst of it.

She taunts him from beyond the grave, her sluttish infidelity revealed for all the world to see. Of course, George knew that she was seeing other men behind his back. She had been punished for it once. But *this!* The goddamn army, navy, and marines!

"Yes, I have dated since I have seen you last," she wrote to one of her innumerable fiancés. *"But most of them disgusted me."*

Ungrateful, scheming bitch!

All right, then.

207

If the papers wanted raving lunatics and werewolves, Georgie Knowlton would oblige.

It was as if Short's death had thrown a switch, unleashed a homicidal whirlwind in the L.A. basin.

On Saturday, January 18, thirty-seven-year-old Mary Tate was found dead on Weller Street in Los Angeles, beaten and strangled with a silk stocking. Tate was black, a resident of North San Pedro Street, L.A. Dr. Newbarr's detailed autopsy notes have not survived, but a coroner's jury listed robbery as the "probable cause of homicide." The panel recommended that Tate's husband, Terry, be detained for further questioning.

Because of the victim's race, to LAPD, it was an unimportant killing, hardly worth a white detective's time. As far as it is possible to tell from spotty, ancient records, the case remains unsolved.

The final corpse for January was a skeleton recovered from a shallow desert grave south of Victorville in San Bernardino County, on the twenty-fifth. LAPD ignored this case until the victim was identified as forty-year-old Irene Weeks, missing from her Los Angeles home since June 1946. Her estranged husband, Orville Weeks, residing in Long Beach, was not considered a suspect. The case remains unsolved.

At 9:30 A.M. on February 10 a coroner's wagon was summoned to pick up yet another body, this one found on Grandview, West Los Angeles, seven miles from Thirty-ninth and Norton. A bulldozer operator discovered the corpse, lying in a vacant lot described as "a sort of lovers' lane." The *Daily News* described what ambulance attendants found: "The body, while not sliced up as was the Dahlia's, was viciously mutilated. One side of her face had been torn open from the lip almost to her ear. One breast was slashed by some instrument which detectives thought was a tire iron or heavy wrench. Part of her hair had been cropped, as in the case of the Dahlia. And the obscenity written on her dead body led police to believe it could have been the maniacal boasting of the Dahlia's mad killer."

The killer had scrawled a message in lipstick on his victim's torso. Press photographer Joe Jasgur, recording the grisly scene for posterity, recalls the message: "Fuck you—B.D. Killer." Years later a retired detective told author James Ellroy that the word "cocksucker" was also printed on the corpse.

Below the infamous "B.D." initials, according to press reports, was written "what appeared to be 'Tex' and 'O.'" Or, given the killer's haste and awkward choice of writing implements, could that *O* have been a *D*?

Tex *Driscoll?*

Someone shifting guilt, perhaps, to an incriminating witness in the Dahlia case?

The Grandview victim was Jeanne Thomas French, age forty-five, a former actress, aviatrix, airline hostess, army nurse. The cause of death was listed as "hemorrhage and shock due to fractured ribs and multiple injuries"—in short, a savage beating. News reports state that the killer not only bludgeoned French but also "stamped with heavy shoes on her breast, hands and face."

A pair of cowboy boots, perhaps?

The victim had a checkered past, including three arrests for public drunkenness. Her blood alcohol level was .30—three times the legal limit for intoxication—at the time she died. Some of her clothing—a burgundy dress, brassiere, and fur-trimmed coat—was dumped atop her naked body in the field where she was found. No panties or stockings remained, but French's shoes had been "carefully arranged" on either side of her head, ten feet from the body. Also recovered at the scene was French's black plastic purse, described by newsmen as "almost identical with one Elizabeth Short carried."

Detectives guessed that French had been dead some two hours when found, at 8:30 A.M., but Dr. Newbarr was more cautious, placing the time of death within twenty-four hours. As with Short's murder, there were no significant traces of blood at the scene, prompting LAPD to surmise that French was stripped and beaten in a car but managed to escape, whereupon the killer followed her, clubbed her repeatedly with a blunt instrument, and finished the job with his feet.

Jeanne's husband, forty-seven-year-old Frank French, already on probation for a wife-beating incident in December 1946, was the immediate suspect. He staunchly denied the crime, and plaster casts of footprints found around the corpse did not appear to match his shoes. Frank's landlady confirmed that he was home during the presumed time of the murder, and a polygraph removed all doubt.

Jeanne's car was found at Washington and Sepulveda on the night of February 10, but there were no incriminating bloodstains in the vehicle, no fingerprints the lab was able to identify. Detectives calculated that a chrome-plated wrench —perhaps the murder weapon—was missing from the car, but it never surfaced. There were vague eyewitness reports of French dining with "a dark-haired man" at a West L.A. hamburger stand sometime after midnight on February 9–10, but there the trail went cold.

The case remains unsolved.

A week after Jeanne French was found, the L.A. Police Commission summoned Chief Clarence "Cowboy" Horrall to give "a detailed report on the city's recent murder wave." Bruno Newman, acting president of the commission, assured newsmen, "We don't want Chief Horrall to reveal any facts which might jeopardize the police investigation, but we do want to know what's going on."

In fact, by all accounts, there was nothing to tell. L.A.'s finest were getting nowhere fast.

Six days later, on Sunday, February 23, they had a new body to cope with. Mary Muldoon, a thirty-seven-year-old stenographer who listed a downtown hotel as her home, was fished out of Fairmont Reservoir, twenty miles west of Lancaster. She had been beaten to death, her sweater-clad body submerged for an estimated ten days before she was found. Muldoon's record included a drunk arrest in 1946, but there were no apparent suspects in her death. The case remains unsolved.

On March 11, LAPD logged two more brutal slayings of women, for a total of five in sixty days. The first victim, found at 1:45 A.M. in the gashouse district, where Ducommun Street crossed the Santa Fe railroad, was forty-nine-year-old Evelyn May Windham, née Winter. She had been clubbed to death by an unknown attacker, the cause of death listed as "subarachnoid hemorrhage and edema of the brain, due to concussion of the brain." In fact, severe blows to the left side of her head—as if delivered by a right-handed man—left portions of her fractured skull exposed. Winter was found with her slip, brown dress, and checkered jacket "pulled nearly off" her body. The victim's underwear and shoes were found a block away, at the corner of Commercial and Center Streets.

A musician and Vassar graduate, once described as a brilliant scholar, Evelyn Winter had been married to Sydney Justin, head of Paramount Studios' legal department, from 1936 to 1941. She, too, had also worked at Paramount, as a music copywriter. In 1942 she had married a soldier named Windham, but they divorced two years later. Lately she had fallen on hard times, including a record of arrests for intoxication, drunk driving, and "resorting." Her blood alcohol level was .28, nearly three times the legal limit of intoxication, at the time she died.

On March 9, two days before her corpse was found, Evelyn Winter had spoken to her mother in the lobby of the Clarke Hotel. She had borrowed five dollars for expenses but refused to say where she was living, remarking that "It's too terrible a place. I don't want to tell you." Her mother reported that Evelyn had once resided at 1850 North Cherokee, a few doors from Elizabeth Short. According to her mother, Evelyn was also known to frequent bars on Hill Street, less than three miles east of Thirty-ninth and Norton.

Police detained George Wickliffe, the twenty-eight-year-old railroad section hand who discovered Winter's body, after they found a woman's blue coin purse in his possession and noted lipstick smudges on his mouth. No stranger to jail, having been arrested for vagrancy in February, Wickliffe had a simple explanation for the lipstick: he admitted kissing Winter when he found her sprawled beside the railroad tracks, before he realized that she was dead. An opportunist. He was subsequently cleared, and Winter's case remains unsolved.

On March 19 fifty-five-year-old Anna Diresio was found with her head badly gashed, lying in a clump of bushes in Elysian Park. A park caretaker followed her moans to the scene of the crime and summoned police. Rushed to the nearest hospital in critical condition, Diresio was described by local papers, with no apparent grasp of simple math, as "the fifth recent victim of murderous assaults on women" in L.A. and its suburbs.

Regaining consciousness, Diresio told police that she "believed" she was assaulted by a "chance acquaintance," vaguely described as a man she met at a downtown market on March 18. She had gone to Elysian Park with the nameless stranger, but rejected his pleas that she follow him home. Beyond that, she remembered nothing more.

The case remains unsolved.

Local police soon had yet another savage slaying on the blotter. Laura Trelstad, a thirty-seven-year-old mother of three, was found dead on May 12 in a Signal Hill oil field twelve blocks from her home. According to the autopsy results, she had been beaten, raped, and strangled with a strip of cotton cloth. There was no mutilation, per se, although various reports describe the beating as "savage" and "ferocious" enough to have fractured her skull.

Trelstad's husband, a truck driver three years her junior, told police he had taken his wife to a neighborhood party on Sunday, May 11, but she left "to go dancing" while he stayed behind to play cards. Detectives tracked down a sailor who was seen leaving a Long Beach café with the victim on Sunday night, but he was cleared of suspicion in the case. Police believed him when he said he had escorted Trelstad to a bus stop and put her aboard a Huntington Park bus at 11:50 P.M. From there, authorities declared, "she kept a date with another girl," but no details were forthcoming. The case remains unsolved.

Six similar slayings in the four months between January 15 and May 12. At least four of the victims—Short, French, Muldoon, and Winter—were known barflies with alcohol-related arrest records. In all six cases, beating and/or strangulation was reported as the cause of death. Each of the bodies was partially stripped; several of them were nude. In each case, the victim was apparently killed elsewhere, then transported to the dump site. Again, in each case, some article of clothing was either lost entirely or recovered a substantial distance from the body. At least one victim, Jeanne French, bore wounds, combined with lipstick writing by her killer, that evoked echoes of the Dahlia case.

The papers didn't find these clues coincidental, and neither, for a time, did the police. Author David Rowan, writing ten years after the fact, noted that each of the unsolved murders included "other elements, best left unmentioned, which suggested that they had been inspired by the manner of Elizabeth Short's death."

Or perhaps they were committed by the same fiendish killer.

And those were just the victims that LAPD knew about.

By mid-February the search for Beth Short's murderer had shifted far afield. On Monday the seventeenth, Bostonian George Poleet ran out of gas in Pittsfield, Massachusetts, and asked for help at a nearby state police barracks. Troopers were suspicious when Poleet could not produce his auto registration, and a license check revealed the car had recently been stolen in Albuquerque, New Mexico. They also found an ax and a shovel in the trunk. They were "taking no chances" with their suspect in the face of rampant Dahlia fever. In fact, Poleet admitted having been in Los Angeles from late December through the greater part of January, working at a restaurant from January 4 to 21. LAPD had grabbed him for suspicion of robbery on New Year's Eve, and again for suspicion of burglary on January 8, but he had been released both times for lack of evidence. His luck would not desert him in the Dahlia case, but Albuquerque had him cold this time, on auto theft.

Five days later, in San Francisco, police jailed an electrician, thirty-one-year-old Phillip Smalley, on the strength of a request from LAPD's Captain Donahoe. According to the *Daily News,* Donahoe wanted to question Smalley regarding the deaths of Beth Short *and* Jeanne French. Lieutenants William Cummings and Lloyd Bang were dispatched to bring Smalley home, but Captain Donahoe played his cards close to the vest, saying only that Smalley's arrest "climaxed a series of guarded investigation [*sic*]." So guarded, in fact, that his eventual release, without so much as an apology for wasted time, was never mentioned by the press at all.

In Chicago on March 6, police detained three women for questioning after one of them, twenty-nine-year-old Marie Grimes, claimed knowledge of Short's murder. Grimes, who sometimes called herself Marie Griene, was held as a material witness after promising to name Beth's killer. The best she could do, in the long run, was to finger a woman named Billy, who had passed through Chicago the previous month and claimed to have murdered Short "in a fit of jealousy during a lovers' quarrel."

Ten days later in Saint Louis, twenty-five-year-old Melvin Bailey was being grilled on suspicion of auto theft when he interrupted detectives with a surprise. "Let's forget about cars," he said. "I've got something hot. Let me tell you about the murder." Which murder was that? Why, the Dahlia's, of course.

Bailey claimed to have met Beth Short in a Los Angeles tavern "just before Christmas." He was vague on details of the murder, blaming his lapse on a surfeit of liquor and goof balls, but he remembered clubbing Beth with the pommel of a Marine Corps combat knife, then severing her torso in a stolen car parked "somewhere in the Los Angeles manufacturing district." After dumping her at Thirty-ninth and Norton, Bailey said, he drove to a friend's home in Long Beach and slipped in unnoticed to trade his bloody clothes for a clean suit. Thus attired, he caught the next bus to Saint Louis, where police had rousted him for stealing cars on George Washington's Birthday.

Back in Long Beach, William Hughes admitted knowing Bailey, but denied having seen him since October or November 1946. No bloody clothes had shown up unexpectedly in his apartment, Hughes declared, and none of his own clothes were missing. Hughes's landlady, Ellen Scaife, however, recalled a man who seemed to fit the suspect's general description, turning up around the time of Beth Short's murder. He had tried to make his way inside the Hughes apartment, but without success. The controversy fizzled, finally, when Captain Donahoe announced that Beth was still in San Diego on the date when Bailey claimed the two of them had met.

Back in Los Angeles on May 6, sheriff's deputies jailed forty-eight-year-old Wallace Fortier, a Long Beach machinist, on four felony counts stemming from the kidnap and rape of a twelve-year-old Buena Park schoolgirl. Classmates had recorded Fortier's license number, and the victim readily identified her rapist at the county lockup. L.A. newsmen called Fortier the "hottest suspect yet found" in the "Black Dahlia murder cycle," noting his resemblance to a man seen leaving the field where victim Dorothy Montgomery was found murdered on Saturday, May 3. In time, however, that case would resolve itself with the arrest and trial of Montgomery's husband. No evidence was found connecting Fortier to any other homicides, but he had trouble enough as it was: he was held in lieu of $50,000 bail, awaiting trial on charges of kidnapping, assault, and child-molestation.

Meanwhile the hunt for L.A.'s resident werewolf went on. Detectives had no way of knowing they had missed one homicide entirely. Chances are, it would have made no difference either way.

It is a sunny afternoon when George and Janice drive to Union Station. Daddy and his little girl. The hunter and his bait. Inside, they find a seat. Georgie opens his paper and begins to read—or pretend to. He keeps a sharp eye on the ever-changing flow of passersby until he sees exactly what he needs: a stylish redhead wearing a green print dress and carrying a cardboard suitcase. Georgie rushes over, exuding charm, offering to help the lady with her bags. Jan follows, trying to remain invisible and make no clumsy errors to produce an angry tirade. She cannot be sure if Georgie knows the redhead, but they seem to hit it off at once. The woman smiles and lets him take her bags out to the tan La Salle. George makes small talk, keeping her amused. Jan's memory gets hazy as they drive away, but somehow they wind up back on Texas Street in Westminster.

George pulls straight into the garage, turns off the engine, sets the parking brake. He gets out, closes the garage door, and gets back into the car. He reaches for the redhead, trying to embrace her, but she pulls away. Her resistance sparks his rage. He locks his strong hands around her neck and drags her out the driver's side. She is unable to escape his grasp as Georgie shoves her toward the little room behind the garage.

Jan's next image: Georgie has the redhead gagged and trussed up in the same chair where Elizabeth was killed. He crosses to his workbench, picks up a butcher knife, and walks slowly back to stand before the woman. Thoughtfully, he runs his thumb along the cutting edge. The redhead strains away from him, secured by her bonds. Jan watches from the car, feeling no conscious fear, the inner numbness overriding her emotions.

Taking his time, Georgie thrusts his knife into the redhead's midsection with one smooth stroke. Blood streams as the woman topples over to her left, chair and all. It is so tidy that George seems pleased. He turns toward Janice with a toothy smile, wiping the blade of his knife on a towel or rag as he circles the car, coming up on the driver's side. He opens the door, leans in, and presses the blade against Jan's throat. Familiar threats of death, evoking promises of silence.

Janice "goes away."

And comes back, in her own good time, to yet another waking nightmare in the charnel house. The naked redhead is suspended by her ankles from the rafters, as news reports insist Short must have been, the way her father dresses out a deer or calf. Georgie stands in front of her, clutching her hips with both hands, his face buried between her thighs. The act seems almost loving, worshipful, despite the grisly circumstances.

Finally sated, Georgie undergoes another sudden change. He fetches back a hatchet from the workbench, muttering and snarling in his rage. He hacks at the suspended body aimlessly, gashing the torso, severing first one arm, then the other. Finally he concentrates on cutting through between the rib cage and the hips. It takes him longer with the hatchet than with his Skil saw, but he seems to like the exercise. At last, the upper body falls away. Dark entrails slither free and wind up on the dirt floor in a steaming heap.

From somewhere, David's dog sneaks up behind George, following the scent of blood. George sees him rooting in among the guts and curses, grabs him by the scruff and takes him back outside. The dog has signed his own death warrant. Fascinated by the blood smell, he will haunt the small garage until his master snaps. Within a week or so, the dog is shot and buried in the yard, his skeleton unearthed four decades later by authorities investigating Jan's recovered memories.

In the garage, George has another plaything to amuse him. Blood is smeared across his chest and lower body, some of it by accident. The crimson dripping from his genitals is a deliberate application. Ghoulish finger painting. Reaching overhead, he cuts the body down. It tumbles into ruin at his feet.

George sips a beer and looks around the slaughter pen, apparently recovering his senses. "Shit," he mutters. "Now I gotta clean up this goddamn mess."

Jan runs to fetch the hose upon command, and Georgie

bathes himself. The redhead is a larger problem, but he has an inspiration. All that prior experience at carving venison will not be wasted.

Georgie goes to work with hatchet, knife, and butcher paper, wrapping parcels, stashing them in the refrigerator. Entrails and the like go into metal buckets, waiting. Georgie has a plan.

Their garbage man is Mexican-American. He drives a flatbed truck, collecting rubbish from the neighborhood. In those days, years before the advent of the Hefty bag, his gear includes a reeking oil drum for the wet stuff.

Georgie walks his buckets to the curb. The garbage man is smiling, happy to accept a cigarette. He doesn't mind when Georgie crawls up in the truck to do the dirty work himself. He empties the buckets into the oil drum, making sure he gets it all.

Before the truck pulls off, he has a bright idea. "Hang on a second." Georgie walks back into the garage, returning moments later with a parcel wrapped in paper. "Here," he tells the driver, "maybe you and your family can use this. It's fresh kill." He breaks down laughing, as the garbage truck pulls out of sight.

Jan doesn't get the joke. She has forgotten all about the redhead.

"Dumb spic," her father says. "I put one over on him. What he doesn't know won't hurt him."

In the backyard, Georgie rinses out the pails. He catches Janice watching him and sprays her with the hose, a little something to amuse himself.

A job well done. "That's the last we'll see of her," he says. Not quite.

There are at least two dozen meaty parcels waiting in the fridge. Jan finds herself promoted to the rank of courier. From time to time, as Georgie may direct, she takes a package with her on her daily walk to fetch the mail. There's a nice big trash can at the branch post office; it is emptied every day. No fuss, no muss, no comebacks.

What they don't know can't hurt Georgie Knowlton one damned bit.

George left his wife and family on May 14, two days after Laura Trelstad's body was found in Long Beach. We know the date from papers filed by Margie in her pursuit of a divorce. The break had been a long time coming—after nearly thirteen years of mayhem and abuse—and still it came as a surprise. Marge had become accustomed to the thought that George might kill her, kill the children, but she had never dared to hope that he would simply leave. She had two women—Beth Short and Kay Cardran, who was now separated from her spouse—to thank for her release. And yet, when Georgie left to live with Kay she was absolutely unprepared.

There were some desperate times on Texas Street after Georgie ran away from home. He left the family destitute, reduced to eating rotten vegetables from the small garden out back. Marge was forced to go on welfare, and she hated it. A few months later, when the house was sold, she made a point of paying back the state.

As a first step toward independence, Marge hired attorney Craig Hosmer—later a congressman from Long Beach, who spent over twenty years in Washington—to help her rid herself of Georgie. Hosmer filed the divorce petition, citing "extreme cruelty" as grounds. That was an understatement, but it did the trick.

Another legal problem was brewing around that time, though crucial details have been lost. We know from Prudence Knowlton, six years old in 1947, that she accompanied her mother on a visit to the police station. She recalls seeing a man staring at her through the bars of a holding cage. Either she did not hear or did not understand her mother's conversation with police, but independent evidence suggests that a criminal investigation was in progress.

Forty-two years later, sorting through her mother's papers after Marge died, Prudence found half of an old business card, torn in two down the middle. The remaining half includes the last name Pool, the legend "ct Attorney," and a Santa Ana phone number.

It was no great leap of the imagination to suspect that Mr. Pool was an Orange County distri*ct attorney,* and, in fact, the Santa Ana telephone directory for 1947 reveals that a Willard R. Pool, deputy D.A., resided at 601 South Birch. From this we may surmise that the matter under discussion must have been criminal in nature, since the district attorney does not concern himself with divorces—nor, in those days, was he likely to care much about the welfare of a mother and her children in Orange County. That was someone else's job. The D.A. is retained to prosecute.

It is entirely possible, as Prudence has suggested, that the card was given to her father during some investigation of suspected crimes. If Marge tore the card in two, asks Prudence, why would she keep half of it like a souvenir and throw the rest away? In retrospect, it seems more logical that Georgie was confronted by authorities, presented with the card, and that he tore it up, contemptuous as ever of the law. Marge found it in the trash—or half of it, at any rate—and kept it through the years, perhaps as a weapon she could use against her husband in the future if things ever got too bad.

But did she ever call that number? Did she ever speak to the authorities about Beth Short? About the violence she endured? About anything at all?

If George was questioned in connection with the Dahlia slaying, would his battered spouse have given him the airtight alibi he needed to escape prosecution?

Jan's records from Westminster Elementary indicate that she was absent four days running, from Monday, May 19, through Thursday, May 22. No one in the family remembers illness in the house around that time, and while we cannot rule it out, there is at least an equal possibility her absence was occasioned by a visit Georgie made a few days after he slipped off to live with Kay. Ostensibly, he came to patch things up with Marge, but his approach was self-defeating—

he rambled on about how he loved his wife *and* Kay so much that he could not bear to lose either of them.

Marge let him talk, but she would not be moved. Not this time.

Georgie saw how things were going, and he gave it up. He still had one more mission to accomplish, though. Plan B.

Alone with Janice in the kitchen, glaring at her with the cold eyes of an executioner, he said, "I hear you've been saying bad things about me."

A damnable lie. Janice was devastated. "Oh, no, Daddy! I've been sticking up for you."

"Well, just remember what I told you. Keep your big mouth shut!"

By that time, Jan had no idea, at any conscious level, that she had been victimized by George or that she had been forced to watch him kill at least five persons.

She could not have told on Daddy, even if she'd wanted to.

The monster was insatiable. He could not rest.

At half past three on Tuesday morning, July 8, postal clerk Newton Joshua was walking to work when he found a woman's naked body lying in the gutter on Elmyra Street, below Elysian Park. A stocking had been tightly wrapped around her neck, her right breast slashed. The only items of apparel left to her in death were bits of jewelry—a religious medal, and a ring.

The latest werewolf victim was Rosenda Mondragon, age twenty-one. She lived on South Crocker Street, about two miles from where her body was found. A New Mexico native, married in 1943, she had been separated from Antonio Mondragon since late April. They kept in touch, however, and her latest visit to Antonio had been at 2:00 A.M. the day she died. Antonio described her as intoxicated, prattling on about a date, and he had watched her drive away in a coupe, not otherwise described. Police did not consider him a suspect in Rosenda's death.

Newspapers quickly jumped on Mondragon as the "sixth victim in the Black Dahlia murder cycle," noting the breast mutilation and police suspicions that she had been murdered elsewhere, then dumped at the curb from an automobile. Dr. Newbarr confirmed death by ligature strangulation, with the notation of a "traumatic subarachnoid hemorrhage" indicating one or more heavy blows to the skull.

LAPD Detectives Finn and Hausman were assigned to work the case, but they never seemed to catch a break. The mystery remains unsolved.

On Thursday, July 17, Canadian divorcée Vivian Newton was found raped and strangled on Torrey Pines Mesa, fifteen miles north of San Diego. That was still municipal territory, and Lieutenant Ed Dieckmann, chief of homicide for San Diego PD, told newsmen his detectives were seeking a white John Doe who had squired the victim around Tijuana on Wednesday. Police had photographs of them together, smiling underneath sombreros, sitting in a donkey cart, and Newton evidently did some shopping in the border town. Her body, when discovered, was still clad in the white peasant blouse and black-trimmed dirndl skirt she had purchased in Tijuana.

The victim had arrived in San Diego on the Saturday before she died and settled in a small downtown hotel. One of her neighbors, Edna Mitchell, told police that Newton's date for the excursion into Baja was a pilot from Los Angeles. When Vivian returned that Wednesday night, she had accompanied Mitchell to a downtown dine-and-dance club in the hope of meeting men. She lingered on at the club, dancing with a new male friend, after Edna left at midnight, and no one could remember seeing her alive beyond that time. Investigators traced her traveling companion to the Fairfield Army Air Base near Solano on July 20, but Sergeant Frank Adams had not seen Newton since their Wednesday outing. Another man, initially believed to be the victim's final dancing partner, was eliminated from the suspect list when Edna Mitchell failed to make a positive I.D.

The case remains unsolved. Another woman raped and strangled in the werewolf's happy hunting ground. It was a short drive south to San Diego from the L.A. basin. Georgie Knowlton made the trip all the time.

Judge Raymond Thompson granted Marjorie's petition for divorce on September 22, 1947. She won the case by default—no response from George pro or con—and she was granted custody of the children and awarded twenty-five dollars a week in spousal support. It would have been premature, however, to suppose that she was free of Georgie yet.

Jan started another school year at Westminster Elementary on Wednesday, September 10. She was present that first day, in Frances Bard's sixth grade class, but things began to fall apart at once. On Thursday, Jan missed twenty percent of the school day for reasons unknown, and she was absent all day Friday. On the twenty-sixth, four days after Judge Thompson granted her mother's divorce, Jan's attendance record notes that she was transferred out of Westminster for good.

The move was Georgie's brainstorm. He and Kay were driving back to Massachusetts. Margie and the kids were welcome to come along for the ride—or they could stay in Westminster and try to make it on their own. The court's decree of child support meant less than nothing to George Knowlton. Once he left Orange County, there was nothing the judge could do about it, anyway.

Marge made her choice. Her family lived back east, and California held grim memories. Her "new beginning" on the coast had ended in defeat, with two of her children planted in Westminster Memorial Park. There was nothing to hold her in the so-called Golden State.

Marge and Kay buried the hatchet, after a fashion, before they hit the road with Georgie's transient sideshow. Kay apologized for breaking up the marriage, and her penitence seemed genuine enough, but Marge refused to hear it. "Don't apologize," she said. "You did me a favor."

They were packing the car and preparing to leave when next-door neighbor Gladine Deal beckoned Marge to one side. Jan drifted over that way, listening, and heard the neighbor say, "Be careful, Margie. He might try to murder you."

They followed Georgie's favorite track, Route 66. Before they left L.A., though, Georgie made a detour to the famous tar pits, off La Brea Avenue. There was no park, no grand museum, in 1947. Just the reeking, crusty pools of tar, with cautionary signs on prominent display. A pit where ancient things had come to die.

George Knowlton's kind of place.

Jan and Prudence have very different recollections of the tar pits. Prudence recalls the stop as an adventure— standing on the crust until it started cracking, leaping back to safety in the nick of time. Her mother worried, but their father was a laid-back, take-charge kind of guy. "Leave them alone, Marge," he ordered. "They'll be all right."

Jan's memory is of a different kind of game: George lifting her, strong hands beneath her armpits, dangling her above the stinking lake of tar, his cold voice threatening to toss her in and let her sink. One way to shut her goddamn mouth for good.

Another stop along the way was the Grand Canyon. Georgie knew the region from his hunting trips to Arizona, but it was a marvel to the kids. Marge played it safe and would not leave the car when Georgie called her to the chasm's brink. Disgusted, Georgie rolled his eyes. "Get your mother to come see this, Janice," he ordered.

Jan hurried back to the car. "Mama, come look!"

Marge shook her head, refused to budge.

Jan understood and tried to make it better. "Mama, he won't try to murder you, I promise."

Margie grimaced and shook her head. No way.

The strange extended family moved on, eastbound.

9

Bloodlines

Why is betrayal the only truth that sticks?
                                    —Arthur Miller, *After the Fall*

ARRIVING IN MASSACHUSETTS, GEORGE DROPPED KAY AND HER daughter in Lynn, then drove on from there to Beverly, where he left Marge and the kids with her parents. Annie Hatch was too "delicate" to cope with four children in the house, and Kenneth was blunt in his suggestion that Margie place her offspring in an orphanage or foster home. Marge tried to stand her ground, found work at the Economy Shoe Company to pay her way, but she could hardly dictate terms beneath her father's roof.

In short order, a compromise was reached. Evelyn and Prudence remained with Margie and her parents, while the older children, Jan and David, went to live with Georgie's sister, Myra. Even then there was confusion. When Janice enrolled at Rial Side School in October 1947, her home address was listed as 7 Winthrop Avenue in Beverly, the home of George Senior and Gladys.

Life was far from perfect—Jan recalls that "the word 'mean' was invented to describe Aunt Myra"—but it showed a definite improvement without Georgie around. The difference shines through in a free-form poem written by sister Prudence years later:

We played
in the henhouse
after the rooster
was gone
The dogs
no longer whimpered
after the rooster
was gone
We became rowdy
in our ecstasy
We blew tin horns
and banged
on pots
and pans
after the rooster
was gone
We built beaches
in the living room
in our merriment
after the rooster
was gone
We cried
in relief
We rode on tricycles
to the farthest stretches
our imaginations
could reach
after the rooster
was gone.

There was no celebration on Winthrop Avenue. Gladys Knowlton was furious with Georgie for the scandal he was heaping on her bleached-blond head. Family legend has it that Gladys took a dusty German Luger from the closet, went looking for the "other woman," and warned Kay to find herself another man or face the consequences. Maybe so, but Gladys never used the gun, and Kay had more tenacity than that. She wanted Georgie, even knowing what he was, and now she had him.

Georgie kept in touch with Margie on the side, though, undoubtedly aware that she was being prodded toward a reconciliation by two sets of parents. That hope was doomed from the beginning, but finally, in late November, Marge agreed to give the marriage one more try.

Those who refuse to learn from history are doomed.

The setting for a most unlikely "brand-new start" turned out to be a weather-beaten farmhouse outside Charlestown, New Hampshire, south of Claremont. It was cold and bleak December, snow heaped in the yard, banked up against the house and barn. In Rial Side, Jan's school record indicates a transfer to North Charlestown, and while she remembers riding a horse down to meet the school bus, there is no evidence of her attending school in New Hampshire. We do find David signing up in Claremont on the fifth of January, but his grades and record of attendance have been lost.

Jan clearly remembers the farm. There was a gentle snow-white draft horse that let her mount him bareback. He took her on tours of the property, but he was stricken with an illness shortly after they arrived. Black water fever, said the locals. Georgie "tried to save" the animal—his remedy included forcing one arm up the horse's rectum—but his veterinary skills had not improved, and soon the horse was dead. Janice watched him stiffen in the snow before the knacker came and carted him away.

It was the same old story with her parents—beatings and abuse from George, their arguments competing with the brutal wind outside. One change had occurred, though: Margie had learned to fight back. Once, she even flung a cast-iron pot of stew at her ex-husband's head.

Marge conjured up a Christmas celebration by sending Georgie out to cut a tree in the surrounding forest, then stringing it with popcorn for adornment. There was nothing in the way of presents, though, and Georgie got his Christmas spirit from a bottle.

The attempt at reconciliation was hopeless. Marge had made her last attempt to satisfy others by taking Georgie back.

Rial Side School recorded Jan's return to Beverly in January 1948. Her home address was still listed as 7 Winthrop Avenue, an upstairs flat above the senior Knowltons, granting Marge a respite from her father's tyranny. Marge painted shoe soles at the plant and brought her meager paycheck home to feed her family.

That May, George Junior startled everyone by buying a gift for Prudence's seventh birthday. His selection was a pink sundress with ruffled hem and neckline, cut to leave one shoulder bare. Marge hated it, pronouncing it "too sexy for a little kid." She knew George well enough to doubt his motives, but he made the normal show of injured innocence: "Oh, Marge, come on."

Afterward, thinking of her mother's comment, Prudence felt guilty whenever she wore the dress.

On rare occasions, Gladys took Jan to her beauty shop to "doll her up." On one such visit Gladys gave the child a perm and then demanded fifteen dollars for her trouble. Jan was stunned, explaining what the older woman knew already: she had no money. Gladys took delight in scolding, sneering at her like a deadbeat off the street, before she did a sudden flip-flop and dismissed the whole performance as a joke. In place of the demand for cash, she now belittled Jan for thinking she was serious.

Mind games. The Knowlton specialty.

Jan tried to do her part by baby-sitting for her uncle Donald's children and by doing child-sized jobs around the house. It was at Donald's that the family discovered Jan could not tell time. Donald's wife, Aunt Dorothea, called out to her from the kitchen one gray afternoon to ask what time it was.

"The big hand is on twelve," Jan answered, "and the little hand's on three."

Aunt Dorothea was aghast. "You can't tell time?"

Jan thought she had.

Her aunt and uncle blamed the shoddy California schools, and no one ever set them straight, but it was not a teacher's oversight that left Jan's memory so nearly blank. In Westminster the lesson had been pounded into her at home when Georgie finished with Elizabeth Short: "You don't know anything, you hear me, bitch? If anybody asks, *you don't know anything.*"

In autumn 1949 she was enrolled at Briscoe Junior High, and she recalls the talent show where Georgie came to hear her sing. He sat in the audience and wept openly at her rendition of "Beautiful Dreamer."

Wake unto me . . . but not yet.

One evening Georgie showed up drunk and weeping on the doorstep, begging Marge to mend some women's clothes that he had torn while beating Kay. Marge grudgingly consented, tucking George in bed with Jan to sleep it off. He stayed awake for some time, crying on his oldest daughter's shoulder, trying to absolve himself. "I don't know what got into me."

Another time, when Georgie dropped by Winthrop Avenue with Kay, his mother wouldn't let the redhead in. Kay waited in the car, and Georgie didn't seem to mind. Upstairs, Marge had declared a truce of sorts with Kay, and had taken advice from her replacement on the proper means of briefing children on the facts of life.

In Kay's opinion, Jan was old enough to know about menstruation. Marge agreed, but she was short on teaching skills. "Janice," she said, "there comes a time when you start bleeding from between your legs. You're reaching that age."

Marge never got around to saying why a woman bleeds at monthly intervals, where all that blood originates, or whether it would ever stop once it got started. Jan was pushing twelve, prepared to hemorrhage any day and bleed until she died.

Thanks, Mom.

Dissociation helped. If it appeared that she was bleeding too much, she could always "go away" until it stopped, or until there was no blood left. She knew about that kind of bleeding. At least, on Winthrop Avenue, Jan reckoned she was bound to have a proper funeral.

Out west, where Finis Brown and Harry Hansen were the only homicide investigators still assigned to Beth Short's case, the Dahlia still made news from time to time. Red Manley still caught dirty looks from neighbors and acquaintances; his mental state was declining as a result of the pressure of suspicion, and in 1948 he sought to clear his name for good. "Truth serum" seemed to be the answer, and he volunteered for one more grilling session, hyped on sodium pentothal. He passed with flying colors, clearly innocent, but he had soaked up too much ink since January 1947. Given time, the Dahlia case would doom his marriage, rob him of his sanity, and ultimately claim his life.

The year 1949 marked a flurry of Dahlia activity, starting with a bellhop's testimony that a fellow worker had killed Beth Short in a hotel at Twenty-ninth and Flower. Detectives shrugged, admitting that anything was possible, but once they nabbed the suspect in Salinas, he was quickly cleared.

October took the prize for zany supposition in the press, when small-time actress Terry Loughlin* disappeared. Last seen in Hollywood on October 7, she was formally reported missing two days later, when her purse was found in Griffith Park. Inside the purse, a note read: "Kirk. Can't wait any longer. Going to see Dr. Scott. It will work best this way while mother is away."

Within the next six days, LAPD investigators questioned scores of Dr. Scotts and Kirks—including one Kirk Douglas —all without result. On Sunday, October 16, two hundred searchers scoured Griffith Park with tracking dogs and came up empty. Homicide detectives were encouraged by their failure to retrieve a corpse, but yellow journalists were clearly hoping for the worst. Before the search of Griffith Park was even under way, reports beamed nationwide were spreading fears of "another Black Dahlia type of mutilation murder." An unnamed LAPD spokesman took a rather different view, suggesting that Loughlin was "recovering from an illness she wishes kept secret"—he meant an abortion—but the answer to this riddle, like so many others surrounding Short's case, remains obscure. At this writing, forty-four years after the fact, there is no concrete evidence that Terry Loughlin was ever found, alive or dead.

Before the year was out, an L.A. grand jury took a long, hard look at unsolved murders in the city, finally deciding that the best solution was a new police chief. Clarence "Cowboy" Horrall was replaced by William Worton, a retired army officer, who would serve until August 1950, when he was replaced by William Parker.

And still, the specter of the "Black Dahlia Avenger" refused to fade away. On Saturday, November 25, 1950, Christine Reynolds surrendered to Oakland police, naming herself as Short's killer. Blond and stocky, thirty-four years old, Reynolds was confessing nearly four years late, she said, "so I can look myself in the face again." Inspector Eric Gustavson of the Oakland Police Department was "frankly impressed" with Christine's "rambling, sometimes incoherent statement," but it proved to be another false alarm. Reynolds had no more to do with Short's death than any of those who confessed theretofore.

Eleven days later, suspect Max Handler, a.k.a. Mack Chandler, surrendered to LAPD and confessed to Beth's murder. For once there seemed to be supporting evidence. Short's personal effects had included a business card for a company where Max was once employed, and she was known to frequent several clubs where Handler told investigators he had gone with her on dates. When Harry Hansen asked his key forensic questions, though, Max didn't provide the appropriate answers. There might be something wrong with Handler's mind, but he was clearly innocent of murder.

On Winthrop Avenue, Marge worked long hours to make ends meet. When she came home from the assembly line, she seemed remote, perhaps as a result of exhaustion, fear, and post-traumatic stress. She had no patience, arguing with Janice over anything and everything. Jan became convinced that Margie didn't love her anymore.

Six miles away, in Saugus, Georgie bought himself a blackened plot of ground on Walden Pond Road. The house had been destroyed by fire, but there was still a basement he could build on. Brother Donald was a carpenter, and even Georgie's father lent a helping hand in the construction.

Janice and the other children went to visit, staying with their father and his new wife, Kay, in the basement underneath the brittle skeleton of what would someday be a home. From one such visit, Prudence recalls an incident that gave the lie to Georgie's change of heart.

A cat had wandered in from somewhere, she remembers, and it settled on the dining table. No one seemed to mind, except Kay. "Our stepmother began to nag and complain about the cat on the table," Prudence says. "Our father lost his temper and threw the cat. It hit the opposite wall. He took it outside and hit its head on something 'to put it out of its misery.'"

On another visit, George and Kay drove Janice to a Catholic orphanage, to visit Lena,* Kay's young daughter from her marriage to Pete Cardran. Pete had placed her in the orphanage—as punishment for Kay, perhaps, or to protect the child from George's abuse—and Jan recalls the youngster perched on Georgie's knee, twitching and scratching herself like a nervous monkey. Lena called him Uncle George. Later, when the house was finished and it seemed the family was settling down, Pete would relent and send Lena back to Kay.

Life didn't seem that bad to Jan, with her ability to filter out abuse as it occurred. In fact, she came to feel that she was better off with George and Kay than with her mother, back in Beverly. She started agitating, begging Marge to let her go. The arguments went on for hours. Finally George and Kay drove to Beverly to plead her case while Janice waited at the Saugus house. They came back after nightfall, Georgie looking glum.

Jan couldn't wait to find out the decision. "Will she let me come?"

George shook his head, apparently dejected. "No."

Kay slapped his arm, rebuking him. "George, quit tormenting her." She turned to Janice, smiling. "You can come."

On her last night in the Beverly apartment, Marge and Janice packed her clothes in paper shopping bags. She heard her mother weeping softly, but she could not understand. Marge didn't care about her, Janice thought, so why the tears? Her mother's crying angered her, as only twelve-year-olds can be infuriated by the unknown, and Jan made up her mind that she would never live with Marge again.

Aunt Dorothea played the mother role and scolded Jan for leaving. "You're a selfish child!" she snapped. "Your mother needs you. You just want what you think *they* can give you."

Janice bit her tongue. And you, she thought, don't want to lose your baby-sitter.

Looking back, sister Prudence recalls that Marge blamed Gladys and George Senior for the latest rift in her family, complaining that they "stole [Jan] away by putting big ideas in her head." George Junior and Kay were living beyond their means—on the buy-now-pay-never plan—and Marge could not compete. Still, in Prudence's view, allowing Jan to leave was "the biggest mistake [Marge] ever made, aside from marrying him."

Briscoe Junior High reports that Janice Knowlton transferred out to Saugus High School on March 13, 1950. Academic records of her eighth grade year have not survived, but she did average work in ninth grade, pulling C's in English, math, science, art, and "foods." Her solitary D, in gym, speaks more of her physical condition and the abuse she endured at home than of any lack of willingness to try.

Jan had begun menstruating, but her graduation into puberty did not put Georgie off. He was an equal-opportunity abuser: any age or sex would do. As Prudence recalls, he even took another shot at Margie, turning up in Beverly one night without an invitation, leading her to the sofa, where he "started to sweet-talk her and get mushy."

"I stuck right there," Prudence says, "because I could see she felt uncomfortable." Soon the nine-year-old began to mock her father, whispering sweet nothings to her mother's foot, until the tension broke and both of them began to laugh. "I stayed there till he left," said Prudence, "to protect her."

There were no protectors in Saugus. In the midst of one explosive argument, George threw a hunting knife at Kay. He missed, but that had more to do with Kay's experience and speed than with Georgie's aim. Their battles rocked the house on Walden Pond Road.

And he raped Jan throughout that spring and summer any time the two of them were alone. He liked to take her in the master bedroom, often brutally but sometimes almost affectionately, possessively. There were times when Janice almost felt like Georgie's wife. He dreamed aloud about another trip to California, leaving Kay behind in Massachusetts. That way, if Jan happened to get pregnant, "no one in the East" would have to know.

Like Marge.

Like Gladys.

That was, in fact, the only one of Georgie Knowlton's fantasies that made the long hop to reality. Jan was pregnant by July.

The worst thunderstorm in living memory struck Marblehead, Massachusetts, on the night of Saturday, November 25, 1950. The entire town was blacked out for hours, with telephone service disrupted over a wide area. Residents huddled in their homes by candlelight or retired early, giving in to the irresistible darkness. Those who had to venture out on business wore their slickers, carried umbrellas, and drove slowly in the face of nature's wrath.

On Sunday morning, bright and early, it was time for taking inventory. Drains and gutters were clogged with fallen branches and wind-whipped leaves. New resolutions were made to repair that leaky roof, fetch up storm windows from the cellar, fix that washed-out flowerbed.

The revelation came at half past eight on Monday morning. Kenneth Phillips was a milkman for the Whiting Milk Company, and Monday was his regular collection day on Sewall Street. He knew most of the people on his route, including Beryl Atherton, the resident at number 57, a white two-story cottage, on the small side, tidy and well kept. Miss Atherton always had a smile for Phillips when she paid her weekly bill.

But not today. The kitchen door was standing open when he got there. Stretched out on the floor, feet toward the open doorway, lay Beryl Atherton. At least, he *thought* it was Miss Atherton. It was difficult to say for sure, with all that blood around her face and throat. Even the globe light overhead was flecked with crimson.

Phillips ran to fetch a neighbor, and police were summoned to the scene. They found the forty-seven-year-old teacher dead, lying on her back in a pool of clotted blood, her throat slashed "half a dozen times." Detectives told reporters that the fatal wounds appeared to form a cross, but later they admitted there was too much tissue damage to be sure of anything. Inspector Raymond Foley of the state police confirmed the obvious, that it was murder, but he found no evidence of sexual assault or robbery. The victim had been fully dressed except for her skirt, which police found neatly draped across an upstairs banister outside her bedroom door.

It was Marblehead's first murder since the unsolved killing of Stephen Hathaway in 1885, and authorities were anxious to improve their record. Still, they had little to work with. Inspector Foley told reporters that no murder weapon was found "where it should have been," and the house had not been ransacked. Furthermore, the victim's reputation made it difficult for friends and neighbors to believe that she would have an enemy on earth.

A spinster, Beryl Atherton was the daughter of Reverend Warren Atherton, pastor of the First Baptist Church, lately deceased. A Connecticut native who grew up in Springfield, Massachusetts, she had taught third grade at Glover School in Marblehead since 1925. Her next-door neighbor, Elizabeth Glass, was the school's ex-superintendent. She described Atherton as "an excellent teacher who never missed a day of class."

Nor did there seem to be any hint of scandal in her private life. The day her corpse was found, neighbors confidently told police that Atherton had "no male friends." She kept a dog and a cat, both found alive inside the cottage, and her habits were predictable. She had few visitors, and walked her dog each night between 10:00 and 11:00 P.M., regardless of the weather. She drove a ten-year-old car, and while press reports described Atherton as comparatively "well-to-do," with an estate estimated at $25,000, her only known bank account had a standing balance of six dollars.

Nevertheless, this semi-recluse with few known contacts outside of her job had clearly infuriated someone. Mortician George Nichols called it the most brutal murder he had seen in thirty years of tending corpses, and Medical Examiner Robert Shaughnessy was inclined to agree. According to his report, Atherton had suffered three broken ribs from a beating or kicking, while bruises and crushed bones in her throat suggested strangulation by powerful hands. Her head was nearly severed, with a minimum of six deep slashes to the throat. The gaping wound, said Shaughnessy, was large enough to hold a baseball. Furthermore, "every drop" of blood had drained from Atherton's body before it was found. Shaughnessy had to pump her heart by hand to obtain a blood sample for laboratory analysis.

Authorities did their best to explain the bizarre, brutal

crime. Atherton was last seen alive at Marblehead Center, shopping for groceries, around 6:00 P.M. on Saturday. She obviously made it home, but from that point on, her movements became harder to follow. She had placed some pork chops and a chicken in the fridge, but left a sack of vegetables and beef sitting on a kitchen chair, apparently while she went upstairs to change her clothes. Detectives found the jacket of her blue suit on a hanger in the bedroom closet, but her skirt was draped across the banister. She went back to the kitchen dressed in sweater, blouse, and slip, to meet her death.

The timing puzzled the detectives. First they speculated that a prowler had crept into the house while Atherton was undressing for bed, but that did not explain the groceries left to spoil a few short steps from the refrigerator. A revised theory had the killer arriving around 7:00 P.M., unlocking two doors as a "possible means of escape." But if that was the case, how did he get in? And why was there no evidence of robbery?

The murder weapon was another mystery. Detectives found a bone-handled bread knife in a kitchen drawer, its blade broken in several pieces, some of them scattered around Atherton's body. The state police lab found bloodstains on the knife and in the kitchen sink, suggesting that the knife was deliberately broken after being washed, perhaps to keep detectives from seeking the real murder weapon.

"There is little question," a Marblehead police spokesman told reporters, "that the bread knife was planted there as a blind. The medical examiner and detectives feel that only a very sharp knife could have caused the wounds that killed Miss Atherton. The bread knife was not sharp enough. Furthermore, the locations of the bits of broken blade were too obvious. We feel they were placed on and near the body to cause investigators to stop looking for any other knife. We haven't stopped looking for another knife, not by a long shot."

Four days later, on December 8, police reversed themselves again. This time they thought the broken instrument —described in revised statements as a carving knife—was, in fact, the murder weapon. Having made that statement, though, they found themselves no closer to finding a suspect in the case.

In fact, despite Beryl's sheltered lifestyle, there appeared to be *too many* suspects. On the day her body was discovered, neighbors gave police the name of a man, described as "a bad actor," who was often seen in the Reeds Hill section of town. The lead went nowhere, and authorities were no more successful in their grilling of a Marblehead merchant, briefly described in the press as a "principal suspect." Another prospect was a twenty-eight-year-old ex-convict, recently discharged "from a southern jail" on larceny charges, who had lived within a hundred yards of Atherton's cottage before moving to his present home in Beverly. The young man was "considered violent," but police could never link him to the crime, and he was finally released. Police Chief Samuel Bradish speculated that the killer might be "skilled in judo," but that quirky angle was another flop. On November 28 a resident of Lynn was routed from his home at gunpoint by detectives, but they set him free on learning that he "positively didn't have a chance to do the job."

By that time the authorities were fishing, some of their unfounded speculation strongly reminiscent of the Dahlia case. Detectives claimed that Atherton had shunned male company "almost entirely" since her father's death, and one department wag told newsmen, "There is a definite possibility that a strong woman could have committed the crime. Give a highly enraged woman a sharp knife, and she can do as much damage as any man."

Indeed, but there was no real evidence to indicate a female killer in the case. And police would soon find out that Beryl Atherton's supposed aversion to the opposite sex was more a facade rather than reality.

By Friday, December 1, police were willing to admit "that while Miss Atherton apparently had lived a quiet life in Marblehead, she probably kept dates with male friends outside this community." An accountant from Lynn was among those who acknowledged having shared "dinners and automobile rides" with her. In fact, it appeared that Atherton had led a kind of double life—prim and proper by day, prone to visiting saloons in nearby Salem, Lynn, and Saugus after dark.

One of the most peculiar leads uncovered by police involved a two-year string of checks that Atherton had written on a weekly basis "to some person who was unknown to her close friends." The checks ranged in amount from seven to ten dollars, and the last one had been written on November 1. Numerous stubs were found by detectives, bearing only a first name which, they said, "could be that of a man or woman." Georgie?

George Knowlton *was* in the vicinity from autumn 1947 through the early days of 1951. He *was* bar-hopping in the neighborhood of Salem, Lynn, and Saugus, where old-timers recall a limited number of nightclubs to choose from. Author Joan Noble Pinkham, after years of research on the case, considers it "real likely" that Georgie and Beryl Atherton would have met if they were both out boozing in the neighborhood. Police files on the case have disappeared, says Pinkham, lifted by an ex-detective who "planned to write a book and never did." After lengthy discussions with Jan, Pinkham considers Georgie's involvement in the Atherton murder a "distinct possibility."

Jan cannot furnish names and dates, but she does recall details that appear to mesh with Atherton's demise.

Jan is lying on a sofa, in a stranger's living room. She has a clear view of the kitchen. Georgie crouched above a woman's prostrate body, both hands wrapped around a knife as he delivers vicious, ripping strokes. Blood pools beneath the woman's body on the floor. On the backstroke, Georgie's blade flings scarlet drops above his head. The globe light begins to drip blood, as if decorated for a ghoulish party.

Afterward, when he is finished, George leads Janice to a bathroom, where he bathes himself and rinses out his clothes. Jan rolls them up in fluffy towels to dry before he puts them on again. Downstairs, he orders her to wash a long bone-handled knife. He seems distracted, mutters something about the state asylum in Danvers, four miles north of Marblehead. At first, Jan thinks they may be going there, but Georgie drops her at an uncle's house instead, returning for her hours later.

Without a file to work from, Marblehead police decline to answer queries on the case. Presumably they have no evidence in hand to compare with Jan's recollections, pro or con.

Another case—this time from Boylston in Worcester County, forty miles from Georgie's Saugus home—involved the murder of forty-year-old Margaret Corrigan. Known as Jackie to her friends, the "comely" widow of eight months, a resident of Worcester, was last seen departing a Shrewsbury saloon on the night of November 19. One news report said Corrigan was asked to leave the bar for being "boisterous and noisy." Taxi driver Arthur Generis recalled that Corrigan and a female friend, twenty-four-year-old Mary Wigmore, had piled into his cab and directed him to another bar, the Happy Hour Club. Generis was about to pull out from the curb when a man stuck his head in the window and said, "I'm going to the same place. Do you mind if I ride along with you?" Descriptions of the man were vague, but Wigmore later told police he was a stranger to her.

Corrigan was still missing on Tuesday, November 22, when police were notified. Eleven days later, at 3:30 P.M. on December 2, Oliver Nelson and his eight-year-old daughter were picking Christmas berries in a lovers' lane near Sewall Street in Boylston when he stumbled on a body hidden under fallen leaves. Police found Jackie Corrigan lying on her back, her face destroyed by heavy blows from something like a tire iron. Although she was fully clothed, her coat and skirt were bunched up around her waist, suggesting sexual assault. A birch bough, four feet long and some two inches thick, lay across her chest. One high-heeled shoe was missing. Detectives found it thirty yards away, beside a cocktail glass. From scratch marks on the victim's legs, they speculated that a car had been parked where the shoe and glass were found, her body dragged from there to its final resting place. Medical Examiner Charles Abbott reported that Corrigan was killed "at least a week" before her corpse was found.

Nine years had passed since Frances Cochran's death, in Lynn, and Worcester police had played no role in that investigation. They were not intrigued by similarities between the dump sites, the ferocious beatings, shoes discarded on a road some distance from the bodies, the creative use of sticks to "decorate" each corpse. They saw no link between a corpse on Sewall Street in Boylston and the murder of Beryl Atherton on Sewall Street in Marblehead.

Detectives spoke of suspects in their latest case—the stranger from the cab and a married sailor whose wallet was found in Corrigan's coat pocket—but both were later cleared. As of September 1993 the death of Margaret Corrigan remained officially unsolved.

There were strange doings in Saugus as well, while women were busily dying or dropping from sight all over the map. By mid-November 1950 Jan was nearly five months pregnant. Kay and Georgie must have known by that time, but she wasn't showing yet. They still had time to get away, before the family caught on.

The cops were after George that winter, busting him for nonsupport of Margie and the kids, but Prudence recalls that he was friendly with the officers who took him in. One of them even apologized for spoiling Georgie's day, and he was soon released. It never crossed their minds, apparently, to question him about the recent deaths and disappearances around his hunting ground.

As in the past, when George planned to relocate, he laid his move out in advance and relied on a friend to help him see it through—in this case, Eddie Tacy, an associate from one of George's foundry jobs. By late October, Tacy, his wife Rita, and their seven-year-old son were sharing quarters with the Knowlton clan in Saugus. Ed and Georgie drove to California that December, scouting out their prospects, and the journey coincides with a peculiar gap in Jan's school records, from December 21 to January 4, 1951.

At a glance, the break—eleven school days—would appear to be a normal Christmas recess, but Jan's academic record in Saugus specifically notes that she "moved [to] Long Beach, California," on December 21 and returned two weeks later, a seeming impossibility that remains unexplained to this day. At that, she would not linger long. On February 6, she left school again. Her records were mailed to Phinneas Banning High School in Wilmington, California.

That first "move" is bizarre, considering the fact that Georgie never lived in Long Beach, but the record stands. We can but speculate about what happened. Jan's memory is largely blank for those days, blighted by continuing abuse.

She does recall a friend from class, Anne Merrill, whose idyllic home life sparked elaborate fantasies from Jan. She wished herself into the Merrill family, with their picture-postcard house and smiling faces, parents who responded to a child with love instead of sexual abuse and violence. Her longing was impossible to hide. Years later Mrs. Merrill told Jan that she had considered asking George and Kay if Jan could stay with her instead of moving west. "But you loved your father so much," the kindly neighbor went on, "I didn't think it would be right."

On Tuesday, February 6, they loaded up the car and started west again. Between the Knowltons, the Tacys, and a dark-haired friend of Georgie's known as Buck, the group consisted of eight people in all.

Another "fresh start" in the West.

10

Tender Prey

Better murder an infant in its cradle than nurse an unacted desire.

—William Blake

JAN'S EARLY MONTHS IN CALIFORNIA ARE A BLUR. FOUR DECADES would elapse before she started to recover even fleeting glimpses of that time, and most of that period eludes her to the present day. School records indicate that she attended Phinneas Banning High School in Wilmington, midway between Long Beach and the Palos Verdes peninsula, from February 19 to March 26, 1951. Her transfer records show straight C's, with the exception of a D in gym. Jan's home address was listed in the file as 2518 Monroe Street in Dominguez, half a mile due north of Wilmington. Repeated visits to the little stucco house have sparked no memories of living there, but Jan does not dispute the public record.

And the memories she has recovered from this period are grim enough to justify dissociation on a massive scale.

It was around this time that Jan gave birth to twins, a boy and girl. Thirty-five years later, Jan would be confronted with circumstantial evidence that the babies were delivered at Saint Mary's Hospital in Long Beach to a mother named as Kathleen Knowlton. That fiction spared Georgie from charges of incest, and Kay predictably blamed Janice for the pregnancy, instead of her pedophile husband.

Jan's memories of the event are fragmentary. Men in green surround her in the hospital delivery room. One says, "She's acting like a wild animal." His companion orders nitrous oxide.

Sometime later Kay sits at her bedside, scowling. "This never would have happened," Kay informs Jan, "if you hadn't flirted with him."

Jan had repressed the memories of Georgie raping her and had no memory of the attack that left her pregnant. To whom was Kay referring? she wondered.

Decades later, even after she recalled the pregnancy and its traumatic aftermath, Jan would absolve her father of responsibility, assuming that the culprit must have been Buck, their traveling companion on the trip from Saugus. Months of therapy were needed to unlock the truth.

A devil's bargain was concocted at the hospital: Jan's baby girl was put up for adoption, the records sealed by law; her son went home with Jan and Georgie to a new house on Eighth Street in Seal Beach. Was it some perversion of paternal pride that made George keep the boy? Or did the dark-haired child remind George of himself?

One little Indian.

In any case, it was a tragic choice for all concerned.

Today Jan refers to her baby as Vincent, though she never had a chance to name him properly. His life was short, a few brief days, and in the Knowlton house, that might have been a mercy in disguise.

His murder is a grim montage of fractured images in Jan's memory—her father's rage, provoked by God knows what, the hammer in his fist, subconscious flashbacks to the killing of Elizabeth Short. Two nightmares intertwined.

Jan tried as best she could to save her child. When tears and pleading failed, she gave herself, providing Georgie with oral sex on demand, as a distraction.

It didn't work.

The hammer fell, and Vincent was another memory repressed from force of habit. Anything to block the pain.

Enduring the unendurable. Surviving in the face of sudden death.

Kay Knowlton and her daughter Lena play no role in Jan's traumatic memory of Vincent's death. All things considered, it would seem that George and Kay were separated for a time, the problems in their own relationship exacerbated by Jan's pregnancy and the delivery of her twins. It would not be the last time Kay left Georgie in a fit of anger, or to save herself from violence in the home. In any case, there is no evidence—and Jan does not suggest—that Kay took part in Vincent's murder or the subsequent disposal of his body.

Two young lives. One crushed, the other thrown away.

Another day with Georgie in the slaughterhouse.

On March 26, 1951, Jan Knowlton enrolled at Huntington Beach High School. Her home address is listed in the file as 318 Eighth Street, Seal Beach, a short walk from the pier where Georgie made his first attempt to dump Beth Short. The eight-mile bus ride from her home to school gave Jan some insulation. It was an escape from Georgie, even if the classroom only sheltered her for a few short hours on weekdays.

It is not uncommon for survivors of prolonged abuse to lose touch with themselves and with the changes in their bodies as they come of age. Maturity is nothing to be cherished in a household where the ultimate taboo of incest is ignored and violated on a daily basis. Despite the recent pregnancy, already filed away in her subconscious, it would take humiliating taunts from classmates on the bus ride home to make Jan realize she had developed breasts.

She turned to Kay for help and was escorted to a local store to buy her first brassiere. That night at dinner Georgie noticed. Jan was wearing a familiar T-shirt emblazoned with a picture of Roy Rogers and Trigger when she caught his eye. The smirk became a leer.

"I notice Trigger is rearing up now," he teased her.

Jan was relieved when he let it go at that, but luck was hard to come by under Georgie's roof.

The sexual abuse continued, with Georgie picking up the porno trade where he had left off with Elizabeth in Hollywood. In time, Jan would remember being raped by George while other men stood by and watched, a tripod-mounted camera capturing the action for posterity. The strangers took turns when George was finished. One of them was a fat Chicano who, in spite of his abuse, may well have saved Jan's life.

It was her father's habit to sedate Jan prior to "parties" with his friends and paying customers. He fed her wine, as Beth had done on visits to the Hawthorn, and its powerful effect made Jan suspect that it was drugged. On this particular occasion, she remembers passing out and waking sometime later, naked, in the bathtub. Georgie was standing above her, also nude, "playfully" shoving her head under water and holding it there. The fat Chicano pulled him off, giving Jan a chance to breathe. But the Good Samaritan felt he deserved a reward. He lifted Jan from the bathtub, dragged her to the bedroom, and raped her.

Another link between George Knowlton and the murky underworld of child pornography existed in the person of his uncle Fred, George Senior's brother, who lived in Bellflower, eight miles north of Seal Beach. Fred Knowlton was confined to a wheelchair by 1951, crippled by tuberculosis, medicating himself with cheap wine, but there was nothing wrong with his hands. Years later, Fred's adoring daughter would admit to Janice that her father spent long hours in his bedroom editing commercial porno reels. A cottage industry of sorts, all in the family.

The frequent visits to Tijuana also mesh with Georgie's interest in pornography. In those days, prior to VCRs and Scandinavia's emergence as the global hub of kiddie porn, most of the smut consumed by Californians came across the border from Tijuana, Mexicali, and Tecate. Then, as now, the border towns were rife with prostitution, donkey shows, and other forms of vice that lured servicemen and college students, husbands, housewives—anyone at all, in fact, who craved a little action on the wild side.

Jan recalls one trip across the border, where her father bought maracas for the children. Driving back, as they approached the customs checkpoint, Georgie passed a pair to Lena, seated just behind him, and said, "How about some music?"

Visibly excited by the opportunity to make some noise without a beating in return, Kay's daughter shook the handmade rattles all the while Georgie was engaged in conversation with the border guard. At length, they pulled away, the border left behind, and Georgie's mood turned like a striking rattlesnake. "Knock off that goddamn racket!"

Lena knew him well enough by now to lay the toys aside. It had been great fun while it lasted.

Back in Seal Beach, he disclosed the reason for the episode with the maracas. From the glove compartment he removed a paper bag and, from the bag, a parrot he had smuggled in from Baja. The maracas were his cover, just in case the bird began to squawk while they were held up at the border checkpoint.

In addition to rapes and beatings, Georgie constantly rehearsed new means of keeping Jan under his thumb. Manipulation was a favorite tactic, learned at his mother's knee and carried to bizarre extremes. He alternated fits of screaming rage and physical brutality with tearful pleas for understanding of his delicate mental condition, guiding the emotional roller coaster with a master's hand. How much of his performance was sincere, and how much crafty show-manship? It hardly mattered to a daughter who craved Daddy's love.

And in the last analysis, if all else failed, the bottom line was blood.

They had a rabbit hutch behind the house on Eighth Street, and Jan was assigned to feed the bunnies. She grew fond of them, and Georgie had a brand-new weapon in his hands. Jan has no memory of what provoked the argument that doomed her rabbits, but the image of her father comes in crystal-clear. He slid the door back on the hutch and pulled a young rabbit out, its legs kicking helplessly. He held a long knife in his free hand.

"It's your choice," Georgie tells her. "I can do this all day long."

When Jan does not respond, he grinds the rabbit's skull to pulp beneath his heel.

That summer at the Seal Beach pier, Jan made her first unconscious stab at suicide. She started swimming out to sea, no goal in mind, oblivious of time and distance. At length, loudspeakers hailed her from the pier, and Jan turned back, treading water, to see who was in trouble. She spotted a lifeguard swimming toward her, a power boat gliding out in his wake.

"Who are you saving?" she called to the lifeguard.

And the answer came back: "You!"

Bemused, Jan let herself be helped into the boat. So much attention from a simple swim!

The famous Seal Beach undertow had failed a second time.

In September 1951 Georgie and his family were compelled to move next door, from number 318 to 316 on Eighth Street. The owners of 318 were returning home from Palm Springs, and they needed the house. Number 316 was newly vacant, and they made the move in record time. It was a smaller house with only one bedroom, but Georgie parked a travel trailer on the empty lot next door, for Janice and Lena to sleep in.

The charade of privacy was nothing more than an illusion. Whenever Kay left the house with Lena, Jan was at Georgie's mercy. One day, following another rape, they sat together on the porch and Georgie waxed nostalgic, staring at his daughter's face, her coal-black hair. "You look more like her every day," he said.

"Like who?" The latest sexual assault forgotten. Simple curiosity.

"Elizabeth."

The name meant nothing to her. "Who's Elizabeth?"

George frowned. "A woman I knew once."

Tenth grade gave Jan her only respite from the house of horrors. Academic records for her sophomore year report a B in driver education, C's in English, glee club, and "world problems," D's in gym and shorthand. Despite the mediocre grade, Jan's favorite class was glee club, where she had a chance to exercise her singing voice and win recognition for her style and talent. She could still make Georgie cry with music, but his tears never lasted long. When Janice needed high-heeled shoes for an impending concert, George insisted that she wear a pair of Kay's. Jan told him Kay's shoes were too small. George punched her out.

One evening Georgie turned up with an unexpected gift for Jan, a wobbly-legged lamb. It was love at first sight, doomed to failure. Penned in the garage, the lamb drank kerosene from one of Georgie's open cans. Its eyes turned white and milky, sightless. Georgie blamed his "careless" daughter, ordered her to make arrangements with a vet to have the lamb put down.

Jan tried to make the call, but could not follow through. When Georgie found the lamb alive that night, he flew into a rage and snapped that he would handle it himself. Jan raced into the bathroom, turned the water on full blast, and crouched beside the bathtub, hands clasped tight against her ears.

In the garage, George scooped the lamb up in his arms and smashed its skull repeatedly against the wall. When it lay dead, he went inside to wash his hands and boast to Jan of his technique. The whole damned mess was her fault, after all.

A few weeks later Georgie came home with a horse. It was a gift, he said, for Jan and Lena. They could share. Jan wasn't interested, and while Kay scolded her for being selfish, Jan had learned her lesson: George would slaughter anything she loved. This way at least the horse might have a chance.

* * *

In January 1952, at age fifteen, Jan found herself pregnant for the second time. Spontaneous repression of her father's sexual assaults prevented her from understanding how it had happened, and the clues were vague. She did not bleed on schedule, but her slender body barely showed the changes going on inside. Kay ignored Jan whenever possible, sporadically fleeing the house with Lena when life became too chaotic. At school, Jan had no close friends, and her natural shyness prevented her from stripping in front of her classmates for gym. Sometimes she slipped inside a standing locker to change her clothes.

You can fool all of the people some of the time, but Mother Nature always gets you in the end.

One afternoon in early April, Jan came home from school with cramps and nausea. She made it to the bathroom, stripped, and hung her school clothes on a hook behind the door. A nice warm bath would help, she thought, but after several moments in the water, she was cramping worse than ever.

Georgie heard her cries of pain and stormed into the bathroom. "What the hell's wrong with you now?" he demanded.

Jan was past answering, gripped by pain that threatened to rip her in two. George watching from the sidelines, seated on the toilet like a sultan on his throne. He made no move to help her, even when the baby slithered free and settled to the bottom of the tub.

The birth was premature. The infant's size and coloring, the cord wrapped tight around, bespoke a stillbirth. Georgie seemed more curious than startled. Rising from his ringside seat, he knelt beside the tub and poked the child, a girl, with a demanding index finger.

No response?

No sweat.

His knife flashed, slicing through the soft umbilicus, and Georgie scooped his daughter-grandchild from the water. Jan was instantly relieved to see him wrap the baby in a towel, convinced her daddy meant to "save" it.

Pausing on the threshold, with the bundle in his arms, he said, "Get up and get your clothes on."

Janice did as she was told, trailing Georgie to the kitchen. She saw her baby lying on the sideboard, near the sink. George turned to face her, let her see the shiny carving knife. "I'll show you what they would have done with her," he said.

The legs were easy for a butcher with experience. Small joints and tender flesh. Before Jan realized what was happening, George dropped them in the sink.

She flung herself across the room and tackled Georgie, tried to knock him down. He laughed at her and let her have a solid backhand, slamming her against the nearest wall. She wound up on the floor, ears ringing, the familiar darkness closing in. The bloody knife was relentless, invasive, shearing flesh from bone.

A moment later he was finished. Georgie bundled the remains up in a towel, considered them for several heartbeats, then suddenly exploded into rage. He turned and flung the bundle across the room into the dining nook. Jan scrambled underneath the table to retrieve her child. She heard George berating her.

The whole damned thing was *her* fault. "If you took care of yourself," he snarled, "she wouldn't have been born that way. You selfish bitch, I'll teach *you* a lesson."

He drove her out into the yard and around the east side of the house, adjacent to their former home at number 318. The wooden fence between the yards was thick with ivy.

Georgie slapped a shovel into her hand. "This time," he said, *"you'll* do the burying. What happens to me, happens to you."

If Georgie took the fall for this one, it would be Jan's fault. Worse yet, for all Jan knew, she might just wind up sitting on his lap in the electric chair.

George never used one threat when he had an opening for two or three. When Jan finished covering the tiny grave and tamping down the earth, he grabbed the spade away from her and gripped her arm, hard fingers clamping like a vise.

"You keep your mouth shut, hear me? I can kill you any time I want to, plant you underneath the house. I'll tell your mother that you ran away. No one will *ever* find you."

Numb inside, she offered no resistance as he led her to the bedroom, stripped her, and threw her on the bed. She barely felt the carving knife against her throat as Georgie raped her, his foul breath in her face.

"You like it, don't you?" Wheezing with exertion now. "You like your old man's cock. Tell me you like it!"

Janice "went away."

In May or early June of 1952, George took another hunting trip. It is impossible to chart his movements through this period, but friends and fellow hunters have confirmed that he often drove as far away as southern Utah in his search for game. Sometimes he took companions with him. This time he went alone and came back with a rather different kind of trophy.

Janice, having seen his pickup pull into the darkened garage, walked out to meet him there. George either did not notice her at first or did not care that she was watching as he pulled a woman's body from the cab.

Georgie found a long electrical extension cord and made a hasty noose to fit around the woman's neck. That done, he tossed the cord across a rafter, muscles straining as he hauled her inert body off the floor. When she was dangling at the proper height, he tied off the electric cord, walked around to stand before his trophy, and pulled at her clothes.

Jan watched her father rape the hanging woman, certain she was dead now. No reaction from the corpse, except to jerk in time with Georgie's pelvic thrusts. It didn't take him long to finish, stoked on death. A psycho power trip.

When he was done, George lit a cigarette and took the body down. He was now aware of Janice watching him, but he did not speak as he untied the noose and dragged his latest victim to the back of the garage, where he folded her into a corner and stacked heavy bags of rabbit feed around her to conceal the body.

Coming back to Jan, he slipped an arm around her shoulders, smiling, and said, "This will be our little secret."

When she walked back to the travel trailer, Lena taunted her maliciously because Jan was crying. Finally, sobbing incoherently, Jan ran into the house. George met her in the living room, scowling, sticking to his standard rule for discipline: punch first, ask questions later. Jan was down before she had a chance to speak, and George was kicking her around the kitchen with his heavy boots.

It hurt too much to cry, and Janice wound up in a fetal curl, her back against the wall. George had run out of energy and slumped in the nearest chair to catch his breath. Kay, sensing that the storm had run its course, finally appeared from her hiding place in the bedroom. She ordered Jan back to the trailer, but did not rebuke Georgie for the violence that was part of daily life.

Was Kay aware of Georgie's latest murder? Was she consciously aware of *any* homicide, except Beth Short's? That one case, which was still making news from time to time, was enough to silence Kay—an obvious accessory after the fact. If she had accompanied Georgie on his outing to Pacific Beach in early January 1947, then she might have been considered an accessory *before* the fact as well. A phone call to police, no matter what she knew, would have wrecked Kay's life. Assuming Georgie didn't kill her, there was still the threat of prison and the certainty of losing Lena either to her father or to another orphanage. The truth that Kay refused to see might echo in her dreams, but she could live with that. You had to be alive to dream, and anything was better than a cold hole in the ground.

As far as Janice was concerned, Kay had no sympathy to spare. The girl was Marge's child and Georgie's plaything. Any time he spent abusing Jan was a reprieve for Kay and Lena. Kay was looking out for number one.

Sometime within the next few days, the latest victim disappeared from Georgie's hideaway. There were no relevant reports of bodies found around this time, but it is difficult to rule out every possibility without specific dates.

Most likely George had found a more effective way of covering his tracks. From all appearances, George Knowlton had it made, but he was still uneasy, conscious of his own guilt, even as the members of his family pretended all was normal in the little house on Eighth Street.

Predators survive by knowing when to fight and when to run away. George sniffed the wind and reckoned it was time to leave.

Jan's last day of class in Huntington Beach was June 13, 1952. A few days later they were eastbound yet again—George and Kay, Jan and Lena, plus a man named Archie who had wandered into George's life sometime within the past twelve months or so. George and Archie had had a brainstorm: they would give up the foundry life to work as partners in a doughnut shop and diner. Their chosen market: southern Maine, in the vicinity of Lewiston and Auburn.

Jan remembers nothing of the summer trek that spanned 3,000 miles from California to New England. Forty years would pass before she came to grips with memories of Archie and her father taking turns at raping her in the garage on Eighth Street in Seal Beach. If the abuse continued on the long drive east, those images have mercifully eluded her.

The would-be doughnut barons entered into partnership, each knowing that the other had a gift for keeping secrets.

Instead of driving straight to Maine, George swung through Massachusetts on a whim and left Jan with his parents for the summer. Despite the hidden snares of life with Gladys, Jan was visibly relieved, relaxing, forging or renewing friendships in the neighborhood. On sunny afternoons the kids would hike out to the Rock, a stony promontory on the nearby coast, then plunge into the ocean to flirt with the undertow. All pain is relative. By August, Jan was starting to believe that she might like to stay in Beverly and finish school there.

Then Kay showed up with marching orders. Jan was told

to pack her things and get in the car. George needed her in Maine to help around the doughnut shop, and it was almost time for school to start.

The twin cities of Auburn and Lewiston, planted on either side of the Androscoggin River, together form the second largest metropolitan center in Maine. Only Portland is larger, founded on shipping out of Casco Bay, and Auburn-Lewiston rivaled Portland in economic significance. Associated with the textile industry and shoe manufacturing since the early nineteenth century, Auburn survived a series of catastrophic fires to hold its rank in the state's economy. During the First World War, 75 percent of all the canvas shoes in the world were produced by one factory in Auburn. Across the bridge, Irish and French Catholics, drawn to Lewiston's thriving textile mills, were standing firm in the face of nativist opposition. By 1970 a clear majority of Lewiston residents claimed French-Canadian descent, and they no longer had to duck or hide from Know-Nothing bigots.

Jan's academic file in Huntington Beach reveals that a copy of her record was sent to Edward Little High School in Auburn, Maine, on September 8, 1952. No documents have survived from that institution, but a second copy of her record was mailed a month later, on October 7, to Mechanic Falls High School.

Mechanic Falls lies ten miles west of Auburn, near the Androscoggin County line. Jan's record lists her father's "full address" as "Minot, Maine," a wide spot in the road a few miles north of town. The Knowlton house was primitive —no plumbing, with a hand pump in the kitchen and an outhouse in the back. A second water pump, a short walk from the house, afforded Jan a minimum of privacy for baths. The actual location of the doughnut shop remains obscure, a problem most of Georgie's would-be customers found insurmountable by autumn 1952.

It was agreed that George would pay Jan for working in the shop, and he did so—at first. Of course, he had his little tricks, like holding money out to buy two horses for the girls. Jan's horse was skittish to the point of being dangerous, a wild one prone to bolt at breakneck speeds. Jan loved him all the same and managed to control him, more or less, with some assistance from a special bit that Georgie purchased. Jan had no one else to love and gave her full affection to the animal. She never took the wild rides personally, even when she wound up sailing headfirst from the saddle.

It wasn't long before declining business prompted Georgie to revise his plans. Jan would continue working at the doughnut shop, but she would not be paid. If schoolwork interfered with business, serving doughnuts took priority. Of twenty school days recorded while Jan was in Mechanic Falls, she missed seven altogether and was tardy for an eighth. George relented, briefly, and released her from the job, then changed his mind again, demanding that she do her part to save the failing business.

Jan tried to reason with her father, and they had a raging quarrel at the doughnut shop. When one of Georgie's customers spoke up in Jan's defense, the pastry master told his daughter to go home. A friend from school was present, and he offered Jan a ride, if she would wait until his favorite song was finished playing on the jukebox. Jan sat on the wooden steps outside, unaware of Georgie coming up behind her until she reeled from the sudden pain of a kick to the small of her back.

"I told you to get the hell home!" Georgie bellowed.

Janice rose to leave. "I'm going, dammit!"

"What did you say?" Raging. "Get your ass back over here! Repeat what you just said!"

Defeated, Jan did so: "I said, 'I'm going, dammit.' "

Georgie slapped her hard across the face, and Janice took off running, blinded by the tears that sprang in equal part from pain and embarrassment. A carload of her classmates overtook her farther down the road, and Jan reluctantly agreed to let them drive her home.

After arriving at the house, she primed the outdoor pump

and washed her face, then went inside to relate the latest incident to Kay. Jan's stepmother, heavy with child at the time, ran true to form by taking Georgie's side. If Janice didn't talk back to her elders, she would get along just fine.

George came home in rage, shouting about the embarrassment Jan had inflicted upon him by "making" him lose his temper and strike her in front of his customers. He found her in the kitchen, whipped off his belt, and flailed at her like a man possessed. Jan fell to her hands and knees and retreated toward her bedroom, but was cornered when he cut her off. The buckle of his belt bit deep into the back of one hand, drawing blood. Jan saw the dripping crimson, stunned.

"Quit whining," Georgie sneered. "You're hardly bleeding."

Kay called out to Georgie from the master bedroom, urging him to stop, but she did not have energy enough to walk across the room and intervene. Besides, she had an unborn baby to protect, and George was whipping *his* brat now, not one of Kay's.

The sight of blood cooled Georgie down a bit. He put his belt back on and left Janice to collect herself, but he could not resist a parting insult. Muttering on his way to the bottle, he accused Jan of trying to make him feel guilty by staring at her wounded hand.

Late that night Jan sat outside the house, one arm around the family's German shepherd. Talking to the dog, unmindful of the open kitchen window at her back, she vowed to run away and take the shepherd with her. Find a place where they could hide from Georgie's wrath.

Next morning over breakfast, George reminded Janice that the walls had ears. "Don't ever think that you can run away from me," he said, "because I'll track you down no matter where you go."

A short time later brother David came to visit for a hunting trip with George. He seemed to have no inkling of the conflict in the house, and Jan did not enlighten him. He knew about their father's violent temper from personal experience, but Jan had repressed the intimate abuse as soon as it occurred.

If David chose to spend his free time with George, his younger sisters did not follow suit. Prudence, for her part, flatly refused to visit her father in Maine. "I was afraid of him," she says today. "He lived too far away. If he'd lost his temper and beat me, I'd have been stranded."

Like Jan.

Around the time that David was supposed to leave, Jan got into another violent quarrel with her father. She may have seen an opportunity to break away, or maybe it was simply Georgie being George. He lobbed a shaving mug at Jan, but she was quick enough to duck and save her face.

"Do you want to go live with your grandparents?" Georgie demanded.

"Yes!" Jan said, not caring that she would be back with Gladys and George Senior. Anything was better than the doughnut shop and Daddy.

Jan packed quickly, tossing clothes and other personal belongings into shopping bags. It didn't take much time. Kay dropped her off on Winthrop Avenue in Beverly and drove away. Jan had to plead her case with Gladys, but she pulled it off.

She had a home, of sorts.

Later, Kay would tell Jan that she found George weeping bitterly on her return to Maine, lamenting Jan's departure. "She was the only one of my kids who wanted to come live with me," he sobbed, "and I drove her away."

He would get over it, of course. A short time later, Georgie sold Jan's horse for dog food. When she begged him to give her the bridle as a keepsake, he refused. Incapable of taking a hint, she asked him for a small allowance. Again, Georgie flatly refused. She had a free home waiting for her, if she wanted to come back and join him.

"Otherwise," he said, "to hell with you."

* * *

Jan spent her first week back in Massachusetts grieving for the loss of Georgie's "love." Though Gladys saw her frequently in tears, she provided no comfort. Simple kindness was a rare commodity on Winthrop Avenue, where even medical necessities were closely rationed.

Back in Maine, shortly before the last blowup, a dentist had drilled one of Jan's front teeth to drain an abscess. Now she begged her grandparents for dental care to save the tooth, but Gladys stalled and stalled until the tooth had to be removed. Another long, humiliating month would pass before the dentist made a bridge to close the gap and stop Jan from lisping when she spoke.

Jan was enrolled at Beverly High School as a junior, working part-time at W. T. Grant's dime store on Cabot Street to help pay her way. Gifts of secondhand clothes from Gladys's friends were enough to remind Jan of her status as a charity case, but she pulled herself together all the same. Bouncing back from a report card full of incompletes in Maine, she finished the school year at Beverly High with B's in gym, art, and advertising and salesmanship, plus C's in English, typing, and American history.

It was a miracle of sorts, considering Jan's mental state by this time. The school nurse had already noted her condition, recognizing symptoms of post-traumatic stress disorder before the condition even had a name, and she gave Jan carte blanche to rest in the school infirmary whenever she felt the need. There was a catch, however: Jan had to tell her grandmother about the deal.

When Gladys heard the news that afternoon, while driving Janice home from school, she flew into a rage. She made it clear that Jan must *never*, under *any* circumstances, air the Knowltons' dirty linen in front of a stranger. "Every family has skeletons in their closet," she insisted.

Some more literal than others.

Janice got the message. "It was clear to me," she recalls, "that I would be homeless if I ever sought help."

At that, the single greatest source of danger had by then

removed himself from the immediate vicinity. A short time after Jan's retreat to Massachusetts, George and Archie quarreled at the doughnut shop and went their separate ways. George opted for another swift cross-country run after stopping by Winthrop Avenue with Kay and Lena, to say good-bye. Janice was walking home when she saw his car approaching. Gripped by sudden panic, she ducked out of sight behind another house and hid until the coast was clear.

The strange reaction left her shaken, feeling guilty and confused. Why should she be afraid to see her father? He had always loved her so.

If Gladys and George Senior grudgingly accepted Jan, Aunt Myra was a different story. She often dropped in when Jan was home alone and berated her for being "selfish," urging and then demanding that she move back in with Margie and her siblings. It became routine for Jan to hide out in her upstairs bedroom with the door locked whenever Aunt Myra came to call.

There were visits to Marge and the kids, of course, at their small apartment on Elliott Street. Marge had graduated from the shoe factory to a clerical job at the General Electric Riverworks in Lynn. She was making better money, but the job and three remaining children left her little time for any kind of private life. She still grieved for her dead children, keeping mortuary photographs of Marjorie and Sandra in a bedroom drawer, living in what Jan describes as "a world of her own."

"There was no talking *with* Mom," Jan remembers, "just talking *at* her. There was no room for me."

Nor was Marge Knowlton anxious to replace her former husband with another man. Prudence recalls Marge describing herself as "a kid's woman, rather than a man's woman." She seldom dated after the divorce, and when she did, Prudence notes significantly, "they were always men old enough to be her father." In Prudence's opinion, Marge "was afraid of younger men," leaning toward aging companions who were "less apt to bother her with sex." As

Prudence explains, "We knew she didn't like sex. She said decent women didn't like it, and only men and women who were tramps like our stepmother did." Ironically, Marge was "always drawn to drinkers" despite her own aversion to alcohol and her habit of pouring her highballs into potted plants at cocktail parties.

Marge was not without prospects, even so. The mayor's brother was interested, but Marge refused to answer the door when he came calling, a tactic that disappointed Prudence "because he was such a nice person." One who did get his foot inside the door was an older man who promised Marge a house, but the girls torpedoed that relationship, in Prudence's words, "by being bratty, because we didn't want her to sacrifice herself to a man she didn't love just so we could have a house and she could stay home with us." Prudence and Marilyn had divined Marge's thoughts "because of the way she talked, like she was going to make the supreme sacrifice of marrying him to give us a home." Looking back, though, Prudence has some doubts. "For all I know," she wrote in 1993, "maybe she actually loved him, but felt apologetic, so she made the marriage idea seem like a sacrifice for us, so we'd accept him. If so, it backfired."

At least for Margie and the kids, once George was removed from their lives, the stakes weren't life and death.

The greatest sacrifice, albeit an unconscious one, was Jan's. She had already given up her youth, her innocence, and her memory, but that was not enough. With Georgie, it would never be enough, as long as any shred of hope remained in Jan's heart.

11

Killing Time

One man's remorse is another man's reminiscence.

—Gerald Horton Bath

GEORGIE AND KAY RETURNED TO SEAL BEACH IN TIME FOR THEIR daughter, Tiffany,* to be born at Saint Mary's Hospital, Long Beach, on November 16, 1952. They found a nice two-story house on Twelfth Street, four blocks from the fateful fishing pier, and Georgie shopped around for work. He also continued taking hunting trips to the Sierras, Arizona, and southern Utah.

By the spring of 1953, Jan had begun to blossom. George Senior and her uncle Donald whistled at her one day when they glimpsed her in a swimsuit, giving Jan the first suggestion that she might be more than average in appearance. Even Gladys bragged about her now and then, but never in Jan's presence. Any compliments from Gladys came back secondhand from mutual acquaintances. Most times, when Jan was close enough to hear her, Gladys was content with snide remarks and insults.

That summer Jan worked full-time at the American Toy Company on Rantoul Street, not far from the factory where Marge had once painted shoe soles. She learned how to dress and act as much from television and the movies as from anyone at home, developing a mild case of the Hollywood fixation that had doomed Beth Short. An avid autograph collector at sixteen, she met Anne Baxter and Tyrone Power at the Somerset Hotel in Boston, where Gladys had one of her beauty salons. A high school advertising class paid off for Jan in 1954, when she was chosen, with a crop of other would-be sloganeers, to visit Eddie Fisher's *Coke Time* television show in New York City.

Janice took the train from Boston and was lodged with other contest winners at a hotel in Manhattan. It was far from elegant, but it meant freedom, if only for a little while, and she made the most of it. Confined to the hotel with other teen contestants on her first night in town, Jan made new friends and sat up half the night luxuriating in the distance from her oppressive family.

Next day, the winners turned out for the *Coke Time* taping. Afterward Fisher signed Jan's autograph book with an illegible scrawl. She asked what he had written, and the singer sneered, "Figure it out for yourself." Jan was pleased, some years later, when Elizabeth Taylor dumped Fisher in favor of actor Richard Burton. Later that evening, the teens put on sophisticated faces for an outing to the Stork Club, but Jan embarrassed herself by putting cream and sugar in her consommé. Instinctively, she made a silent vow to keep the incident from Gladys at all costs.

New York was a diversion, but when Jan returned to Beverly, the daily tedium of life went on. She graduated from high school that June with a B in English, straight C's in bookkeeping, economics, office practice, and business law. On the eve of graduation, Gladys broke the news that she and George Senior would not be attending the ceremony, since "You didn't invite us." Stunned, Jan burst into tears, and Gladys relented after several hours of pleading. Her assessment of the ceremony was a terse complaint that almost no one had applauded for Jan.

Despite Jan's average grades, a counselor encouraged her to take a shot at college. Gladys, always preferring criticism to inspiration, offered no encouragement. At last, in something close to desperation, Janice turned to George for help.

He and Kay agreed to take Jan in while she attended Orange Coast College in the fall.

At that, Jan almost missed her opportunity to suffer more abuse from George. Recalling the events of their explosive separation in the wilds of Maine, she penned a letter threatening to have him jailed if there was any repetition of the single beating she remembered. Georgie went berserk, perhaps anticipating further threats, but Kay eventually calmed him down with a reminder that he *had,* in fact, assaulted Jan in Maine. The letter Jan received in answer to her ultimatum was remarkably sedate, considering the source. George wrote that if she wasn't happy living with the family, in Seal Beach, he would help her find new lodgings and provide her with a cash allowance till she found a job.

That left the trip itself, and Janice caught a break when Nancy and Dexter Radison showed up, visiting relatives in Lynn. They offered to drive Jan back to California when they left, and she accepted. Only then, when the arrangements were complete, did Gladys question Jan's desire to leave the house on Winthrop Avenue. Jan answered frankly that she did not think she would be welcome to remain. The years of being treated as a burden had convinced her it was time to leave. Grandmother Knowlton feigned amazement, saying she had "always planned" for Janice to enroll at Salem Normal Teachers College in the fall. Unfortunately, she had kept the notion to herself, apparently expecting Jan to read her mind.

The drive from Massachusetts back to California is a total blank to Jan. The Radisons were always kind to her, but Janice managed to repress that whole week on the road, perhaps because of who was waiting for her at the other end . . . and because of what came next. If Jan had not been so adept at burying the past, she might have known what lay ahead.

Life on Twelfth Street was a brutal echo of Jan's earlier sixteen-month stay in Seal Beach, four blocks to the west, in 1951 and 1952. George beat his wife and daughters any time the spirit moved him, and the threat to turn him in rang hollow, since Jan repressed each incident the moment it occurred.

One neighbor from the period was Velma Jackson, Eddie Tacy's married sister. She cared for Tiffany from time to time at her home, and Velma still remembers Georgie stopping in to fetch his daughter after work. He seemed affectionate enough, except when Tiffany began to walk and George told Velma not to hold her hand. He wanted all his children to be "independent" from the cradle up.

No physical abuse took place in Velma's presence, but she does recall one incident that occurred when she visited the house on Twelfth Street. George and Jan were in another room, behind closed doors, and while she witnessed nothing, Velma would remember Jan's heartrending sobs for over forty years.

The sexual assaults also resumed on Twelfth Street, in the upstairs bedrooms, in the garage, and sometimes away from home. Kay feigned ignorance and made a point of never catching Georgie in the act. From time to time, when he had Janice in the master bedroom, Kay would call to Georgie from the bottom of the stairs, as if attempting to distract him, but she did not have the heart or the nerve to interfere.

And there were times, as at the Eighth Street house, when George brought his buddies home. Despite his open bigotry and frequent talk of "spics," he played no favorites when it came to choosing drinking partners or men with whom to share his oldest daughter's body. Most of them, in fact, were Mexicans or Mexican-Americans, perhaps reflecting Georgie's frequent trips across the border and the way he seemed to feel at ease in lawless border towns.

One graphic memory, from the garage on Twelfth Street, has Jan tethered to a rack of shelves. A rope is tied around her neck, but George has not secured her hands, since she needs both of them to keep the noose from choking her. George rapes her first and is immediately followed by a Mexican. Another image, seemingly a separate incident, finds Jan suspended by her wrists, stark naked, while

Georgie and at least one other man rape her. In yet another scene from the garage, she sees her father kill and mutilate a cat.

The summer blurred into an endless nightmare: Georgie stalking Jan across the patio, a shotgun in his hands, threatening to blow her brains out if she tries to leave him; Georgie raping Jan in the garage, half strangling her with the rope, then showing her a coffee can lined with cellophane and filled with "white stuff," presumably illicit drugs; a day trip to Orange, with another Chicano, both men taking turns with Janice at Hart Park; a naked woman tethered in the rest room, Jan unable to determine if she is dead or simply drugged.

One of the most disturbing memories from 1954 involves a trip to Arizona with her father in July or early August. Portions of the memory remain elusive, but the details Jan has managed to recover during therapy include a desert campsite, firelight—candles or a campfire, she is still uncertain—and a dead man stretched out on the ground. The corpse is smeared with blood, a gaping wound dead-center in the chest. At least two other men are present, chanting words she does not understand. Jan's father squats beside the corpse with knife in hand, a crazed smile on his bloody face.

A gang rape follows, Georgie leading off, berating Janice even as he violates her flesh. "You little bitch! That's all you're good for! And you love it, don't you? Slut! Tramp! Bitch! You're just like *her!*"

Jan does what she must do to save herself.

She "goes away."

As with Jan's memories of ritual abuse in Pasadena, it is easy to dismiss the Arizona trip as lurid fantasy . . . until we spend a moment pondering the strange events of April 1989. On April 9 a smuggler by the name of Serafin Hernandez drove through a police roadblock in the neighborhood of Matamoros, Mexico, without stopping. He likewise ignored the squad cars that trailed him to a sun-baked ranch in the middle of nowhere. Hernandez was surprised to find himself surrounded by a ring of uniforms and guns when he stepped from his car, since he believed himself to be invisible. No matter, though, for he was also bulletproof.

A night in jail not only shook Hernandez's faith; it also loosened his tongue. He led detectives back out to the ranch and helped them excavate the shallow graves of fifteen mutilated victims. One, a gringo college student named Mark Killroy, had been the object of a sweeping search along the Tex-Mex border ever since he disappeared from Matamoros during spring break. Besides the corpses, Mexican authorities retrieved a cauldron filled with human blood and brains, assorted dead animals and insects, and numerous sticks and bones. Hernandez told them they had found the cult's *nganga*—the cauldron of blood—used to communicate with "spirit slaves" in the land of the dead.

The man behind the Matamoros cult was Adolfo Constanzo, a Miami-born American of Cuban ancestry. Trained by his mother in the arts of Santeria and its dark counterpart, Palo Mayombe, Constanzo had moved to Mexico in 1984, working his way up from the rank of fortune-teller and celebrity witch doctor to the leadership of his own murderous drug cult. Competitors were sacrificed, their hearts consumed in cannibalistic rituals designed to protect Constanzo's disciples and bring them success in their illegal business. By the time police got wise and broke up the cult in 1989, Constanzo's ghouls were known to have been responsible for at least twenty-five ritual murders in Matamoros and Mexico City.

But surely, some will suggest, such aberrant behavior is a fluke, unparalleled in modern history.

They would be wrong.

At the time Constanzo died in a shootout with police, Mexican authorities were investigating the ritual murders of sixty adults and fourteen infants in Mexico City alone, with a similar spate of killings reported from Veracruz. As prosecutor Guillermo Ibarra told the press, "We would like to say, yes, Constanzo did them all, and poof, all those cases are solved. And the fact is, we believe he is responsible for some of them, though we'll never prove it now. But he didn't commit all those murders, which means someone else did. Someone who is still out there."

From Florida to California, wherever drugs are smuggled into the United States from the Caribbean or Latin America, investigators find evidence of black magic at work, employed by the smugglers to protect themselves or to intimidate their enemies. In Houston, Texas, Detective Jaime Escalante says of ritual magic, "It's just like guns are a part of the drug trade. Cocaine dealers carry weapons—it's part of the business. These cults have evolved as part of the drug traffic world, too." Vernon Parker, chief of the Drug Enforcement Administration in San Antonio, reports that Cuban and Colombian smugglers "are heavily involved in black magic religion. They believe it protects them from police and rival gangs. Mixing drug dealers with black magic gives you an organization that is more loyal and willing to do whatever the cult leader says. For them, moving drugs is a spiritual act, not just a business." And from Brownsville, just across the border from Matamoros, DEA agent Armando Ramirez says, "Every arrest we make on the border, the suspect has some kind of black magic pouch on his person. [They're] about as common as driver's licenses."

Nor should it be supposed that drug cults and ritual murders are a 1980s phenomenon spawned by viewing *Miami Vice*. Human sacrifice in Latin America dates from the time of the Mayan, Inca, and Aztec cultures. Sacrificial slayings have been documented in Peru from the 1940s to the present day. Practitioners have included merchants, farmers, miners, brewers, and smugglers—all intent on winning favor from the gods. Next door in Chile, human sacrifice is so familiar that criminal courts recognize "compulsion by irresistible psychic forces" as grounds for acquittal in cases of ritual murder.

Jan's gruesome memory of rape and human sacrifice aside, we have good reason to believe that George, in 1946, was linked to Los Angeles–area sex-cult rituals that included elements of Satanism. His family and friends confirm his fascination with the seamy border towns, then as now hotbeds of prostitution, kiddie porn, narcotics, bestiality, and every other vice. His favorite Arizona hunting ground included the Sierra Vista region, roughly equidistant from the Mexican drug dens of Nogales and Agua Prieta. His involvement with pornography and prostitution fall in line with cult activities described by modern law enforcement, and his willingness to kill, for business or for pleasure, would have done Constanzo proud.

Too many years have passed for us to ever prove beyond a shadow of a doubt that Georgie Knowlton was involved with drugs and homicidal cultists on the border, but we know the kind of man he was, the crimes that he committed on his own.

On balance, Jan's memories are easier to accept than the claims of embarrassed family members that Georgie wouldn't do a thing like that.

He would. He could. He did.

The only thing that stopped him, finally, was death. And in the early fall of 1954 he still had eight more years to live.

Sometime that winter, after Jan enrolled at Orange Coast College, Georgie moved the family eight miles east, to Garden Grove. He borrowed the down payment for a house on McDuff Street from new neighbor Jim Farrow,* brother of Rita Tacy, thus cementing yet another friendship with roots in New England. Of all the Farrows, only twelve-year-old daughter Glenda* thought there was anything strange about George from the start. She made a point of avoiding him, and forty years have not erased her first impression that he was "an icy person," radiating "cold and meanness." He treated his dog "very cruelly" in Glenda's presence, and while she never witnessed any physical abuse of family members, Glenda "didn't get a good feeling" about Georgie's relationship with Kay and the children.

Among adults, he was the same old charming George. When neighbors got together on a Friday night or Saturday, he always stopped in for a beer or two, but he would never hang around for very long. It seemed that smiling Georgie always had someplace to go and something to do after dark. Nobody asked for details at the time. It would have been unneighborly.

Orange Coast College is in Costa Mesa, six miles south of Garden Grove. It is a two-year junior college, offering an associate degree or transfer to a four-year institution when a student has disposed of all the basics. Midway through her first semester, Jan took a battery of IQ tests, and the results were interesting enough to rate a one-on-one meeting with her psychology instructor.

The IQ tests confirmed a first impression of Jan's intelligence gleaned from her participation in class, but there were gaps in the data, presumably resulting from her spotty education and frequent transfers from one school to another. Because repression, dissociation, and the resultant attention deficit disorders were unknown or poorly understood by most psychologists in 1954 and 1955, Jan's instructor offered a more mundane prognosis: Janice didn't follow certain trains of thought, he assumed, because she must have missed that week in school. He had no way of knowing things that Jan herself was not aware of. He could not have known that certain memories, responses, and thought processes had been tortured, raped, and beaten out of her from infancy.

As the teacher won Jan's confidence, she told him more about her home life, including Georgie's violent fights with Kay, his physical abuse of Tiffany and Lena. Sometimes, she said, both adults would storm out in a fit of anger, leaving Jan to baby-sit with the younger girls. Jan still did not believe, as late as 1991, that she too had been a target of abuse even after she had dropped her ultimatum in the mail, but things were clearly bad enough at home to justify a change.

Jan's teacher recommended that she move away from Georgie, find a job, and continue her education in night school. She was instantly agreeable, sensing another whiff of freedom, but the news sent Georgie into a rage. Jan was "selfish" he insisted, thinking only of herself. If she was set on quitting school, she ought to get a full-time job and help pay Georgie's bills. She *owed* him, dammit! Anyone with half a brain could see what he had done for Janice out of the goodness of his heart.

She took the bus to Long Beach and moved in briefly with the Tacys. Georgie came around to threaten and cajole, refusing Jan's requests for cash until she finally recalled his promise of assistance if she failed to make a go of it with him and Kay. The mention of their summer correspondence brought a sudden change of heart, reminding Georgie of her threat to see him jailed. For all he knew, if Janice started talking, she could put him on death row.

On second thought, he said, a small allowance was no problem, after all.

A few days later, Jan nailed down an office job and found herself a small one-bedroom cottage on Lime Avenue, a block from Ocean Boulevard in Long Beach. Thirty-five years would pass before she recognized the close proximity between her flat and the hotel on Linden Avenue, where Beth Short had lived from mid-July to early August 1946.

And while the years dragged on, the Dahlia case refused to die.

In 1954, Red Manley was committed to a mental institution by his wife, who claimed that "he hears voices, writes foolish notes and has a guilt complex." Red had been cleared of Beth's murder, but that made no difference. Hounded by the voices in his brain, he ultimately killed himself.

In 1955, a self-styled Hollywood producer advertised his plans to make a movie that would tell "the real truth" of the Dahlia case. He kept the details vague, saying just enough to interest gullible investors. The "producer" had $100,000 in his bank account when someone tipped off the bunco squad, and he received a prison term upon conviction for grand theft.

In 1956 there came another false confession, this one with a twist. Dishwasher Ralph von Hiltz, age forty-four, told homicide detectives in New York that he had witnessed Beth's demise, though he was not responsible for killing her. She had been murdered by "a friend" as von Hiltz watched from the sidelines. He later pitched in to help dismember Short for easier disposal. Sergeants Brown and Hansen read his statement and dismissed it as a phony, citing various unspecified discrepancies.

Four years later, Pasadena lawmen thought they had a live one when a woman strolled into the station carrying a black silk dress and declared it had once belonged to Short. Examination of the dress disproved that claim, and after sitting through their suspect's rambling monologue, detectives sent her to the nearest hospital for psychiatric observation.

Shakespeare would have loved the Dahlia case. All sound and fury, signifying nothing.

Jan's first semester of college was also her last, for a while. She came out of Orange Coast Junior College with B's in typing and introductory psychology, C's in English, stenography, and physical education. Orange Coast also gave Jan her first real boyfriend, a young man named Jerry. Their relationship was serious enough to include discussions of marriage, but Jan was frightened by Jerry's desire to "go all the way." Kay must have been surprised at first, when Jan confided her misgivings about losing her virginity, but Georgie's second wife was smart enough to keep her mouth shut. Anything that Janice managed to forget was best left buried. That way it would never surface in a court of law. A few more years, at that rate, and the statute of limitations would run out.

On every crime but homicide.

When Jan and Jerry finally made love, she was confused and frightened by the lack of pain and bleeding she had been conditioned to expect. All virgins bleed, she had been taught, and now the man she loved would think she was a tramp. He tried to put her mind at ease, but the relationship was doomed from that point on.

Jan's first priority was work, but there was time for singing. In the spring of 1956, she was referred to Arthur Bradley Codd, a voice teacher in Long Beach. Though Jan regarded herself as "too old," at age nineteen, Codd began grooming her for an operatic career.

George visited the Codds on one occasion, near the end of 1956, ostensibly to see how Jan was doing with her lessons. Mary recalls him as a "slight swarthy man," soft-spoken and morose. Before he left, he told Arthur, "You have probably been more of a father to her in six months than I have all her life."

Mary had heard Jan describe fights and violence in her home, including Georgie's favorite method of "disciplining" his children by killing their pets. Once, when Mary asked her point-blank if Georgie had molested her, Jan answered she "didn't think so." In Mary's opinion, recorded three decades later, Jan was "always looking for something from her father that he couldn't give."

In 1956, the movie *Picnic,* starring William Holden as a maniac, transient Georgie clone, cast Jan into an unexplained depression, marked by panic attacks and thoughts of suicide. She gave up eating, lost weight, and caught herself on more than one occasion crossing steets against lights, with traffic racing past. The Codds supported her through all of it, and by age twenty, Jan had pulled herself together.

By 1957, Jan was in an apartment on Chestnut Street, Long Beach, and that year's city directory lists her as an employee of Seaside Hospital, five blocks from her flat.

Oddly, she retains no conscious memory of the apartment or job, learning of both only in November, 1992, after perusing the old directory. We can but speculate on the events that marred Jan's life on Chestnut Street. Most twenty-year-old women can remember where they lived and worked at any given time, but Jan had learned to "lose" whole months, if there were events she needed to erase.

A single blurry fragment is her legacy for early 1957: Janice lying ill on a bed, with Georgie standing over her, asking, "Why didn't you let me know?" and Jan informing him, "You're the cause."

Another suicide attempt or sudden illness? We may never know, but it is safe to say that Jan did not repress those months without due cause. She still lived close enough for George to drop in unexpectedly, and he was always in the mood for violent sex—or worse. Without the Codds around, she had no witnesses and no defense against her father's twisted brand of love.

The Codds suggested Jan move into a small cottage diagonally behind their home in the spring of 1957. Mary, some twenty years her husband's junior, recognized a "kindred soul" in Jan and happily befriended her. She became "Aunt Janice" to the Codd offspring, David and Margaret.

A heart attack killed Arthur Codd in September, 1957, and Mary continued Jan's singing lessons.

In early 1957, Jan found a new job as a secretary at the autonetics division of North American Aviation in Downey. There she met George Kachikas, twelve years her senior, a soft-spoken doctor of physics who chaired one of the company's major departments. He lived in Sunset Beach in a lovely oceanfront home he had designed for himself, and spent his weekends on a sailboat of his own construction. Jan began to date him, cautiously at first, but in a short time they were lovers.

This George seemed to have it all: respect, compassion, empathy, a natural capacity for caring. Despite the glaring difference in their personalities—his introversion versus Jan's manic compensation for the nightmares she had witnessed—they appeared to complement each other. George gave Jan her first taste of emotional stability, and he encouraged her ambitions as a singer. She joined the Long Beach Civic Light Opera singers workshop, eventually progressing from the chorus to an occasional leading role and understudying the lead in *Kismet*. She was gaining confidence, but still lacked any solid faith in herself or her talent. Above all, she avoided Hollywood and any intimation that she might be suited for movie roles. On rare occasions, when essential business forced her to enter Tinsel Town, she caught a ride with friends, unable to remember the directions on her own.

One weekend, Kachikas invited Janice and another couple to the beach house. They were swimming in the ocean—George and the Pacific Ocean juxtaposed—when Jan tipped into sudden shock, complete with seizures, hyperventilation, hives. Kachikas scooped her from the surf and carried her to the house, where a warm bath gradually put things right, or so it seemed.

That episode went unexplained for over thirty years.

In Garden Grove, the Knowltons moved twice more, first to a new house on McDuff. They remained in Garden Grove for as long as George had ever settled anywhere.

By 1958 the old, familiar patterns were apparent in his life. He cheated openly on Kay with any woman who would give him half a chance, and he sometimes made advances to the boys and young men who accompanied him on hunting trips. At home the violence was routine, spontaneous. A word or a look might set him flailing with his fists, boots, belt—whatever came to hand.

Eleven years after the Dahlia, Kay had found her place at the bottom circle of hell. By May she was pregnant again, carrying Georgie's son, but that made no difference. George was never one to hide his infidelity, and age made him increasingly boastful, as if recounting his conquests made him more virile. Jim and Lynn* Farrow's daughter recalled her parents description of a particular trip to Tijuana with the Knowltons, where Georgie gave his wife and friends the slip. Rejoining them near sundown, he proceeded to describe in loving detail his adventure with a group of local prostitutes. Kay listened stoically, but the Farrows were frankly shocked. From that day on, they would see less and less of Georgie, finally breaking contact altogether.

Back in Massachusetts, daughter Prudence recalls that she "got lonesome for a father" in the latter part of 1955 and wrote to George. His answer, when it came, amounted to a plea for sympathy because of recent problems with his back. As Prudence describes the note, "He said he hoped I wasn't writing only because I'd heard about his back and felt sorry for him."

That Christmas, George sent "gifts for everyone" back east, including a blue sweater decorated with pearls and pink flowers for Prudence. As she recalls, "That was the only time he bought gifts through the years."

He came to visit, though, from time to time. The same old Georgie, clocking up the miles along Route 66 from coast to coast. The highway was his only constant friend, as emotionless as George himself. It took him anywhere he longed to go and asked for nothing in return.

On one trip east, to celebrate his parents' wedding anniversary, George spent some time with eighteen-year-old Prudence and her close friend Marian Dunbar.* He was drinking at the time and kept a bottle in the late-model white El Camino he had driven east from California. Marian told George about her infant daughter, and he offered her a ride back home when it was time for her to leave. Prudence went along for the ride and witnessed what she later described as Georgie's "drunken pass" at her teenage friend. George opened with a rambling joke about an old man who had trouble dancing, then proceeded to "demonstrate" by grabbing Marian and whirling her around the baby's room. Marian la   'in an embarrassed sort of way," and Georgie's pickled brain eventually got the message. "On the way home," Prudence recalls, "my father told me I shouldn't hang around with Marian because she was a tramp."

Another thirty years would pass before Prudence noticed Marian Dunbar's physical resemblance to young Elizabeth Short.

And if he failed to score in Massachusetts, Georgie didn't

really mind. There was a whole wide world out there, and he had lots of prospects in his own backyard.

The last thing anyone expects to find at baseball practice is a woman's corpse—a few skinned knees and elbows, certainly; sore feelings on the losing team; perhaps a fistfight now and then—but the three coaches from California's Babe Ruth League were looking forward to a normal practice session on Sunday, June 22, 1958, as they trudged along King's Row, a private access road that served Arroyo High School's athletic field in suburban El Monte. Burdened with equipment, they were talking shop when one of them stopped dead in his tracks, pointing to the base of an acacia thicket on the left side of the road.

The glitter of a broken necklace caught his eye, pearls scattered in the dust, and then he saw the woman's supine body, lying with her skirt bunched up around her waist. She wore no slip or panties, and her shoes were missing. Her right stocking was in place; police would find the left one wrapped tight around her neck, along with a cotton cord.

There was no question of an accidental death or suicide. The woman's purse was also missing from the scene. A coat that seemed to match her dress was spread beneath the body, almost as a courtesy, to spare her flesh from contact with the soil. The victim was completely naked underneath her dress, but homicide detectives later found a bra beneath her body. El Monte Police Captain Orval Davis told the press she had been murdered elsewhere and transported to King's Row, 150 feet due east of Tyler Avenue.

The red-haired, blue-eyed victim was a nurse, Geneva Ellroy, though the press and medical examiner would stubbornly refer to her as Jean. Newspapers also shaved six years from Ellroy's age, reporting it as thirty-seven, but that hardly mattered in the circumstances. Five feet five and busty, she could have passed for a younger woman.

Dr. Gerald Ridge, a deputy medical examiner for L.A. County, performed the autopsy on Monday, June 23. The cause of death was strangulation, with "intense paratracheal soft tissue hematoma, level of ligature." Geneva had also been beaten over the head, as evidenced by multiple "deep scalp focal ecchymoses." Lesser injuries included a bruised right eyelid, superficial abrasions on the left hip and both knees, and deep purple bruises on the inside of both thighs. The victim was menstruating when she died, and Dr. Ridge found a tampon in place, along with quantities of semen. (Curiously, despite the bruising and presence of semen, the L.A. *Times* declared that Ellroy's autopsy disclosed no evidence of sexual assault.) Geneva's blood alcohol level, at .08, was slightly below the legal limit for intoxication.

Aside from the semen—still decades away from the science of DNA "fingerprints"—and a few streaks of "apparent dried blood" on Geneva's right palm, there was nothing left to help police identify her killer. Subsequent reports made much of skin and tiny hairs allegedly recovered from beneath her fingernails, but Dr. Ridge's autopsy report is unequivocal: "The spaces beneath the fingernails, which are rather long, are grossly clean in appearance, with no visible debris."

Divorced, with a son to support, Geneva Ellroy had been on her own that weekend, while ten-year-old James spent time with his father. James learned of the murder when a taxi dropped him off in El Monte on Sunday afternoon. The yard was full of detectives, and patrol cars were lined up at the curb.

It was a tragedy, of course, but James was not exactly prostrate with grief. He would have preferred to live with his father, but a divorce court had decreed otherwise, leaving James with the woman he described as "sharp-tongued" and "bad-tempered," "a boozer, lazy, and semipromiscuous." "I found her in bed with men," he recalled, years later. "I had a lot of uncles." On hearing the news of her death, James says, "I felt relieved. I remember forcing myself to cry crocodile tears on the bus going back to L.A."

Police, meanwhile, were busy looking for Geneva's killer. They had nothing of substance to work with, but an informant seemed to recall seeing Ellroy on Saturday night, June 21. She had been drinking at a bar on Valley Boulevard, and he had seen her "for a short time" with a couple who might or might not have escorted her out. The male half of the nameless duo was described as swarthy, dark-haired, forty-something, wearing a dark suit with a sport shirt open at the neck. His female companion was blond, age thirty-five to forty, five feet six, 135 pounds and wearing her hair in a ponytail.

Four decades would elapse, without another useful clue, before the first suggestions of a link between Geneva Ellroy's murder and the Dahlia case were aired. At that, the notion should have come as no surprise. Between her sleazy lifestyle and her striking physical resemblance to Kay Knowlton, Ellroy made a perfect victim. In FBI parlance, she was a prime "target of opportunity."

And Georgie always did his best to answer when opportunity knocked.

Almost precisely two months later, Southland homicide investigators had another unsolved murder on their hands. This time the victim was a bona fide celebrity—or had been, in her prime. Helene Adele Jerome was a New Yorker who had been raised in England, where she studied at the Royal Academy of Dramatic Art. Oscar winners Paul Scofield and Lord Laurence Olivier were RADA alumni, and while Helene Jerome never achieved their status, she had enjoyed a successful stage career in the 1930s, touring the Far East with several British companies. At fifty, she was statuesque, and full-bosomed, with a fine aristocratic air, and could have passed for a younger woman. She was planning on a comeback via motion pictures, which explained her lodging at a small hotel on North Las Palmas Avenue in Hollywood.

Helene Jerome had been separated from her husband, sixty-five-year-old character actor Edwin Jerome, for "a couple of years, off and on," but they kept in constant touch. That Wednesday, Edwin was concerned about his wife, her recent illness, and the fact that he could not get through to her by telephone. The line was busy every time he called, and mild concern rolled over into worry when the hotel switchboard operator told him that Helene's phone had been off the hook for hours.

Edwin reached the flat around one-thirty and found the screen door slashed, its latch undone. The front door of Helene's apartment stood ajar. Inside, he found her stretched out on the bed, face up, completely naked, stone-cold dead. The small apartment's air conditioner and an electric fan were both turned on full blast.

LAPD investigators learned that Edwin had come calling on his wife the night before. She was alive and fully dressed when he went home, around eleven, but now her robe lay crumpled on the floor, pajamas, her bra and panties wadded up in a nearby chair. Besides the slashed screen door, detectives found a bathroom window screen torn and pulled out of its frame. Bruising on the dead woman's throat implied death by strangulation, and the autopsy confirmed that suggestion. According to the coroner's report: "A sex killer committed the crime inflamed by a murderous lust, a sadist who got his sexual kicks from strangling naked women."

Nor, according to author John Austin in *Hollywood's Unsolved Mysteries,* was this the only crime of its type recorded by LAPD in recent months. "Still wide open on the Hollywood police blotter," Austin writes, "were the unsolved sex stranglings of two lone women in their apartments by a nighttime sex maniac or maniacs." Regrettably, no further details are provided in Austin's account, and LAPD refuses to comment on the existence—much less the current status—of any unsolved homicides from 1958. These unsolved murders, if in fact they ever happened, are another tantalizing mystery, perpetuated and exacerbated by Los Angeles police.

As for the case at hand, a night clerk told police that he had noticed Helene's phone was off the hook at 4:00 A.M. He walked around the garden path to reach her flat, knocked softly, found the door unlocked, and entered quietly to see if she was ill. Inside the lighted room, he saw a man in bed with Ms. Jerome. Both of them were nude, and he retreated unobserved. Approximately half an hour later, he saw a man departing from the flat, apparently in haste. Despite the darkness, he described the visitor as twenty-five or thirty years old, tall and slim, and dark-complexioned, with prominent ears and "a full head of hair." Playfully, the clerk called out to him, "Next time you'd better lock the screen door," but the stranger hurried off without a backward glance.

According to the clerk, a man of similar description had phoned Ms. Jerome from the front desk earlier that evening, giving his name as George. Edwin Jerome had fielded the call, telling the stranger that his wife was asleep. Much later, around 2:00 A.M., a neighbor had seen a man knocking at Helene's door, but she could offer no description to police.

Edwin Jerome told police that it was not uncommon for his wife to take a "purely motherly interest" in some young actor or writer. One recent visitor, described by Helene as her "protégé," was supposed to be an electronics technician and part-time actor-producer, but Edwin could never recall his name. He had encouraged Helene's pastime, Edwin told police, in the belief that her involvement with other performers would help "get her out of herself."

Hotel employees told a very different story to Detectives Robert Beck and Jimmy Close. In fact, they said, the matronly Jerome had led a very active nightlife. She was out late almost every evening, often after Edwin had come and gone. She patronized a number of saloons on Hollywood Boulevard, often bringing younger men back to the flat for one-night stands. "It was a standing joke around here," the night clerk told police. "Mrs. Jerome evidently thought she was being very discreet, that nobody knew what was going on."

Edwin Jerome confirmed the report of a man named George phoning from the lobby on Tuesday night, but he had never seen the man and could not help police identify him. Homicide detectives traced Helene's "protégé" and swiftly cleared him of involvement in the crime. He bore no resemblance to the swarthy visitor observed on Wednesday morning, but he did corroborate the tales of Helene's indiscriminate love life. While he and Jerome were "just good friends," the young man described her as "practically a nymphomaniac when she was drinking."

And that, apparently, was most of the time.

Detectives ran down several of her part-time lovers, questioned them, and called for polygraph examinations if their alibis were fuzzy, but each in turn was finally released. As for "George," he might have been a phantom, there and gone. Police never even came close to finding him. Come October, a coroner's jury returned an open verdict in the case, and Helene Jerome's murder remains unsolved.

In the midst of death, Jan tried to go on with her life. In the spring of 1959, she entered a talent contest for the title of "Miss Welcome to Long Beach," and while missing the crown, she was hailed in the local daily as a "statuesque beauty." That November she played the female lead in the Long Beach Civic Light Opera's mini-revue of *Oklahoma*— the same role played by Shirley Jones (of whom more later) in the movie musical. Her singing lessons continued with Mary Codd, but there was change in the air.

Mary Codd had been teaching at Long Beach State College since her husband's death, but now she had an opportunity to move back east. Her sister-in-law was married to Boris Goldovsky, head of the New England Opera Company, and a job was waiting for Mary in Brookline, Massachusetts.

Around the same time, Jan began to think that she might profit from a change of scenery. Her relationship with George Kachikas had reached an emotional stalemate—no retreat, no surrender, more attrition than affection. They would always be good friends, but Jan was kissing off the fairy tale.

That fall she auditioned for Professor Wolfgang Martin, a

visiting conductor from the Metropolitan Opera. His assessment of her talent was encouraging, and he prepared an introduction to Bob Herman, assistant to manager Rudolph Bing, in New York City. All Jan needed was the nerve to pack her things and leave.

In January, George and Kay presented Janice with a new half brother, Kevin Lee. Another golden child with fine blond hair. A blessing and a curse for Georgie, all rolled up in one small package.

Three weeks later, Jan was in Saint Mary's for a tonsillectomy. She was conscious for the surgery, performed with local anesthetic, and went into shock immediately afterward, perhaps as a result of a combination of the hospital setting and the scalpel near her face. Oxygen and emergency treatment brought her around, another near miss with the Reaper.

In August, Mary Codd was on her way to Massachusetts and a brand-new life. She packed up her children and her worldly goods, with room enough for Jan to ride along. It was good-bye to California, to her father, and to the blighted family he ruled through fear. Jan hoped it was good-bye forever, but she had no way of telling what tomorrow held in store, when she could not remember yesterday.

The toughest part of running away from yourself is the frustration. You learn over time that you can never really break away. Some nightmares must be faced before they can be laid to rest.

But at the moment, everything seemed bright and clear to Jan. Unknowingly, she was reversing Beth Short's pilgrimage to fame and fortune, bound for new beginnings in the East.

12
Death Wish

*A man, when he burns, leaves only a handful of ashes.
No woman can hold him. The wind must blow him
away.*

—Tennessee Williams, *The Rose Tattoo*

A SHORT TIME AFTER JANICE LEFT FOR NEW YORK CITY, GEORGIE
"found the Lord." Or maybe God found him. In either case,
they didn't have a lot in common, but a yearning for divine
approval is a fairly common trait among psychopaths.
Some, like Heinrich Pommerenke in Germany, kill on
orders from a vengeful deity, while others, like Henry Lucas
and assorted members of the Manson tribe, are born again
in prison, with an eye toward gaining sympathy from a
conservative parole board.

Georgie bought his ticket to the afterlife from the Jehovah's Witnesses, a controversial Christian sect that deviates
from mainstream Christianity on several major points.
Organized as a theocracy, presumably directed by Jehovah
through his spokesman, Jesus Christ, the Witnesses draw
much of their inspiration from the teachings of Arius, a
theologian whose beliefs were officially declared heretical by
the Council of Nicea in A.D. 325. The sect believes that
Christ was Jehovah's first creation rather than a member of
the triune godhead. Human beings are saved by faith and
obedience to Jehovah in the form of good works, primarily

the sale of books and magazines published by the Watch Tower Bible and Tract Society. At death, humans go to the grave—that is, to hell—and their only hope lies in future resurrection. In the wake of Armageddon, a select 144,000 Witnesses will go to heaven and reign with Christ, while the vast remainder will dwell on earth eternally. As agents of Jehovah's earthly government, the Witnesses eschew all manner of "idolatry," as in saluting the flag and singing the national anthem.

It is a startling image: Georgie Knowlton, with his bloody hands, traipsing from door to door in search of souls to save.

George and Kay's conversion cut their last remaining ties to Jim and Lynn Farrow. Returning from their final trip to Garden Grove, the Farrows told daughter Glenda that George was "acting weird and preaching to them" all throughout their visit. Faith in God was one thing, but they couldn't shake the echoes of Tijuana, and they'd sensed an oppressive hypocrisy when Georgie launched into his pious spiel.

The Lord works in mysterious ways, we are told, and it would be wrong to suppose that he changed Georgie's life overnight. When George wasn't out peddling tracts or soliciting handouts for Jesus, he was still a tyrant on the home front. Sudden violence was his stock in trade, presumably supported by some bit of Scripture that was long on discipline and short on love. He beat his wife and children when it suited him, and Lena has described one incident where Georgie hurled a cast-iron ashtray at Kay, missing her by inches and striking infant Kevin in the head.

Georgie's crowning achievement, in terms of emotional abuse, was the reunion he arranged between Kay and her estranged father. Farmed out to relatives and foster care as a child when her mother was committed to a mental institution, Kay had been disowned by her father, a devout Catholic, when she divorced her first husband. They went years without speaking, until Georgie tracked the old man down and conned his way into a pseudo-friendship. At

Georgie's request, Kay's father agreed to resume a normal relationship with his daughter as long as she remained with George. Thereafter, any time Kay mustered up the courage to resist abuse at home, she faced the additional threat of losing her father a second time. The family talent for manipulation was thus elevated to a new plateau of cruelty.

On occasion, the mania for control extended even to the children George had abandoned back in 1947. When daughter Evelyn got married, Georgie somehow found the cash to bring the newlyweds out west and get them started in a house next door to his in Garden Grove. It was a thoughtful gesture on the surface, but it came with strings attached. George and Kay made daily visits, criticizing Evelyn for the way she ran the house. When Evelyn's health took a turn for the worse and her housecleaning suffered accordingly, the folks next door increased their nagging, but declined to lend a helping hand. At last, a few months after they arrived in Garden Grove, Evelyn and her husband moved back to Massachusetts, explaining that George and Kay had been "too intrusive, too bossy."

Christian or not, Georgie was still playing by the same old rules. Anyone who didn't want to do things his way could get the hell out of Dodge.

Arriving in Manhattan, Jan settled in the Studio Club, an East Side YWCA residence for young women active in the arts. A fellow resident and future friend, Shirley Hall, noted that Jan seemed "troubled by emotional problems," but because of memory gaps spanning much of her life, the problems eluded definition, much less solution.

Jan's first paying job in New York was a secretarial position at Burns and Roe Consulting Engineers in lower Manhattan. Her immediate boss, remembered by Jan as a lecherous "twerp," made a habit of groping her breasts and displaying nude snapshots of his wife around the office. No one had heard of sexual harassment in the 1950s, much less codified a remedy, and Jan was too frightened to report her boss, preferring to keep her distance whenever possible, and thus keep her job.

Her salary went for rent, necessities, and singing lessons. Bob Herman, at the Met, was impressed enough with Wolfgang Martin's praise of Janice that he referred her to voice teacher Rosalie Miller. Sadly, Jan caught up with Miller near the end of her career, when age had largely robbed the teacher of her hearing, but Jan stuck it out through aimless lessons that included slaps across the knuckles with a ruler whenever the aging coach detected a sour note.

On the side, Jan nailed down her first professional singing job at Chez Lucy, a supper club on Fifty-ninth Street in Manhattan. Between her day job and the endless music lessons, she suffered a precipitous decline in health. A bout of flu, complicated by stress and missed meals, degenerated into severe anemia. Iron injections and dietary supplements saved Jan's life, and she eventually found the nerve to terminate the knuckle-rapping sessions with her aging vocal coach. New problems with a deviated septum led to plastic surgery, and while the nose job improved Jan's breathing, it also enhanced her resemblance to another would-be star, deceased since January 1947.

Marge's father, Ken Hatch, died suddenly in August 1959, leaving his widow, Annie, to board with a sister, but Jan still had other friends and family in Massachusetts. Mary Codd had settled on the outskirts of Boston with her new husband, Eli Rabkin, and Jan enjoyed seeing them from time to time. While she was in the neighborhood, Jan also visited with Gladys and George Senior in Beverly, picking up some belated—and most unwelcome—sex education in the process. According to Gladys, her husband had lost the ability to sustain an erection. George Senior, for his part, insisted it wasn't *his* fault; he was simply repulsed by the sight of Gladys's sagging breasts. This was more than Jan had ever wanted to know about sex in the golden years.

In 1961, Jan escaped her job at Burns and Roe after a

successful audition for summer stock at the Cape Cod Melody Tent in Hyannis, Massachusetts. Those were heady days in the Bay State, the first year of John Fitzgerald Kennedy's New Frontier, and Jan performed in six shows as the summer wore on. The results were encouraging, but Jan's self-confidence was still a fragile thing, stunted by Georgie's lifelong admonition to expect defeat on every front. She found auditions difficult, and dance lessons alarmed her so much that she often froze in her partner's arms. She had no conscious memory of Georgie dancing her around Short's deathbed back in Westminster, but she was haunted by it all the same.

Despite her stress-related limitations, that November found Jan singing at Max Loew's Viennese Lantern on East Seventy-ninth Street in Manhattan. Press reviews called her "a distinct asset" to the program and "a little girl with a fine, big voice," but Jan still had her doubts. She was put off by men who tried to guide her new career, and gradually drifted toward the nonperforming side of show business, serving as executive secretary for some major theatrical companies in New York.

It was success, of a sort, and it kept her away from the spotlight that so often made her freeze like an animal trapped in the high beams of an onrushing car.

Out west, meanwhile, her father's hectic life was starting to unravel.

George could almost see the writing on the wall.

The fickle finger, when it paused at last, was pointed not at Georgie, but at Kevin Lee. That spring of 1962, the three-year-old was diagnosed as suffering from rare and deadly myelogenous leukemia. George gave permission for emergency transfusions, flying in the face of declarations from his church that blood transfusions are akin to vampirism and are banned by God. The decision cost George his salvation, in the opinion of most Jehovah's Witnesses, and it was all in vain. By June, physicians gave young Kevin one chance in 100,000 of surviving through September.

Somehow Kevin's case became a local cause célèbre. Paul Chapple wrote a front-page story for the *Register,* painting a portrait of fatherly love at its finest. Georgie had given up an unspecified job, Chapple wrote, because Kevin would accept his frequent doses of Purinethol from no one else. Beyond that, he was bent on selling off the Yoak Street house to pay for one last trip to Massachusetts, George and Kevin on their own, while Kay remained behind with Tiffany to work and pay the bills. George had selected Massachusetts for their getaway, said Chapple, because his son loved to romp in the woods and watch furry animals at play. Nurses at Hollywood's Cedars of Lebanon Hospital were said to "marvel at [the] inseparable bond between the boy and his father."

A cynic might regard the story as a calculated ploy, complete with a two-column photo of George and Kevin peering skyward, "as if seeking a ray of hope for the boy's life." What they got instead was a pair of Disneyland tickets purchased by sympathetic neighbors, plus a surge of private donations that enabled Kay to leave her job and join the eastward trek.

For all the journalistic hype, there was another side to Kevin's life that few Orange County residents were privileged, or cursed, to see. According to reports from daughter Lena—married now, but still a frequent visitor on Yoak Street—George still "hit Kevin with his belt." George also told a number of his neighbors that he did not plan to let a blood disease deprive him of his precious fair-haired son. When he believed that things were truly hopeless, Georgie said, he would kill the boy himself. Put him out of his misery.

The Knowltons started driving east on Saturday, July 7. They took two cars, George in the point vehicle with Kevin, Kay, and Tiffany bringing up the rear. A week on the road brought them to Beverly, and they spent several days on Winthrop Avenue before moving on to Amesbury, near the New Hampshire line, where Gladys and George Senior had a summer cottage on Lake Attitash. When Kevin wasn't playing in the woods, George drove him in and out of Boston for radiation treatments at Children's Hospital.

It was a death watch, never mind the trappings of a summer idyll in the great outdoors. Physicians were unanimous in their belief that Kevin would be dead before the leaves began to change for autumn.

They could not be absolutely sure, of course . . . and thereon hangs a tale.

Jan saw her father for the last time in mid-August 1962 at the Lake Attitash cottage. The purpose of her visit was twofold: to offer her condolences on Kevin's illness, and to see if George could help her make sense of the distance that she felt from Marge, a void that left Jan feeling like an orphan.

She dressed in basic black, à la Elizabeth, unconscious training from her childhood kicking in. George had not seen her since the operation on her nose, and now he found himself confronted with the spitting image of Jan's mother, plus a fair approximation of Beth Short. The three-year difference in their ages—Jan was twenty-five by then; Beth had died at twenty-two—may well have helped impress George with the march of time.

It may be that Jan's final visit was the trigger to what followed, or the match that lit a long, slow-burning fuse. The "resurrection" of Beth Short, together with the impending loss of Georgie's son—another failure and perhaps his last chance to erase the "taint" of nonwhite blood—may well have tipped him into fantasies of self-destruction.

At the moment, though, he seemed at ease. He and Jan sat outside the cottage on a pair of folding camp chairs, staring off across the lake toward distant trees. Without admitting anything, George did his bumbling best to help explain Jan's strained relationship with Marge. "Your mother loved you as much as the rest of the kids, Janice," he said. "But when you were born, she was so sick she had to stay in the hospital. I took you home and I took care of you."

No mention of the sexual abuse included in that "care,"

or any of the grim atrocities that followed. Georgie made it sound like simple infant bonding with one parent in the other's absence. Jan's very questions may even have reassured him that her mental block was still in place. She could not testify to things she didn't know. Amnesia was a blessing, all around. It kept George out of prison and prevented Jan from stewing over things that she had witnessed or experienced in years gone by.

As their conversation drifted onward, Jan remarked on the recent death of Marilyn Monroe, reported to the world on Sunday morning, August 5. George sneered at mention of the famous actress. "She was nothing but a tramp," he told Jan. "She deserved to die."

A matter of opinion, or an observation from the early days of 1946, when Beth and Marilyn were tricking for the swells in Hollywood? To Jan, the comment smacked of vintage Georgie.

Six weeks later he would take his secrets to his grave.

The doctors said it was impossible, but Kevin did it anyway. September passed, and he was still alive. More to the point, his health seemed to be improving. His physicians shook their heads in wonder. Relatives began to speak in terms of miracles.

And Georgie told his brood that it was time they went back home, to Garden Grove. If Kevin Lee could beat leukemia, all things were possible.

For her part, Kay was less than thrilled at the idea of going back to California. As much as she loved Kevin, she had come to hate his father. Continual abuse, the pain and guilt of life with George, had combined to take their toll by autumn 1962.

A plan was hatched before the family left Lake Attitash, but Kay would keep it to herself for almost thirty years: as soon as they were back in Garden Grove, she meant to shoot George with his own deer rifle and arrange the scene to make his death seem accidental.

It was perfect, but she never got the chance to pull it off.

George stole the show again.

The two-car caravan reversed its course along Route 66. In their Buick sedan, piled high with toys and luggage, George and Kevin watched the miles slip by. Behind the Buick, Kevin's latest gift, a pony, was securely tucked inside a U-Haul trailer. Kay and Tiffany rode in the second car, sometimes ahead of George, sometimes behind.

They were ahead of him on Friday evening, the fifth of October, when Georgie stopped to gas up the Buick in Claremore, Oklahoma, seat of Rogers County. Kay drove on another dozen miles or so and stopped outside of Tulsa on the Will Rogers Turnpike, waiting for George to catch up. She had been waiting ten or fifteen minutes when another female motorist pulled up and rolled her window down. All breathless with excitement, she inquired if Kay and Tiffany had seen the "terrible accident" a few miles back on the turnpike, between Tulsa and Claremore. A car had "blown up," she explained, with people inside.

A few more details, and the truth hit home with Kay. She turned the car around and started back toward Claremore and her husband's funeral pyre.

As reconstructed by police, the Buick was a few miles west of Claremore, moving at a rapid clip, when it unaccountably swerved to strike a concrete bridge abutment. Freshly filled, the gas tank burst on impact, and the car went up in flames. A long-haul trucker stopped and tried to save the passengers, but he was driven back by the searing heat. He emptied his extinguisher, but failed to quench the fire. At last, he settled for rescuing the pony, which escaped with minor burns. Another hour passed before firefighters could extract the shriveled bodies of George and Kevin from the blackened, twisted wreckage.

Dr. Orville Holt, the Rogers County medical examiner, was notified of the accident by highway patrolmen at 7:30 P.M. Three hours later he examined George and Kevin at the Musgrove Funeral Home in Claremore. Kay identified the bodies, and no autopsy was performed on either victim. Dr. Holt ascribed George Knowlton's fate to "Accidental death

—probably skull fracture." A handwritten notation at the bottom of the death certificate read: "Same for his 3 year old son Kevin Lee."

Single-car fatalities are questionable at the best of times. The weather, road conditions, automotive factors, and the driver's health and state of mind may help explain each crash. We know the skies were clear that Friday evening, and an item in the *Register,* reporting Georgie's death, described the Will Rogers Turnpike as "Oklahoma's finest highway." George had left a rest stop moments prior to wrecking the Buick. There is nothing to suggest that he was drinking or fatigued. The smoking wreckage yielded no apparent evidence of a vehicular malfunction on the road.

It had been several months since Georgie spoke of his plan to kill his son before leukemia could do the job, and while it seems that Kevin Lee's surprise recovery would logically have squelched those plans, we must remember who and what his father was and the pressures Georgie faced as he began the long drive back to Garden Grove.

We may presume that seeing Janice at the lake contributed to the stress. She had become the very living image of one woman George had murdered and another whom he still professed to love. Their conversation must, inevitably, have revived old memories—for George, if not for Jan.

And there was Kevin Lee. Although the leukemia was in remission at the moment, he was still in limbo where the future was concerned. The same physicians who expressed amazement at his recent turnaround were adamant in their belief that no one could ever really beat leukemia. He might have gained a few more weeks or months, through some amazing fluke, but death was surely coming for him sometime soon.

Could Georgie look at Kevin, see him dying day by day, without remembering the deaths of Marjorie and Sandra sixteen years before? Now a third child was slipping through his fingers, emphasizing Georgie's failure as a father even when he tried to help.

It is a fact of life that random psychopathic killers

sometimes turn on themselves when they have reached a private nadir of depression and depravity. It would have been totally in character for George to kill himself, and simultaneously put Kevin "out of his misery."

On balance, no other explanation rings true.

Georgie covered his tracks to the end, fooling some of the people all of the time. The Beverly *Times* described his final months as "A heartwarming story of human kindness and feeling . . . brought to a tragic end by the untimely accident." Back in Orange County, the *Register* covered the crash in a front-page story headlined "Brave Kevin Comes Home to Rest." Newsprint memorialized George Knowlton as a selfless father who gave up his job, his home, and finally his life to buy Kevin a few happy weeks at the end of the road.

Janice, for her part, was in no position to contradict the sticky-sweet obituaries. She remembered George in different terms, of course, but she could not recall his string of ghastly crimes.

It cost $261.66 to fly the bodies home from Tulsa on American Airlines. A memorial service was held at Peeks Family Colonial Funeral Home, in Westminster, with Kay requesting donations to the Cedars of Lebanon Hospital cancer fund in lieu of flowers.

Jan did not attend the funeral. She could not bring herself to stand at Georgie's casket, even with the lid closed on his charred remains. The service might have sparked new memories, but Jan had no idea her brain was hiding anything. The average person will not search for something unless it is known to be lost.

George Knowlton went into the ground with Kevin at his side, Kay and Tiffany mourning their loss of the child, if not the man. For Kay, at least, the grief at Kevin's death was doubtless tempered with relief. There would be no more rapes or beatings, no screaming arguments. She had some ugly memories to live with, but she found a semblance of release through alcohol. At least this way she did not have to kill him herself and risk life in prison if she got it wrong.

For Janice, in Manhattan, knowing George was dead provided only marginal relief. He was a lifelong trickster. What if he had staged the accident somehow, with someone else—a hitchhiker, perhaps—to take his place?

And even if he *was* dead, his most intimidating threat remained, sealing her lips and clouding her recollections: *It would kill your mother, if she knew.*

A secret part of Janice knew that it was safer to forget.

13
Echoes

*I am still of the opinion that only two topics can be of
the least interest to a serious and studious mood—sex
and the dead.*

—William Butler Yeats

THE BIG APPLE WAS SLOWLY, INEXORABLY GOING SOUR FOR JAN
by the time her father died. In 1963, while dining at a small
sidewalk café, she heard a screech of brakes, glanced up in
time to see a yellow taxi hit a pedestrian. Jan nearly fainted
as sudden nausea washed over her.

Jan's eyes and conscious mind were focused on a New
York street scene, but her brain, adrenalized by shock, was
coughing up childlike reactions to the homicide in Lynn
some nineteen years before. She still had no concrete mental
images of murder or of the basement grave, but the accident
made one small crack in the retaining wall she had erected
to confine her memories.

New York was never really safe, all things considered, but
its swift decline toward something that resembled anarchy
clearly dates from the 1960s. And every day, it seems, the
headlines offered Jan some new grisly shock.

In 1967, twenty years after Short's murder, Jan experienced her first real incident of acting out unconscious
memories. It started with a minor bit of home repair and
almost claimed her life.

She had a straight-backed chair in her apartment. Jan decided to replace its torn seat cushion, choosing as her tools a kitchen knife and a claw hammer. Kneeling in front of the mutilated chair, its stuffing on display, she was reduced to childlike stature. Little Janice, staring at Elizabeth across the years.

Next morning, Jan was stricken with a rash of giant hives, a symptom of anaphylactic shock. Some individuals are prone to hives, but Jan had suffered from them only once before, in 1957, on her date with George Kachikas at the beach. Much of the swelling was internal. Jan was close to suffocation when a doctor saved her life with massive doses of adrenaline and antihistamines. Another twenty years would pass before she learned that adrenaline was critical in the suppression of traumatic memories.

There was another jarring incident in 1967, though Jan managed to ignore it at the time. Her gynecologist remarked on changes in the entrance to Jan's womb that she had seen before only in women who had given birth. Jan knew she had no children, and she shrugged it off as a mistake.

Around this same time, Jan was working for composer Mitch Leigh's company, Music Makers, at the Warwick Hotel in Manhattan. Directly opposite the Warwick was a restaurant owned by a friend of Jan's. One afternoon the friend introduced her to actor Jack Cassidy, husband of Oscar-winning actress Shirley Jones. Cassidy intimidated Jan with his aggressive, "cocksure" attitude, but at the same time, he was easily the most magnetic man she had ever met. They lunched together, and as Jan was walking back to work, she turned and found Jack watching her, still seated at the window table they had shared.

Within a few days they were lovers. Cassidy told Jan that he was separated from his wife, and friends corroborated the report. She felt uneasy with a married man, but she found him irresistible.

Their first weekend together, Cassidy drove Jan to Pennsylvania, stopping at the home of longtime friends. Jan was prepared for Cassidy to act like "a Svengali of sex," but the scene was surprisingly domestic, and she felt her initial trepidation starting to dissolve. At one point Jack noticed a broken chain on Jan's shoe. She followed him to the cellar, where he repaired it.

"That's probably the moment when I fell in love with him," she wrote, years later. "He was sexy and disarming as he put my shoe back on. It wasn't Cinderella's slipper, and he wasn't Prince Charming, but it's as close as I'll ever get to the story."

There was a dark side to the fairy tale, however.

Jack had a sly sadistic streak, evoking memories of Daddy George. He could be cruel in bed. On one occasion, as they were embracing, he drew back without a hint of warning and slapped Jan across the face. Another time he made her scrub the bathroom on her hands and knees, evoking tremors that stopped short of flashbacks to the Culver City American Legion post.

But Jan was getting there. She simply didn't know it yet.

The sick relationship broke up in August 1969. Jack was preparing for a flight to California when he briefed Jan on the massacre of Sharon Tate and her friends. The predators were still at large, but there was ample ghoulish evidence to panic Jan: a pregnant actress in her twenties, hog-tied, mutilated; an apparent effort by her killers to remove the fetus from her body; butchery times seven, when the deadly prowlers struck a second time.

Jan fled New York, fled Cassidy. Her choice of a sanctuary seems peculiar, but it was almost certainly predictable: she ran to California.

Harry Hansen retired from LAPD near the end of 1968 and moved to Palm Desert, California. Finis Brown was close behind him, bound for Texas when he "pulled the pin," and their departure marked the end of any but the barest pretense that the Dahlia homicide was still an active case. The files would be maintained by aging caretakers from that point onward, but investigation of the case, as any normal person understands the term, had long since been abandoned.

Still, Short's murder preyed on Hansen's mind. At his retirement party, as reported in the *Times,* Hansen got drunk and "wept like a baby because this is the one case he wanted to solve, the one killer he wanted to find." The one who got away . . . with a little help from his friends.

Over the next fourteen years Hansen received more than four hundred "clues" to the killer's identity, sent by murder buffs from around the country and around the world. None of them came close to the truth. If we accept Hansen's words at face value, he still had no hint of the killer's identity by September 1977, when he told *Cosmopolitan* magazine: "I suppose I allow myself to lean slightly toward the theory of a male murderer, someone with medical training. I based that merely on the physical aspects of the case. Still, you have to have an open mind to anything, can't close your eyes to any evidence. In other words, it may have been somehow possible that the killer didn't have any medical background."

By that time, according to various sources, the Dahlia files at LAPD headquarters had been "picked clean" by morbid souvenir hunters, making a solution to the case doubly improbable. Official statements typically refer to "6,000 pages" of documentary evidence in Short's file, presumably ready and waiting for trial if her killer happened to stroll in someday and surrender, but discovery requires a search—or at least a willingness to see. In LAPD's case, where Beth Short is concerned, the blinders have now been on for almost half a century.

Arriving on the coast, Jan spent some time with Kay in Garden Grove. One evening, in her cups, Kay spilled the details of her own abortive plan to murder George and stage an accident in 1962 when he returned from Massachusetts with their son. She told Jan that she would have left him years before had it not been for Georgie's leverage with her father. Finally, with Kevin on the verge of death, it didn't seem to matter any more.

From Garden Grove, Jan traveled north to San Francisco, where she settled on Green Street, close to the Presidio. Ironically, another random killer—this one known as the Zodiac—was stalking San Francisco and environs in those days. On October 11, 1969, he shot and killed his sixth victim, cabbie Paul Stine, less than two miles from Jan's apartment. Taunting letters filled the press.

Jan would repress the memory of her days on Green Street, for reasons that were unrelated to the Zodiac murders. More than twenty years elapsed before old Social Security records confirmed the San Francisco residence and before Jan, in therapy, recalled the link between Green Street in Pasadena and the incidents of ritual abuse from 1946.

Another link, unconscious at the time, was Jan's 1970 fixation on a magazine advertisement promoting highway safety. The ad depicted a man being struck by a car, as viewed from inside the speeding vehicle. It was another nudge toward Georgie's crosswalk killing in Lynn, but Jan wasn't ready to remember.

In San Francisco, Jan met Olaf Sandberg,* a Norwegian who had moved to the United States and worked as an executive with a domestic steamship company. She found him bright, attractive, charming. They were married on the day before Thanksgiving 1970, with Lena Tiffany serving as matron of honor.

As with Jack Cassidy, a short year earlier, the fairy tale went sour. Despite his endearing qualities, according to Jan her husband was an alcoholic who became "a monster when he drank." Jan's letter to Marjorie, dated April 13, 1971, sounded happy enough, with its chatty information on the couple's new address and Jan's new job, but the relationship was already showing signs of strain.

And in the meantime, scattered pieces of the puzzle Jan had yet to recognize were falling into place.

Gladys Knowlton died in Beverly on January 8, 1971. The call reached Janice moments after she and Olaf returned to their apartment from a dinner celebrating her thirty-fourth birthday. She flew east for the funeral, and may have seen a touch of irony in the poem that accompanied Gladys's obituary in the local newspaper.

> With each day that passes by
> We miss you more, for sure
> We miss your gentle smiling face—
> And will forevermore.

Jan remembered few smiles on Winthrop Avenue, but she remembered none of the abuse she suffered, either. Visiting George Senior, she was treated to a glimpse behind the brick wall of denial. Looking back across the decades, Grandpa Knowlton told her briefly of the incident "down south" that had marked her father's first known homicide.

Wheels turning, gaining speed.

A few months later, Georgie's old friend Freddie Denno committed suicide. From Prudence Knowlton come reports of incest in the Denno family, a scandal brewing, but there seem to be no charges on the books. Carl Conrad, once a traveling companion, merely notes that Denno suffered "a series of tragic events in his life" before he shot himself.

Was Denno the town character or a pedophile?

In 1972, Olaf Sandberg followed the lure of a new job to Portland, Oregon. It didn't seem to suit him, however, and he grew increasingly abusive, even more so after Jan resumed her singing career part-time. Winter found them back in Alameda County, but Olaf kept falling off the wagon, bringing his anger home in a bottle. Jan enrolled in driver's education at the local night school, biding her time until she had her license and enough self-confidence to hit the road. In April 1973 she struck out on her own in a battered red Toyota, taking only her personal things and her beloved dog Bamse—Norwegian for "teddy bear." She drove to Orange County in search of a brand-new life—unaware of the old one lying in wait for her there.

Olaf made a stab at reconciliation, but Jan was determined to resist his efforts. He made it easy for her when he showed up at her door half drunk and spoiling for a fight. He returned to San Francisco and filed the divorce papers. Jan was notified of the action on January 28, 1974, and the marriage was formally dissolved on February 21.

By that time she had found a job as an executive secretary at Disneyland. Hired on the last day of July 1973, she rented an apartment near the old family homesite in Westminster, but found herself unable to live there. The place gave her fits, and she was forced to move, with no idea of why the flat evoked such negative reactions.

Daily work at Disneyland was far removed from the adventure enjoyed by millions of excited tourists every year. In fact, it proved to be a boring grind, despite good pay. As a diversion, Jan auditioned for a talent show at work, thus revealing her trained singing voice. The next thing she knew, she had been tapped for an "employee appreciation show" at the park. The response was encouraging enough for Jan to try out when the Disneyland Employees Drama Club held open auditions for *The Sound of Music*. She landed the role of Mother Superior, and suddenly, without half trying, she was back in show business.

She auditioned next at Mario's, an Italian restaurant in Newport Beach that featured show tunes and arias with its pasta. She began to moonlight with some of the other "Mario Singers," landing a job at the Five Crowns Restaurant in Corona del Mar, where the ensemble would sing two nights a week for the next five years. The group incorporated as the Showcase Singers and Jan began to handle bookings as vice president of promotions, making a short step from the stage into public relations and management. By the time she left Disneyland in July 1978, Jan was well on her way to self-employment in the entertainment industry.

The future looked golden, but her past was sneaking up behind her, one step at a time.

Seven years after Harry Hansen's retirement, there had been no further progress on the Dahlia case. LAPD still described it as an active case, but the activity was limited to ducking questions from the press and public, solemnly declaring that the files were sealed and would remain that way until the case was tried in court.

It may not be the most transparent scam in L.A. history, but it comes close.

In March 1971 retired newswoman Aggie Underwood told Tod Faulkner and *West* magazine that detectives had "very grave suspicions about one guy who was questioned in the case." In fact, she said, "the evidence at hand [in 1947] was almost conclusive" against the male suspect, whom Underwood described as "not a well-known person." He was "no longer alive" by the date of her interview, however. The same article declared that Harry Hansen "figures the killer himself is dead," but Hansen seemed confused by Aggie's reference to a suspect. "I know for certain," he told Faulkner, "I never met the killer face to face."

So much for "inside" knowledge on the case.

In 1975, NBC produced a made-for-television movie on the Dahlia case. *Who Is the Black Dahlia?* featured Lucie Arnaz as Elizabeth Short, with Efrem Zimbalist Jr. as Harry Hansen and Ronny Cox as Finis Brown. Joseph Pevney directed the film, and ex-Detective Hansen drove in from his desert hideaway to serve as a technical adviser. Zimbalist's stand-in for the movie was actor Paul MacWilliams, who had dated Beth for several months in 1946.

With Hansen and MacWilliams on the set, and so much history to draw on for the story's background, NBC could have produced a film that separated fact from fiction. As it was, an *L.A. Times* reviewer praised screenwriter Robert Lenski's "well-researched script," and another article described Arnaz's resemblance to Short as "disturbingly uncanny."

In fact, the script was riddled with deliberate inaccuracies, beginning with the shift of Beth's childhood to "a small town in Maine," where she lived with a "bewildered, old-fashioned grandmother," played by Mercedes McCambridge. That change was prompted by Phoebe Short's refusal to sign a release for the film, which reportedly left Beth's mother open to harassment from Hollywood. According to word from the family, someone linked to the NBC production telephoned Phoebe after the program had aired, sneering, "Just wait till you see what we say about you after you're dead."

Reviews of the NBC movie were lukewarm at best. Critics called it "a pretty conventional police procedural mystery" and a "fair" period piece, "strongest in its costumes and its cars." Even so, it was too much for Jan. She instantly repressed the program, and would not remember seeing it for almost fifteen years.

Other movies were giving Jan problems as well. In 1972 there was *Prime Cut,* wherein Gene Hackman plays a Kansas City mobster with the unlikely name of Mary Ann. His stock in trade is human flesh, young women drugged and sold at auction in a barn, like cattle. Rival gangsters are disposed of in a slaughterhouse, where a sadistic thug named Weenie—Hackman's brother in the film—grinds hit men into hot dogs. Tough Lee Marvin saves the day, but he had not been there for Jan in 1947.

Scratch *Prime Cut.*

Ironically, the film that Jan worked hardest to repress was *It's a Wonderful Life,* the classic Christmas movie released in 1946. James Stewart stars as George Bailey, addressed in one scene as "Georgie." His wife, Mary *Hatch* Bailey, is played by Donna Reed. They live in Bedford, an amalgam of Beverly and Medford. Georgie's heroic brother is written up in the paper, as Babe Knowlton was at his death. Bailey's guardian angel is played by an actor named Travers—the name of the family that owned the old homestead on

Hollingsworth, in Lynn, with its rotting secret in the basement. In the movie, George becomes abusive to his family as his life disintegrates. In one scene, Mary scolds her husband, "George, stop torturing the children." Worst of all, though, was the happy scene where George and Mary fall into the swimming pool and come up dancing.

Just like Georgie Knowlton and Elizabeth.

Jan resumed contact with Jack Cassidy around the same time Lucie Arnaz was making her Dahlia debut on NBC. He was divorced from Shirley Jones by then, and trying to put his chaotic life in order. Jan was willing to forgive and forget, but they would never be more than close friends. Janice's fatal attraction—to Jack, at least—had worn off.

And so had her tolerance for Disneyland. The office job seemed increasingly tedious by 1978. Jan split from Disneyland, symbolically, on Independence Day, and struck off on her own, performing and doing public relations work.

Jan was scheduled to visit Palm Springs with Cassidy over Christmas that year, but they never made it. On December 12, following completion of a major film—*The Eiger Sanction,* with Clint Eastwood and George Kennedy—Jack was burned to death in a residential fire. Aside from the loss of a friend and onetime lover, Jan was stunned by the similarity of Jack's death to Georgie's, a comparison all the more jolting in light of their similar personalities.

Well after the fact, on September 12, 1977, Jan received a letter of condolence on Jack's death from his friend James Cagney.

Dear Miss Knowlton,
    You may be sure I feel very badly about Jack Cassidy. As you know he was terribly befuddled the last few years of his life, and I am afraid he showed little patience with his desire to "set things straight. . . ."
    He was essentially a good person and had a great career staked out for him, when he burned himself up.

It bothers me greatly that I had not got my letter off to him before he took "the long meander."

With all good wishes to you.

Sincerely,
Jim Cagney

Three weeks later, on the thirty-first anniversary of her sojourn at the Hawthorn, Jan moved without apparent reason to a new apartment, seeking an address as close to Orange Street, in Anaheim, as she could get. Oddly, after moving in, she could never recall the name of the cross street, telling potential visitors, "If you see Broadway [the next major intersection], you've gone too far." It would require a dozen years and some intensive therapy to break the mental logjam, freeing memories of Beth Short at the Hawthorn, which a younger Jan had tucked away to save her sanity.

Remembering, when it began, would mean reliving all of the buried nightmares time and time again.

The first full-length book on the Black Dahlia case was published in 1977. Cast as fiction, *True Confessions* is a strong, compelling novel, and it marked author John Gregory Dunne's introduction to the best-seller lists. As fiction, it was bound to take some liberties with history, but Dunne retained as much of the recorded evidence as art allowed.

Jan has no memory of reading *True Confessions* prior to 1991, but she could scarcely have escaped the movie version, ten years earlier. Filmed in Hollywood, depicting L.A.'s most sensational murder mystery with fine performances by Robert Duvall and Robert De Niro as the Spellacy brothers, *True Confessions* was a shoo-in for publicity and rave reviews. The *L.A. Times* ran full-page advertisements for the movie in October 1981, a rose-tattooed leg in fishnet hose facing another full-page ad for the movie *Tattoo,* which displayed the lower half of a naked woman's supine body, severed at the waist, ankles bound, hips and legs heavily tattooed. *Tattoo's* punch line: "Every great love leaves its mark."

Jan Knowlton was among the Angelenos who saw *True Confessions* shortly after its release, but she "tranced out" through every scene related to the murder, automatically blocking painful images as she had learned to do in childhood. Afterward, her conscious mind remembered only bits and pieces of the film, but nothing had been truly lost. That autumn she was dogged by vague anxiety, increasing stress, and unpredictable crying jags. She also found herself compelled to buy a cheap bone-handled carving knife, even though she had expensive cutlery at home. She kept the relic of Beryl Atherton's murder in a kitchen drawer even after the blade snapped in half. She also began to collect clothing decorated with roses; and stationery with the lower half of a body.

In 1982, Jan Knowlton made a brief appearance on the Op-Ed pages of the *L.A. Times*. Still three and a half years away from surgery, more than seven years removed from any conscious memory of Beth Short's murder, she was sparking—catching brief subliminal glimpses of the truth.

This time the subject was a dog whose masters were estranged and whose ownership was up for grabs, with legal action pending. Jan sat down to pen a note with tongue in cheek, but the result, printed on March 29, 1982, was something else: "I have a solution for the legal question of ownership. Drawing on the wisdom of Solomon, I suggest that rather than severing the dog into two equal halves, divided between the owners, the owners should be severed and given to the dog."

Jan didn't know it yet, but she had just described a nightmare scene from Westminster, observed when she was barely ten years old.

It may be said that Harry Hansen gave the best years of his life to Elizabeth Short. Granted, he could never clap the handcuffs on her killer, but he never strayed far from the Dahlia's shadow in his final years on earth.

In January 1979, when a reporter for the *L.A. Times* asked Hansen's opinion of the Dahlia killer's whereabouts, Harry replied in one syllable: "Dead." He was a bit more eloquent in reference to Short herself, describing the butchered woman as "a bum and a tease." As for an ultimate solution to the case, he said, "We had some good leads, but they never panned out. Oh, sure, I wonder—but I don't lose any sleep over it."

Some three years later, in December 1981, Hansen got a phone call from an L.A. broadcaster who thought he had a hot tip on the case. A rather ghoulish confidential source was claiming to possess a souvenir of Beth Short's murder, more specifically a severed ear, which the informant carried with him always, in a jar. The former homicide detective heard his caller out, then punctured his balloon. "You can file that one in the round file," Hansen said. "She had both ears."

Another Dahlia anniversary rolled around in January 1982, and Hansen stood by for the inevitable nostalgia interview, this time from UPI. The murder would now "be practically impossible to solve," he said, "because the physical evidence would be dissipated, disposed of and destroyed." As for a possible link to other unsolved crimes, Hansen insisted that "It was the killer's first and last killing. He never killed before and he hasn't killed since." His reasons for drawing that conclusion would remain, as always, under wraps.

Harry Hansen was eighty years old and suffering from lung cancer when a stroke took his life in October 1980. By that time, the Dahlia case evidence—described by the *L.A. Times* as filling "three or four file cabinets"—was being supervised full-time by Detective Buck Pearse. A few years later, when Pearse died, the "active" case was handed over to an aging LAPD legend, John St. John.

But shifting personnel was not to be mistaken for a change in attitude where Beth Short's murder was concerned. The

Dahlia files were sealed, and they would stay that way until the case was "legally resolved in court."

In April 1983, Jan's dog was stricken with a lethal ailment. Veterinarians declared that Bamse's only hope was liver surgery, a risky process in itself, compounded by the patient's age. The sure alternative was death. Jan made the hardest choice since leaving Olaf and had her sole companion euthanized, after the surgery destroyed Bamse's liver.

From the day of Bamse's death, Jan started sliding into melancholy that would force her to seek psychotherapy by early 1985. At that, the sessions would provide no great relief. Without the normal well of memories to draw on, something to attack, the psychoanalyst was helpless to explain Jan's deepening depression. There was clearly more involved than simply grieving for a dog, but what was it?

The therapist had no answers.

In the meantime, Jan had business to conduct. Long-buried memories to re-create.

In July 1983 she signed up for a television acting class at Tepper-Gallegos Casting on Sunset Boulevard, just around the corner from the old Hawthorn Hotel. Three months later, Jan flew to Hawaii for a vacation, unconsciously re-creating her trip to the Hawthorn with George and Beth Short. The season was right, and she helped the mood along by setting up an automatic camera in her hotel room, snapping pictures of herself in a kimono hand-painted with *hawthorn* blossoms. She even managed to collect a stand-in for her father, a smooth-talking sleaze who favored blue jeans, a cowboy hat and boots.

By year's end, pseudo-George had followed Jan back to California, where he asked her if he could spend "a few days" at her flat before he moved on to a brand-new job in Phoenix. Jan agreed, but had a private-eye acquaintance check him out. The background scan revealed a pending charge of auto theft arising from his failure to return a rental car. When Jan confronted him about it, he smiled and promised it would all be taken care of. He was still around at

New Year's, drinking constantly, and while he had displayed no signs of violence yet, Jan lived in fear, her tension surfacing in rashes and insomnia. A few days into January 1984, she rose near dawn, dressed all in black, and ordered him to leave. The rascal did as he was told.

Unknowingly, Jan had reversed the Hawthorn scene where Georgie gave Elizabeth her walking papers, leaving her to walk the streets.

Another victory, or maybe just a warning shot. And Janice didn't even know that she was in a war.

By 1984, Jan Knowlton Associates Public Relations was thriving. Her major client was Barron Financial Services, and she was writing radio commercials for Minolta Office Copiers. She also presented her singing act, Broadway Plus, on the college celebrity series, and at national conventions.

She was on her way.

Unfortunately, she had no way of predicting where the road would lead.

In 1984 she wrote a poem that would wind up on her custom-made Christmas cards that year. Accompanied by a photograph of Jan at four years old, taken a few weeks after Frances Cochran's death, it read:

> The child you see still lives in me,
>   As your child lives in you.
> Newly-formed by God's own hand,
>   Hope-filled . . . yet timid too.
>
> Let's set aside all doubt and fear,
>   And celebrate our birth,
> Along with him . . . who bids us sow
>   Peace throughout the earth.

For Jan, there seemed to be no hope of peace on earth by the following winter, 1985. The circumstances of her surgery, the side effects of medication, and her breakdown are recounted elsewhere in these pages. While her mind and body were in turmoil, there were also haunting fears of future disability and unemployment, which she voiced—albeit with a deprecating smile—in a May 1986 interview Jan gave to Forest Kimler at the *Orange County Register*. "Women in my business can't afford to be too much of a soft touch," she explained, "because as you get older you become more conscious that the expression is always 'bag ladies' and never 'bag girls.'"

Another curious event around this time involved a phone call from a woman in her mid-thirties, whose name Jan has regrettably forgotten. The caller, who had been adopted, was seeking her birth mother. After running all the hurdles required for unsealing court records, she had traced her mother as Kathleen Knowlton, but Kay had long since remarried Gene Bryan and was no longer listed under Georgie's surname. The stranger was calling every Knowlton she could find in southern California, hoping for a break.

In 1986 Jan had no memory of Vincent or his female twin, no evidence beyond a doctor's passing comment nine years earlier that she had ever borne a child. Jan readily admitted the coincidence of names, but she could not recall Kay ever giving up a child to an adoption agency. It must be a mistake. The caller thanked Jan for her time.

Somehow Jan never got around to mentioning the call to Kay.

While pushing Broadway Plus as best she could, Jan fell prey to a form of compulsive behavior well known among victims of post-traumatic stress disorder and dissociation. She began unconsciously collecting memory aids, common-place items that echoed details of her long-repressed night-mares. She collected gnarled sticks, for example, and displayed them in her apartment years before she recognized the link to Frances Cochran's murder. She could not pass a cast-off plastic comb without retrieving it from the sidewalk or gutter, and she discarded the colored ones at home till only black remained, an echo from the Culver City

Legion post. An enamel lapel pin, depicting a woman's face marked with musical notes, closely mimicked Beth Short's mutilations.

Even Jan's artwork displayed clues to the atrocities she had witnessed as a child. One painting of a sunny field recalls the Cochran murder scene, a brooding thicket on the right-hand side. Another shows four-year-old Jan peering out of a cave surrounded by garish red flowers resembling fresh bloodstains. The imagery was even more explicit in a 1987 poem, "Postponed Lessons":

> How very much alike we are, my little dog and I,
> When e'er a "bone of wisdom" comes our way.
> We take it out and bury it,
> And secretly we treasure it,
> Saving it for the proverbial "rainy day."
>
> Rejecting all the lessons in the meal we're served.
> We hide our gifts beneath the moldy earth,
> Then scratch and dig some later date,
> Searching and whining with self-hate.
> For postponing what was ours by right of birth.
>
> The next bone that we're offered is gobbled up and gone.
> We've learned from past experience not to delay.
> We chew on it and savor it,
> We worship it and favor it.
> If only it could always be this way.

On January 20, 1987, Jan signed up for a $250 repetition of the TV acting course she had already completed at Tepper-Gallegos Casting, around the corner from the Hawthorn, back in 1983. Gene Bryan died in early February, and Jan suppressed her anxiety and fatigue long enough to sing at her "good daddy's" funeral. On March 12 she taped an episode of the June Cain Miller television talk program, in Anaheim, on the perils of hysterectomy. Before the month was out, she flew back to New York for a visit with friends, then went on by bus from there to Boston, where she was met by sister Evelyn. Jan stayed at the *Hawthorne* Hotel in Salem while visiting her mother in neighboring Peabody. By then, however, a series of strokes had left Marge senile and debilitated, unable to explain or relieve her eldest daughter's pain.

In Massachusetts, Jan "felt like a ghost returning to the places I had been." She drove a rented car and found herself in the proximity of Frances Cochran's murder, unaware that anything unusual had happened there. She did not yet know that she had watched her father dump a woman's mutilated body there in 1941.

Back in Anaheim, Jan's life was a whirlwind of activity: speaking on behalf of the Society for Hysterectomy Education, promoting a new YWCA hotel for homeless women, singing, and obtaining two new clients: a Merrill Lynch office and the mortuary next door.

Anything to keep her mind and body occupied around the clock.

It didn't help.

The darkness was upon her, closing in. It did not have a name or face, as yet, but they would come with time.

There was nowhere Jan could hide.

For all the waking nightmares she had suffered since her surgery, Jan still had no visual memories of rape or murder prior to her mother's death in July 1989. Jan flew east for the funeral, to Salem, the shrunken family coming together once more in extremis. Prior to the memorial service, Jan carefully polished a silver dollar she had received from George in 1959, on the eve of her move to New York, and she placed it inside Marge's casket. Standing over the box for a last good-bye, she kissed her mother's forehead, as she had Beth Short's in January 1947, squinting through the ordeal like a child with "tiny eyes."

After the funeral, before flying home, Jan rented another car for an unscheduled drive to Marblehead. She didn't know where she was going or why she felt compelled to visit

Washington and Green Streets. It would take another two years, revelations from the media, and endless hours of therapy, to forge a link between Beryl Atherton's murder in 1950 and the identical street names in Marblehead, L.A., and Pasadena.

One of those who counseled Jan before she met Jim Frey was Father John Lenihan, at Saint Boniface Catholic Church. In fact, their talks would continue even after Jan recalled her father's murder of Beth Short. By 1991, however, Lenihan had plummeted from grace and had nearly taken Jan's faith with him in the process. Curiously, as his case unfolded, it provided even more support for the concept of repressed memories as valid evidence of criminal activity.

Mary Staggs was twenty-six years old and married in October 1989 when she opened a newspaper and found herself staring at a photograph of Father Lenihan, printed in connection with a fund-raising drive at Saint Boniface. An instant flood of graphic recollections plunged her life and that of family into turmoil. Staggs had remembered specific incidents of sexual abuse by Lenihan that spanned four years, from 1976 to 1979. She had been thirteen years of age when Lenihan began molesting her. The abuse had stopped, at last, when she was seventeen. The thirty-something priest had been supervising Mary's youth group at Saint Norbert Catholic Church in Orange when the incidents occurred.

Mary's first stop was the nearest police station, where detectives informed her that the statute of limitations had run out on crimes from the seventies. Next, she filed a civil suit for damages. Her case was strengthened when Lenihan, in a sworn deposition, admitted one incident of fondling Mary and another of undressing her when she was fifteen, in 1978. Lenihan also admitted sending the teenager love letters, but described himself as a changed man, thanks to eight months of therapy in 1982 "to resolve sexual conflicts." The Diocese of Orange settled out of court for $20,000 in 1991, but Lenihan retained his post as senior pastor at Saint Boniface, still defending himself to the public.

"I'm not proud of it," he told the press, "and I'm not denying it. I'm not guiltless. But it's nothing on the scale being indicated." Lenihan maintains that Staggs was "at least fourteen and a half when we met," as if that made all the difference in the world for a thirty-two-year-old man on the make. "This fifteen-year-old was not totally unaware," he insists. "She was no child. It was like my adolescence too—a very sad thing I had to go through at that stage of my life. I was trying to help her, took her under my wing. I've suffered a lot morally and financially."

The pedophile's lament: "Poor me."

More shocking than a sex offender's rationale for criminal behavior is the way in which the Catholic church closed ranks behind Father Lenihan. The Archdiocese of Los Angeles had been privy to Lenihan's transgression since 1978, when Mary's father complained about the priest writing love letters to his adolescent daughter. Years later Norman McFarland, bishop of the Diocese of Orange, would tell newsmen the problem was "addressed adequately" in 1978, with no further problems from Lenihan. But in fact, Lenihan's 1982 therapy sessions were admittedly prompted by a new sexual escapade, this one involving an adult parishioner.

"Since then," McFarland told the press, "there has not been the slightest hint of wrongdoing or scandal connected to Father Lenihan. He has led an exemplary life of dedicated service to the church and community. I can only stand amazed and chagrined when people can be so certain of their own righteousness as to have no hesitancy in casting the first stone." The bishop reserved special barbs for the *Orange County Register,* which had covered Lenihan's story in detail.

Editor N. Christian Anderson spoke for much of the community at large, when he replied in print: "I'm disappointed that the bishop chose to attack the *Register* rather than address the facts of the case and answer questions that would help you understand how the church deals with matters such as this. On a personal note, I wish he had expressed some compassion for Mary Staggs, who is important to this story, too."

Indeed.

Within another year the Roman Catholic church would stand accused of covering for pedophiles from coast to coast, silencing victims with cash or appeals to doctrinal loyalty, spiriting clerical child-molesters away for "retreats" and church-sponsored "counseling" before they were set loose among helpless victims in another diocese. Hundreds of cases have now been exposed. Civil suits and criminal indictments are piling up against the rapists who hide behind surplice and collar.

For Jan, one instance was enough. Revelation of Lenihan's guilt came at a critical period in her recovery and in the corroboration of her memories, and for the first time Jan seriously considered abandoning her life-saving therapy.

Jim Frey would pull her back from the abyss.

In the fall of 1989, a friend of Prudence Knowlton loaned her a paperback copy of James Ellroy's novel, *The Black Dahlia*. Prudence never finished the book—"I didn't like his writing style," she recalls—but the cover, featuring a stylized portrait of Beth Short, immediately captured her attention. To Prudence, the black-and-white Beth was a dead ringer for Marian Dunbar, the friend her father had embarrassed with a drunken pass in 1958.

She turned the novel over and read on the back that Short's "torture-ravished" body had been found on January 15, 1947, in Los Angeles. And something clicked—the face. The date. The city.

Daddy George.

Jan telephoned a few days later from the coast to brief her sister on the content of emerging memories from childhood. Their conversation bridged the decades as they recalled

George's violence and their mother's suffering. Prudence told Jan about the incident in Saugus when she had watched George kill the family cat in 1949 or 1950. Jan's recollections were more personal. She had already summoned images of rape and molestation, of the fatal hit-and-run in Lynn, and of a shallow basement grave.

No, Prudence said, she couldn't remember anything like that. But suddenly, out of the blue, she commented, "I wonder if Daddy could have killed the Black Dahlia."

Jan was shocked by the suggestion. Even though the "Black Dahlia" label rang a distant bell, she had no conscious knowledge of the case. "Why would you think that?" she asked.

"Well," said Prudence, "we lived out there at the time, and we were just talking about how cruel he was." Besides, she could recall their mother saying that George went out to bars at night and danced with other women. And the Dahlia was a kind of barfly, wasn't she? A tramp, in fact.

Jan had no answer for her sister. The memory of sudden death in Lynn was light-years distant from the Dahlia murder, with its ghastly mutilation and the media reports of torture that had dragged on for days. Prudence's suggestion would require some thought, and thinking had become a painful burden. It would be easier for all concerned if she could just forget about it, but the days of blissful ignorance were coming to an end.

That night Jan dreamed of a redhead in a two-piece blood-red dress being cornered by a madman who resembled Georgie Knowlton. At the woman's feet lay a mutilated human carcass. It had been cut in two and stacked, one half atop the other. The dream-Jan thought herself invisible, and therefore safe, until the redhead pinned her with accusing eyes and said, "How could you leave me alone all night with this maniac?"

She woke up in a sweat, oppressed by guilt, the nightmare images as clear as any television broadcast. With the TV, though, at least you had a chance to switch the channels or turn the damned thing off and pull the plug if it offended you. Not so with memories unleashed after years of remaining hidden in the dark.

Death cuts both ways.

For Jan, the graphic images of murder and her father's constant threats had placed a lock on her subconscious.

I'll kill you if you tell.

Don't make me use this knife, this saw, this ax.

George's death had been a blessing, but it did not free Jan's mind. The worst of Georgie's threats had lingered with her: *It would kill your mother if she knew.*

Too late. The threat rang hollow after all those years. Whatever Janice might recall and tell the world, it could not harm her mother now.

Another cautious step toward freedom, creeping toward the finish line.

The rest would come when it was ready.

Jan could only watch and wait.

Kay Bryan had begun disintegrating mentally around the time that *True Confessions* hit the theaters. It may have been coincidence or a result of haunting echoes from the past, but her relationship with her current husband, Gene Bryan, grew worse than ever. At the VFW hall, Gene's friends dismissed her as a carping bitch, but they had only glimpsed her angry, shrewish side. They never understood the brooding fear.

Kay had grown paranoid and was convinced that Gene was poisoning her food. One of her daughters took a yogurt sample, promising to have it analyzed, but never followed through. Besides the imagined poison, which Kay thought explained her failing health and hypertension, she believed that Gene was having girlfriends over to the house at night after she had gone to bed. Gene's plot, she believed, was nothing short of diabolical, in fact. He *wanted* her to see the women, Kay decided, hoping that the shock of meeting one of them would cause a fatal heart attack or stroke.

Kay fooled him, though. She was tenacious, swallowing the poison, dodging shadow-mistresses until she forced a separation, stopping short of actual divorce. She clung to life, where Gene could not. He died in February 1987, but his passing brought Kay no relief.

Instead, she had her memories. And loneliness.

The TV, tuned to gospel programs all day long, helped a little. Kay sat and watched the preachers looking for salvation in between appeals for cash. She scribbled checks to keep the message rolling in a godforsaken world, and prayed for some return on her investment.

Anyone could be forgiven. Jimmy Swaggart told her so.

Tenacious as she was, Kay did not live to see Jan's memories emerge. She had dismissed Jan's breakdown following the hysterectomy as unbelievably dramatic, but the shortage of compassion did not put Jan off. She doted on Kay, affirming her love by word and deed, still repressing the years of neglect and abuse. It was Jan who finally persuaded Kay to get another checkup, using Jan's physician. When she found Kay's body riddled with inoperable cancer, Jan's grief rivaled that of Kay's own children.

Kay spent her last days in the hospital, Jan slipping in after hours to spend more time with the woman she thought of as her mother. When Kay died, on October 12, 1989, Jan was at her bedside. She went out to fetch the nurse and later made arrangements for a priest to officiate at the funeral. Before Kay went into the ground, Jan delivered a heartfelt eulogy and sent her on her way with a hymn, "Amazing Grace."

Five weeks later Jan attended yet another funeral service. George Kachikas had been fading at the time Kay died, and Jan had worked in several visits with her friend and onetime lover. This time she sang Ave Maria.

George and Margie. Kay and George. All gone. The last restraints thrown off.

By year's end Jan had looked into the pit of hell and found her child-self shackled there, a hostage to her father's savage crimes. She had not seen the whole truth yet, but it was coming.

She had seen enough to know she needed help.

14

Breaking Cover

We are healed of suffering only by experiencing it to the full.

—Marcel Proust

IT SEEMS NAIVE IN RETROSPECT, BUT JAN'S FIRST IMPULSE, AFTER recognizing Beth Short as a victim in her memories, was to alert LAPD. Police are paid to solve crimes, after all, and L.A.'s finest carry the motto "To Protect and Serve" on their patrol cars. They are courteous, professional, efficient. *Dragnet* tells us so.

Jan's first call, in December 1989, was automatically referred to Detective John St. John. The longest-serving homicide detective in Los Angeles, St. John had spent four years on the job when Short was killed in 1947, and he had become a legend in the past two decades. Known as Jigsaw John because of his uncanny knack for solving murders, he had bagged the Freeway Strangler and a host of other real-life monsters in his years of service. He had also been the subject of a book and a short-lived television series in which gravel-voiced Jack Warden played the lead.

Still, every legend has his weaknesses, and no one is immune to passing time. With forty-six years on the force, St. John might wear badge number 1, but his assignment as custodian of the Black Dahlia files was a sinecure, requiring little or no effort in the last few years before he retired. St.

John took phone calls on the case, appeared on tabloid television shows from time to time, but publicity was risky. Dawdling in the greenroom prior to one appearance, St. John told a fellow guest, straight-faced, "I'm senile, and I wonder what I'm doing here."

At first, St. John appeared to take Jan seriously, promising to check her information out and call her back with the results. When two weeks passed without a word, Jan made the call and found herself confronted with a very different Jigsaw John. He had decided it would be a waste of time to check the details of her memory against his files, or even to speak to Jim Frey on the telephone. In fact, St. John declared, he saw no point in budging from his desk until Jan came up with "more corroboration" on her own.

The challenge was, in Jan's own terms, like "waving a red flag in front of a bull." If Jigsaw John desired corroboration, she would get it for him, but she was not giving up on the police establishment. If one detective put her off, perhaps another would be more receptive to a logical solution for the homicide division's longest-running mystery. Jan tried to keep in touch with LAPD through that winter, but the final brush-off came from Captain W. O. Gartland, commander of Robbery-Homicide, in a letter dated January 19, 1990: "Thank you for your information about your father and your concerns that he may have been involved with the 'Black Dahlia' case. I know that you have spoken to Detective St. John and he has explored the possibility that your father was involved in this case. Unfortunately, the death of your father in 1962 prevents us from carrying our investigation further. I am sorry to report that the information you provided has not resulted in any connection between your father and this case."

In fact, Captain Gartland was wrong on two counts. First, St. John, by his own admission to Jan, had not explored anything. Quite the opposite, he refused to investigate Jan's memories, demanding that she handle the detective work herself. And second, while George Knowlton's death precluded an arrest or trial, it certainly did not prevent LAPD from mounting an investigation of the case. No link was found between Jan's father and the Dahlia homicide because St. John and his superiors refused to look.

Across the continent, in Massachusetts, Beth Short's relatives were not surprised by the reaction of St. John and company. To date, the family has never been officially permitted access to the LAPD's Dahlia file, autopsy documents, or any other fruits of the investigation. They are "not impressed" with St. John's efforts on the case, and note that he was "very quick" to reject Jan's information out of hand.

Although he had no time to investigate the murders, St. John did find time to smear Jan's reputation with the press. Once she went public with her memories, reporters started calling Jigsaw John for his impressions, and he never failed to advise them that he had "checked it out" in detail and that her memories had "no connection" to the Dahlia homicide. St. John would cling to this version of the truth for the next two years, until he finally retired and left the case in other hands.

We may assume that Jigsaw John and company believed their flat rejection of Jan's memories would silence her or, barring that, reduce her to the status of another hopeless crackpot dwelling on the case in private. They could not have been more wrong, however, for she took the challenge from St. John quite literally. She would find corroboration for the doubters, even knowing—as she did by February 1990—that no evidence on earth would be enough to satisfy LAPD. She would not quit, but neither could she do the job alone. And that meant going public.

Collecting evidence on unsolved homicides is difficult enough for the police. For a civilian working independently, the stumbling blocks are multiplied tenfold. Most private investigators are ex-policemen with a working knowledge of investigative methods the average citizen does not possess. Nor are regular citizens funded by a government or a wealthy client if their research calls for travel, lab analysis of evidence, or bribes for a reluctant witness. A civilian can't force anyone to talk, much less surrender private property that may, in fact, be crucial evidence. Surveillance of a suspect may itself be viewed as criminal harassment if the watcher does not wear a badge.

And those are just the problems of an average citizen attempting to investigate an unsolved crime. Once a prestigious law enforcement agency has branded that civilian as a fraud or mental case, the odds against success are astronomical.

Jan launched her retroactive manhunt on three fronts at once: potential witnesses among her family and friends; the public record, as preserved in media reports and other sources that police could not manipulate; and the world at large, where unknown sources might be tucked away, just waiting for the proper question to be asked.

She advertised in Massachusetts papers, seeking anyone who had known her parents in their younger days, and came up with a high school classmate of her mother. He was getting on in years, but had a knack for tracing genealogy, and volunteered to trace the Hatch and Knowlton lines through various directories and other public records Jan might otherwise have overlooked. His efforts documented Georgie's movements in the Bay State and New Hampshire, giving Jan a collection of dates and addresses that would later help her search newspaper files for other similar crimes in the vicinity.

Going public helped. A total stranger in New York reached out to Jan with information on the Dahlia cover-up, collected for a book that never made it off the drawing board. That information led to Vincent Carter, James Ahern, and Archie Case. Closer to home, in Orange County, a retired newspaper editor described his private struggle to defeat the local gamblers led by William Robertson, and one more fragment of the puzzle fell into place. A local newsman, close to Jigsaw John, dismissed Jan's memories as "a mistake," but let it slip that Short *was* killed with a claw hammer, exactly as she described. A mutual acquaintance introduced Jan to fireman Bill Nash, the witness long ignored and seemingly forgotten by police. A former L.A. County sheriff's deputy provided Jan with copies of the Dahlia autopsy report, his detailed notes from 1947, and a sheaf of photographs the media had never seen. Officials at the Skil Corporation confirmed that their portable rotary saw, like the one Georgie used on Beth Short, had been on sale since 1934, thereby negating arguments that Jan had been "imagining" a futuristic tool.

Most major daily papers are preserved on microfilm, and with the newfound evidence of frequent moves from town to town and between the East Coast and the West, Jan started tracking bodies. Everywhere that Georgie went, it seemed, the girls were sure to die. In Salem, Marblehead, Los Angeles, and San Diego. Even in Arizona. In a time when the United States produced two serial killers a year— compared with its present annual crop of thirty or forty— *someone* had been dumping strangled, slashed, and battered female corpses from coast to coast. Each crime had been committed within a few miles of the Knowlton residence or Georgie's favored hunting grounds.

In addition to the bodies, there were solid pointers to her father in the press, suggestions that authorities knew more than they were telling. Five acquaintances of Short named "George" as her fiancé on the very day her body was identified, but there was no apparent follow-up by the police or journalists. The medical examiner referred to Beth's assassin having used a saw before he placed her pitiful remains in a refrigerator. One detective thought the corpse had been bisected so that it would fit inside a duffel bag. Lieutenant Freestone said Short's body had been carved the way a hunter dresses out a deer. Beginning in the latter 1960s, Harry Hansen, Aggie Underwood, and others spoke of the elusive killer's death as an established fact.

The public record also validated Jan's emerging memories of specific buildings. Jan had sketched a floor plan of the Culver City Legion hall from memory, a building modern owners understandably deny has any link to Beth Short' murder. When the blueprints were retrieved from storage and compared with Jan's sketches, however, the locations of the rec room, showers, and the basement swimming pool were all a perfect match. Old members of the Moose lodge, reminiscing about their days of sharing quarters with the Legion, even confirmed the presence of a mounted moose head on the wall above the billiard table.

Jan also sketched the small apartment at the Hawthorn where Beth Short had roomed with Georgie and assorted other men in 1946. The Hawthorn blueprints turned up long after Jan had completed her drawing and passed it on to Jim Frey for safekeeping. Once again, she had prepared a nearly perfect drawing of a flat her critics say she never saw.

In addition to validating Jan's memories, the public record also filled in some yawning gaps. An old directory for Long Beach, dated 1957, listed Janice Knowlton as a resident of Chestnut Street and an employee at Seaside Hospital. In fact, she had no memory of where she had lived or how she'd earned her keep that year, when she was twenty, but the listing spelled it out in black and white. On impulse, Jan dropped by her former address, and the present tenant was kind enough to show her through the flat. The sunny rooms evoked no images, however, leaving Jan to wonder what had happened there, so close to George and Kay in Garden Grove, that would erase most of a year from conscious memory.

For all her independent research, working day by day with strangers who were often sympathetic, sometimes hostile or indifferent, Jan received some of her strongest corroboration from friends and family. Some of her contacts had no faith in the emerging memories, and few really understood the process or the way in which their bits of information helped complete the portrait of a monster, but they talked.

That February, Jan called Glenda Farrow, daughter of old-time neighbors Jim and Lynn Farrow, who had loaned George the money for one of his Garden Grove houses. While Glenda Farrow had shied away from George instinctively, avoiding him whenever possible, she recalled the stories that her parents told of Georgie's flagrant whoring in Tijuana and his boozy infidelities at home. She had not witnessed any violence in the family, but she knew that George was cruel to animals. "I was always afraid of your father," she told Jan. "I got a feeling of coldness when he was around. Icy cold. Evil. I remember he used to hit his dog."

Aunts and uncles, cousins, nephews, friends, and onetime neighbors all contributed pieces to the puzzle: George's foray into horse theft at sixteen, his violent arguments and fistfights in a string of Massachusetts foundries, threats to kill his foreman, boasts that he had killed at least two men and beaten the rap each time on a plea of self-defense, Georgie's homosexual advances to a young boy on a hunting trip, the fact that he had owned a Skil saw in the 1940s and had later given it to friends who lost it in a move three decades later. Even Billy Sexton's homosexual affair with George was confirmed by members of the late hairdresser's family.

Jan met with resistance too, but not as much as she expected. She got angry silence and denial from Aunt Myra, who refused to besmirch her brother's memory or to admit that she, too, had abused Georgie's children and her own. There was a furious response from Kay's daughters, in defense of Kay. From one of Billy Sexton's sisters Jan received the unkindest cut of all. "You're just like your father!" she wrote in a letter to Jan.

The strangest family memento came from Nancy Radison. It was a homemade record from the latter 1950s featuring the voices of Nancy, her brother Pete Cardran, George Knowlton, and Kay. The record seems innocuous enough, and yet it opens with Pete Cardran playing the emcee. "Quiet now," he demands, speaking across the years. "Record's on, folks. Record's on. Quiet now. Quiet. Everybody's quiet. George . . . George . . . George is gonna take Kay home and stick her in bed. Okay, George, take it home."

The next voice does not literally issue from the pit of hell.

It has been etched in plastic and recorded on tape. Its owner has been dead for thirty years, but the effect on Jan is staggering. When she first heard it, she did not recognize the nasal, nerdish voice, but in another moment she felt the tremors starting.

Georgie opens with a rhyme. "Had a little bird, he was chock full of turd. Stepped on his neck . . . is that thing goin'?"

And the monster starts to sing about his youthful hobo days, before he tasted blood.

All gathered 'round the water tank
A-waitin' for the train,
A thousand miles away from home
Just a-waitin' for the train.

I walked up to the brakeman.
I give him a line of talk.
He said, "If you've got money, boy,
I'll see that you don't walk."

"Well, I haven't got a nickel,
Not a penny can I show."
"Then get off, get off, you railroad bum"
And he slammed that boxcar door.
Now, he put me off in Texas,
The state I dearly love,
With the great, wide open spaces
And a sky of blue up above.

A woman's voice takes over then—Nancy Radison managing one stanza of another railroad song before she is replaced by Kay. The second Mrs. Knowlton takes it to the finish, with perhaps a hint of irony in her selection. She sings "Little White Lies."

Jan won a victory of sorts in March 1990, when Dr. Norman Beals—the physician who overdosed Jan on estrogen—agreed to the revocation of his California license, thereby dodging an administrative hearing before the California Medical Board. Kathleen Schmidt, the board's senior special investigator, wrote to Jan on March 19, expressing thanks for her participation in the case. "Without it," Schmidt admitted, "I don't think we would have achieved this result."

The news that Beals had lost his license broke nine days later, in articles that noted the El Toro physician was "accused of administering a hormonal treatment that posed a public danger and caused harmful side effects to at least eighteen women." According to the press releases, Beals "admitted that the California Medical Board's allegations were true and declined to contest the charges at an evidentiary hearing." The fifty-six-year-old Beals further "admitted negligence in following usual medical practices in administering hormones to women with postmenopausal depression."

Jan was quoted in the press as being satisfied with the results of the investigation. Jackie Marian, a free-lance writer from Marina del Rey, went further, proclaiming: "It's about time. That man is dangerous." As if to prove that charge, Beals admitted treating Sheryl Massip, lately charged with manslaughter for killing her baby in a fit of postpartum psychosis, but he was quick to note that he injected Massip with hormones only *after* the killing. The judge directed a verdict of acquittal in that case, finding Massip innocent, and that verdict was confirmed on appeal.

Alan Bock, a senior columnist at the *Orange County Register,* broke Jan's story on November 18, 1990, in an article titled "Memories of a Murder." He gave a brief sketch of the Dahlia case, for any readers who had spent the past half century in quarantine, filled in the gaps with some material on Jan, her background and her memories, and the evidence she had accumulated in the past twelve months. The piece was generally sympathetic and resisted any impulse to denounce Jan as a crank. "Whether what she remembers is the Black Dahlia murder or not," Bock concluded, "it was traumatic. She hopes she can figure it out, put it behind her, and resume her life. Maybe some reader can help."

But not at Parker Center, where the stock response from Jigsaw John St. John and company was uniformly negative. The truth lay in their files, said files were sealed, and Jan's explicit memories were "unrelated to the Dahlia case." Police believe that civilians who presume to question LAPD's Dahlia expert are delusional, and they will not be trusted to examine any of the evidence themselves—a Catch-22.

On January 12 an article by Erik Espe in the *Anaheim Bulletin* aired for the first time Jan's report of her father's incestuous abuse of her. Jim Frey told Espe, "I think the flashbacks are memories of a murder she saw as a child. I don't know if it was the Black Dahlia murder, but obviously it sounds very familiar." At the Westminster Police Department, Lieutenant Larry Woessner said, "I don't have any reason to disbelieve [she saw a murder]. I've had contact with people who have repressed things before. It's not uncommon. All the information she does give us we're not going to ignore. If there was a homicide so many years ago, we've got a victim out there." Still, as Woessner admitted, "It's just difficult for us to do a whole lot with it."

LAPD, predictably, warned Espe of "confidential information on the Black Dahlia case that doesn't jell with Knowlton's story." Jigsaw John allegedly received two to five calls every month about the case, including "several women" naming fathers or assorted other relatives as Beth's assassin. "The case is still unsolved," St. John told Espe, confidently. "The facts that [Janice Knowlton] gives don't relate to this case."

A month later, on February 19, Jan's story went nationwide with an article in the *Globe,* headlined "I Watched My Father Kill the Black Dahlia." Jim Frey was quoted once again, describing Jan's flashbacks as "truly repressed, buried memories." Detective St. John took a breather, the tabloid noting that LAPD "won't comment on the case," but an unnamed spokesman for the department confirmed that Short's body was dumped "a few blocks" from the American Legion post in Culver City.

All in all, Jan's story made a splash. The TV talk shows wanted in, and spring would see Jan's graphic memories relayed from coast to coast. She had experienced trepidation at first, as she considered how her family might react, but the time was coming when she would have to face them, one by one.

With all the principal adults deceased, Jan's siblings were her best hope for corroboration, and they remain her most exacting audience. To date, none have acknowledged memories of homicide or molestation, but they are unanimous recollecting their father's violent temper, his sadistic punishments, his cruelty to animals, his drinking binges, and the way he flaunted his adultery.

It may be more significant to note the many things Jan's siblings *don't* remember from those childhood years. Sister Prudence illustrates the point. Years after her parents' divorce, while constructing a dollhouse modeled after their Westminster home, Prudence found that she "had to guess about most of the inside" details. She had one interior photograph to guide her, depicting the Westminster living room. "Since I could see knotty pine in the photo," she recalls, "I made that room knotty pine, and I got sick while drawing the knots on the fake wood. Now knotty pine always makes me feel sick, but it never did before I made that dollhouse. Later, I found a Realtor's listing and found out the whole interior was knotty pine, with pine floors."

And what, we are tempted to ask, went on in those rooms with the knotty pine paneling that caused a mere glimpse of wood to evoke such a reaction after almost fifty years?

"I used to try very hard to remember those days, [to remember] if I saw anything," Prudence wrote to me in January 1993. "A few times, I'd be ready to fall asleep and I'd see something in a flash, the way people do. One was a vampire getting ready to bite a woman on the neck, super-imposed on our bedroom wall in the Westminster house. The woman was in a straight-backed chair"—the kind of chair Beth Short was sitting in, her face slashed and bleeding, on the night she died. Jan recalls her sister walking in on George and Beth in the garage that same night while George was standing over Beth, with a claw hammer in his hand. "There were a few more occasions when I'd 'see' something that way," Prudence recalls, "but then I got my mind on other things."

She has no special memories of George and Janice going off together on their own, Prudence says, "but I do think there is something to that, because of the early pictures of our father always holding [Jan] instead of our brother." Watching Jan on television, Prudence said, "I was stunned to see her trembling and crying. I have never seen [her do] that except on TV, because we live on opposite coasts and can't afford to travel."

Prudence later wrote, "A cousin I'd never remembered meeting came to see me the night after our mother's funeral. He was our brother's age, six years older than me, and he mentioned he had spent a couple of weeks visiting us in Westminster. He stunned me by saying our father took the clothes off the two youngest girls, which, at the time, would be me and Marjorie. So that was another thing that made me wonder about our father. Later, when I hugged [the cousin], I had the suspicious thought of 'Did he come because he remembered our father stripping us and thought we were raised to be easy?' Did he have an ulterior motive?"

Even when she could not corroborate Jan's darker memories, Prudence rose to her sister's defense against other doubters in the family. "Donald's wife [Dorothea Knowlton] said she only met our parents a couple of times before we went to Westminster," Prudence recalls, "yet she doesn't believe the tales of molestation and murder. It is one thing for us kids in the family, if we don't remember, but for the rest of the relatives, they don't know what they are talking about. They didn't live with us."

In fact, Prudence has no conscious memories preceding the birth of her youngest sister, when Prudence was herself four years and four months old. Between that point and the divorce, her childhood memories are shattered fragments. "I don't think that is normal," she admits. "I think I put memories that were too painful into little compartments in my head and locked them up."

When the sisters sat down in 1993 to play the ancient record of their father singing, neither one could recognize his voice.

"I have post-traumatic stress disorder," Prudence said, "and never knew what it was until last year. It was caused by our father, and I've had it all my life, along with chronic depression. If it all did really happen, and I did walk into that garage, I wish I could remember."

In the meantime, like Janice, she writes poetry:

> I had my childhood
> Where was Jan?
> I made myself forget
> The way to school
> After the rooster was gone

By March of 1991, Jan had recovered the memory of being forced to cut and paste the January 1947 message to authorities that accompanied Short's effects. She publicly requested that the LAPD fingerprint division match her prints against those lifted from the package, which were published in the press and scrutinized in vain by agents of the FBI. It stood to reason that the Bureau had no record of her fingerprints, since she was only ten years old.

LAPD made no reply, but the Westminster police were more open-minded. They interviewed Jan and Jim Frey for the first time in early 1990. "We talked with them off and on for over a year," Lieutenant Larry Woessner recalls. "It was our opinion that much of the information she was providing didn't match the information LAPD gave us regarding the death of Elizabeth Short, though we did feel that she may have witnessed some traumatic event at the Westminster location." With George Knowlton dead and Short's file in the hands of LAPD, Woessner deemed it "pointless" to pursue the case in Westminster.

One who disagreed was Harry Francisco, a professor of archaeology at UCLA. Jan got in touch with him in 1990, after reading about his work in the newspaper. They developed a rapport as Jan explained her problem and her suspicion that important evidence—perhaps a body—might be buried at the old Westminster homesite. Francisco was initially reluctant to participate, between his busy schedule and the fragmentary nature of Jan's memories, but her sincerity convinced him to proceed.

"The principle of repression and what it can do was entirely familiar to me," Francisco explains, "and nothing in the development of the ideas [Jan] expressed over a period of time was incompatible with the way this phenomenon occurs. The process of discovery was patchy, painful, fragmental, and not in any order of chronological happenings. Jan became more and more convinced that something might be found, and I grudgingly agreed with the idea that she had indeed witnessed some cataclysmic event, with the result that I agreed to excavate."

Before he started digging, the professor had to satisfy himself that the police were not opposed to excavations and that nothing he unearthed would damage Jan or hinder her recovery. Jim Frey put his mind to rest on the latter score. As for the cops, Francisco says, "After numerous inquiries, it became evident that the police in Los Angeles, Seal Beach, and Westminster were not the least interested in pursuing the case." Marcos and Sarah Gonzales, the present owners of the property, raised no objection to the search.

In April 1991, Jan and the professor were joined by volunteer archaeologists Cynthia Schneider and Don Tryon for the Westminster dig. Jan's childhood home had long since been demolished, and the lot was vacant, but surviving trees, old photographs, and established property lines gave the team their point of reference for the excavation. After working for two days, they uncovered the red brick walkway that had once linked house and garage.

Jan had once watched her father dig a pit beside that path. "What are you digging, Daddy?" she had asked.

And Georgie had replied, "Your grave."

Reopening the pit, Francisco's diggers found an animal bone, perhaps from a cow, a cache of bottles, glass containers in various sizes, and other homely items—an antique doll's hairbrush, a marble, an old mustard jar. Jan would later trace the labels from two of the bottles to L.A.'s East Side Brewery, confirming their 1947 pedigree, but Francisco and his volunteers had limited time and resources. The vacant lot would have to wait.

Jan still had other work to do, spreading the word.

Jan's first television interview aired on *A.M./L.A.* on Wednesday, May 22, 1991. The night before her live appearance, the producers booked her into the Universal Hilton, with a view of the famous Hollywood sign from her window. Standing in that room and staring out across the city, she experienced a strong impression of Beth Short, viewed from an almost childlike perspective.

Elizabeth should be where Jan was, looking forward to her television debut—a clear shot at the spotlight. Jan could almost feel the thrill "Aunt Betty" would have felt in such immediate proximity to lights and cameras.

The feeling carried over to the morning of her interview, but Jan had trouble getting to the studio on time. *A.M./L.A.* was broadcast from a studio not far from Short's North Cherokee apartment house, and Jan got lost en route, weaving aimlessly through the crowded streets, unable to get her bearings. Fortunately she had brought a friend along for the ride, and they got back on course in time for the program.

Waiting backstage in the greenroom, Jan was introduced to actor Charles Durning, a veteran movie star whose film credits include the role of mobster Jack Amsterdam i

1981's *True Confessions.* Jan had seen the film, but she had instantly repressed all scenes related to the central murder plot. And so it was again with Durning after that Wednesday morning. When they met again weeks later at a party hosted by Dom DeLuise, Jan had no conscious memory of meeting Durning at the TV studio.

On camera, Jan described her memories of Beth Short's murder, then stood firm when first one host and then the other tried to draw a line between "real" memories and recollections of events that she had only heard about. Both hosts implied that a ten-year-old would store up details of the Dahlia case from media reports and then, four decades later, produce a fabricated "memory." Jim Frey was at her side to note the difference between spontaneous regression to a concrete memory and the elusive one-dimensional domain of fantasy. He had no doubt that Jan's emphatic recollections were legitimate.

Nine days later, on Friday, May 31, the syndicated tabloid program *Hard Copy* aired excerpts from an interview with Jan conducted by reporter-producer Dean Vallis. The questioning took place in Jan's apartment, where she sat in a straight-backed chair, evoking memories of Short, while Vallis grilled her under glaring lights. Between takes he was frankly skeptical and made no secret of his disbelief, but he later told Jan's sister Prudence that he believed Jan's memories were legitimate. Jim Frey, who was filmed behind his desk, expressed confidence in Jan's "classic clinical symptoms" and declared himself "convinced that Janice is having real memories."

All things considered, when she had a chance to view the final tape, Jan thought Vallis had produced the best, most even-handed of her television interviews. Unaccustomed as she was to pleasant surprises, it made a refreshing change.

Jan's televised appearances in May revived the Westminster Police Department's interest in the case. Detective Mike Proctor had questioned Jan twice the previous summer, but LAPD had discouraged any action by the small suburban police force. If Jigsaw John said there was nothing to it, why should Proctor or Lieutenant Woessner disagree?

In June they had a sudden change of heart, however. The impetus, as Woessner told the press, was Jan's emerging memory of a *second* murder in the Westminster garage. The Beth Short case lay well beyond his jurisdiction, but the murder of the nameless redhead was another story. There was still a chance of finding evidence in that case, but Lieutenant Woessner would have to watch his step. For one thing, excavating vacant lots would take time—and that meant it would cost money, since official personnel would have to man the shovels. But Woessner caught a break when a team of volunteers from San Diego State volunteered to do the spade work, supervised by a representative of the Orange County coroner's office and Dr. Judy Suchey, a forensic archaeologist. The dig was set for Saturday, June 22.

That left only the press, and there was no way Woessner could control the headlines or the content of the articles that would be written about the dig. "We excavated the site in Westminster looking for a murder victim," Woessner explained after the fact. "Our digging of the site had nothing to do with the Black Dahlia, though that is what the media played upon."

Indeed, though every Californian knew Short's body was discarded in Los Angeles some forty-four years earlier, the press appeared to think that Woessner's team was seeking Beth's remains. The *L.A. Times* reported Westminster's "Black Dahlia dig," while the *Californian,* in Bakersfield, headlined its story from the Associated Press: "Dig Fails to Uncover Clues in Black Dahlia murder." In Long Beach, the *Press-Telegram* regurgitated that wire service story with a twist, finding room for a passing mention of the redhead who was murdered after Short.

The latest dig began at 8:00 A.M. and ended at 7:30 P.M. Some two dozen spectators and journalists turned up on Texas Street as fifteen volunteers dug pits and trenches, concentrating on the old garage site. Early finds included a dog's skeleton, a horseshoe, and the jawbone of a cow. Soon after lunch the diggers found some costume jewelry and a cache of "unusual farm tools" that "resembled claw hammers," buried two feet down. A short time later they unearthed a five-inch folding knife.

Lieutenant Woessner found the buried items "very interesting." The burial of farm tools and a knife, in his opinion, "was unusual" and puzzling. "We don't know how significant this is," he told the press, "but it is definitely interesting. Why would anyone put [those things] that far underground?" As for bone fragments recovered at the scene, Mike Proctor told reporters, "We're really not sure what they are right now, but they're probably from an animal."

Jan did her part to help out with the papers, whipping up a press kit to distribute at the dig. Each packet contained copies of press clippings from 1947, complete with references to the elusive "George"; eyewitness descriptions of the tan car from Pacific Beach; a reference to the close proximity of George Knowlton's haunts on Linden Avenue in Long Beach and the Washington Hotel, where Beth had spent a portion of her final summer; a discussion of Beth and Jan's common roots, in Massachusetts; and a brief synopsis of the 1940s gambling scene that had spawned so much corruption in southern California.

In closing, Jan asked several pointed questions that reporters managed to ignore: Would LAPD provide Westminster police with a full autopsy report to confirm or refute Jan's description of injuries suffered by Short? Would LAPD permit Jan to view Beth's snapshot collection so as to check the faces of unidentified boyfriends for a photo of her father? Was LAPD willing to cross-check George's fingerprints, or Jan's, against the package they received in January 1947? Would police in Lynn, Massachusetts, examine the basement of Georgie's old home on Hollingsworth Street for a possible grave?

Lieutenant Woessner was caught in the middle, still

sounding sympathetic to Jan as the diggers packed up their gear. "All we can say at this point," he told reporters, "is that we didn't find anything to support her story. That doesn't mean it didn't happen. It just means we can't prove it at this point. We're convinced she did suffer some type of traumatic incident when she was ten years old. This doesn't corroborate or disprove what Ms. Knowlton has said."

One item from the dig that never made the papers was a scrap of fabric stained a rusty brown. A few days later, Woessner called Jan at home to say that he was sending the fabric, on his own initiative, to be tested for bloodstains at "a lab in Canada." We have no way of knowing what those tests revealed or if they were even performed, because the door abruptly slammed on Jan in Westminster. A short time later, Woessner recalls, Jan was sent a letter informing her that "our investigation is closed and that since her father is dead we will spend no more time on a case that we can't bring to court."

Henceforth, all inquiries to the Westminster Police Department would be referred to Jigsaw John.

Soon after the Westminster dig, Jan flew to Boston for an appearance on the TV program *People Are Talking*. The questions were routine, but what occurred immediately following the show was not. A local reporter waited for Jan backstage and thrust photocopies of an article about the Francis Cochran murder in her face.

New images to cope with, barriers disintegrating in a fraction of the time they might have taken otherwise. Jan had no conscious memories of Cochran at the time, but she was interested enough to seek more information on the case. Disjointed images that clearly did not fit the California murders now fell into place: a field of butterflies, the crooked phallic stick she had fetched for Georgie on demand, her father's square-backed car.

In time, Jan telephoned police in Salem. They were noncommittal, but they taped the call and played it back for author Joan Noble Pinkham, resident expert on the

Cochran murder who had been researching details of the case for a possible screenplay. Pinkham spoke with Jan at length and came away impressed with her sincerity and with the striking similarities between some injuries sustained by Francis Cochran and the violence done to Beth Short in Los Angeles a few years later. It was also Pinkham who alerted Jan to the unsolved murder of Beryl Atherton in Marblehead, which unleashed another flood of memories. By mid-December 1992, Joan Pinkham had "no doubt at all" of Jan's sincerity. There was, she noted, "a distinct possibility" that George Knowlton had been involved in both unsolved murders.

The first week in July found Jan in New York City for a TV interview with Sally Jessy Raphael. The night before that taping, Jan walked the streets where she had spent a decade in show business. She strolled past the spot on Fifty-seventh Street where she had taken singing lessons, then walked along Fifty-ninth Street, where she'd gotten her first professional singing engagement at Chez Lucy. It was a haunting experience, retracing the steps of a stranger, inhabiting a mind and body burdened with so many horrors that the younger Janice had never recognized.

A few days after her appearance on *Sally,* Jan's answering machine picked up a call from a close relative. Even with the venom in her tone, Jan had no trouble recognizing the familiar voice. "Here's my message," the caller snarled. "Back off, or I'll kill you!"

Jan filled out an incident report with the police and let it go. She was saddened by the call, but she had been threatened all her life by an established master of the art, and she had more important matters on her mind than running scared.

On Tuesday night, July 16, Jan told her story on *Larry King Live,* fielding questions from King and members of his nationwide audience. Beth's niece, Valerie Reynolds, had declined to appear on the program, but she sent a statement on the family's behalf. "If what Jan Knowlton claims is true," she wrote, "and I believe that it warrants serious investigation, then it needs to be continued using the evidence collected at the time of the original investigation."

Dr. Terence Keane, head of the National Center for Post Traumatic Stress Disorder, also appeared on the program. He referred to Jan's experience as "a very clear-cut case of a dissociated memory or a repressed memory." Short's murder was, in Dr. Keane's professional opinion, "the kind of event that could actually have been dissociated." Furthermore, when King asked whether the Los Angeles police should take Jan seriously, Dr. Keane replied: "I think they should pay attention. I think that they should look at the whole context of clues surrounding the murder and see where this information that Janice is presenting fits in."

One of the callers who responded on the air was Texan Jim Ammerman, nephew of the late LAPD Detective William Ernest Harmon, and he told of his uncle's personal experience with the Dahlia cover-up. Another link was forged, new avenues of exploration and investigation opened.

Back in L.A., Jigsaw John St. John was having none of it. No wet-behind-the-ears psychologist from Boston, Massachusetts, or whatever, was going to tell *him* what he should investigate. On Friday, August 16, St. John got his chance to rain on Jan's parade when he posed beside his dusty file cabinet for the cameras of *Inside Edition*. Jan had already appeared on that show. She had described what she witnessed in the Westminster garage, and Jim Frey had told the interviewer, "I'm convinced that what Jan's remembering is a memory." But Jigsaw John preferred to play it cagey. "The only thing that I can comment about that," he said, "is that the facts, as she's told them to me is not compatible with the way the Black Dahlia, or Elizabeth Short, met her death." St. John neglected to inform his audience that he had never actually heard Jan's memories, but the announcer set things straight with a notation that the great detective "refuses to meet her" in person.

As for Dr. Terence Keane, on September 22 he told the *Houston Chronicle:* "Janice Knowlton is worth listening to.

Her story could be feasible. I have no way of knowing whether what she says is correct, but, as bizarre as it sounds, it's possible. We deal with cases of lost memory all the time. Vietnam has taught us something about the recurrence of traumatic memories."

That lesson failed to reach the leading minds of southern California law enforcement, though. Lewis Rosenblum, deputy district attorney for Orange County, managed to brush Jan off "without speaking to the merits of the case" when he wrote to her on October 18: "Although I can sympathize with your frustration, my assessment is that it would be unproductive and ill-advised to continue to investigate the filing of criminal charges on a man, who all the evidence suggests is no longer living. Again, I certainly sympathize for the pain and suffering caused you and the entire Short family due to Elizabeth Short's untimely death."

Case closed. Again.

In the fall of 1991 veteran L.A. newsman Will Fowler published *Reporters,* a memoir that had taken several years to write. The book includes a twenty-one-page chapter on the Dahlia case, and while Fowler makes no mention of Jan Knowlton, he does take shots at several others who were operating on the fringes of the case. There is substantial evidence that Fowler deviates from the record in his Dahlia chapter. He has privately admitted fabricating the time of every major incident, perhaps to supplement a failing memory, and his repeated claims of being first upon the scene are refuted by Jim Richardson's report from 1954, naming Sid Hughes as the reporter who first telephoned a description of Short's corpse to the *Examiner.* In fact, Richardson's memoir makes no mention whatsoever of Fowler, and the touted photographs of Fowler posing solo with Short's severed corpse are missing from *Reporters.*

If Fowler's treatment of peripheral issues seems dubious, his handling of Beth Short's remains is downright bizarre. Before pathologists arrived at Thirty-ninth and Norton,

Fowler tells us, he was busy closing Beth's eyelids, poking her vital organs, and measuring her wounds. (His book records the measurements in metric terms, unknown to California coroners in 1947, since, in Fowler's view, they sound "more medically proper.") He notes that her liver and colon "were palpable and soft to the touch. Neither organ had been invaded by a scalpel." So precise were Fowler's observations, in fact, that he made note of evidence that even Dr. Newbarr could not find when he performed Beth's autopsy. According to the medical examiner's report, there were no "neatly severed" vertebrae, and Short's right breast, while gashed, was not "cutaneously excised [severed] along with its nipple." Fowler's source for the mention of Short's "infantile vagina," meanwhile, is identified as a postmortem surgeon other than Dr. Newbarr who asked that his name be withheld. Again, the autopsy report contains no reference to a genital deformity of any kind.

Fowler did score a coup of sorts, though, by leaking Harry Hansen's "secrets" for the first time. Even so, he managed to insert at least one error. Fowler notes the ball of pubic hair retrieved from Short's vagina and the tattooed skin extracted from her rectum, but he can't resist inserting one more detail. "It seemed to me," he writes, "that her ear lobe was missing. It's been so many years now, I can't recall which one it was." In truth neither earlobe was missing, a fact announced by Harry Hansen ten years before *Reporters* went to press.

Finally, having failed to catch the killer himself, Fowler is more than happy to leave the case open forever. "Elizabeth Short's slaying might be solved in the distant future," he writes, "but I sincerely hope not. It's like an unopened present. The present always remains a wondrous thing, as long as it remains unopened."

At that, Fowler's most valuable contribution to the Dahlia literature is his gloating description of the *Examiner* staff at work, tampering with vital evidence, illegally impersonating lawmen, bribing and harassing crucial witnesses, bullying LAPD's chief of detectives into one shady deal after another. The portrait that emerges from *Reporters* is one of a police department more concerned with image than performance, and a newspaper more interested in sales than in the truth.

Daryl Gates retired as chief of LAPD on the last day of September 1992, leaving the department racked by controversy and dissension in the wake of summer riots and the drawn-out Rodney King affair. Gates's new position, on an FM talk show, gave the former chief an opportunity to vent his famous spleen, while Willie Williams, late of Philadelphia, stepped in at Parker Center and attempted to bring order out of chaos.

All of which meant nothing where the Dahlia case was concerned.

LAPD had ample problems in the present tense, without exhuming fifty-year-old mysteries to make things worse. The city shelled out millions every year to settle the complaints of citizens who'd been roughed up by L.A.'s finest, and LAPD veteran Mike Rothmiller was blowing the whistle on illegal procedures in the department's ultra-secret Organized Crime Intelligence Division. There were new files to shred, bare asses to cover.

My first direct contact with LAPD on the Black Dahlia case came as a result of a letter I wrote on October 14, 1992, requesting a copy of the autopsy report for comparison with the document supplied by an ex-sheriff's deputy. On November 4, Lieutenant R. B. Lewis, acting commander of Robbery-Homicide, replied that "It is the policy of this Department to keep the files of all unsolved homicide cases confidential until they are either adjudicated in court or resolved by some other legal means." Since Short's murder was unsolved, "We regret we cannot assist you in this matter."

I wrote back to Lieutenant Lewis on November 17, trying a new approach. This time I told him I had a solid suspect in the case, but I withheld George Knowlton's name. If I provided photos of the suspect, would Lieutenant Lewis take the time required to thumb through Beth Short's scrapbook and attempt to match the face?

While I was waiting for an answer, I approached the L.A. County sheriff's office, which had helped me out with files and photos in the past when LAPD was unwilling to cooperate. A sergeant in the LASO homicide division told me that the sheriff's Dahlia file had "disappeared" within the past twelve months or so, but he suggested that the coroner would probably be willing to release a copy of Short's autopsy report once certain fees were paid. The coroner, in fact, while happy to release the files on half a dozen *other* unsolved cases for a flat $240, balked on Short and cited special orders from Los Angeles police that nothing in her file should be released for public scrutiny.

An unexpected call from Jigsaw John came in on Tuesday afternoon, December 1. He mouthed the standard LAPD line about withholding files on open cases, but he was intrigued by my mention of a suspect and my offer of specific photographs. He asked me for the suspect's name, to "run a check through records," and I told him that the FBI had done that job already. There was no existing rap sheet on George Knowlton, and I held his name back with the honest explanation that my "contacts" in the suspect's family had been brushed off in the past without a hearing. Would St. John agree to view the photographs, compare them with Beth's stash, and proceed from there?

He was surprised at mention of Beth's trunk and luggage, noting that "that hasn't been mentioned or published in a number of years." He asked if my suspect "had access to cars," and he seemed interested in my response that Georgie was, in fact, highly mobile. Finally, grudgingly, he promised to review the photographs and "keep in touch."

Next morning, I mailed half a dozen photographs of Georgie Knowlton, spanning some two decades, and prepared to wait a month or more for Jigsaw John's reply. Instead, he called back on December 7, sounding rather agitated. He could not examine any photographs, he said, without the suspect's name and "full criminal record." I reminded him of our conversation five days earlier and asked him why he needed names to look at snapshots. Turning gruff, St. John informed me that he was in no position to "give anything away." Again, I asked him how confirming or denying the existence of a matching photo in the Dahlia file would compromise a fifty-year-old manhunt. Finally, with obvious reluctance, he agreed to have a word with his lieutenant and "get back to me" when they decided on a strategy.

That was the last I ever heard from Jigsaw John. On January 4, Captain W. O. Gartland, commanding Robbery-Homicide, delivered a combination scolding and kiss-off.

This is in response to your most recent letter of December 2, 1992, and your telephone conversations a few days later with Detective St. John, regarding the Elizabeth Short murder case. As previously indicated, this Department will not be able to conduct an investigation into your specific request unless we receive full cooperation from both you and/or the people you represent.

It is evident that you possess information that leads you, or the people you represent, to believe you have a potential suspect in this murder. The Los Angeles Police Department continues to maintain an open investigation into the murder of Elizabeth Short and anyone withholding information could preclude us from advancing our investigation. It would be most appropriate to have the people you represent contact this Department direct in order that there be no misunderstanding. Should this not be acceptable or possible, we will need the full name and description of their alleged suspect, how or who [sic] determined he was a serial killer, a list of the victims and the identity of any and all law enforcement agencies involved. If they have had previous contact with this Department

regarding the Short case, we would also request the
name of the officers contacted and the approximate
date or dates involved.

Your total cooperation in this matter is appreciated
and necessary. We are looking forward to your response. Detective St. John will thoroughly investigate
whatever information is provided.

My two-page reply, dated January 8, repeated everything
that I had previously told St. John and questioned the need
for such airtight security on one particular murder, forty-six
years after the fact. St. John retired on March 8, 1993, and
Captain Gartland still had not responded four months later,
when I wrote again, this time directly to Chief Williams,
asking him to reconsider LAPD's rule of silence on the
Dahlia case. The common courtesy of a reply, apparently,
was deemed to represent a violation of "security."

The nationwide rash of prosecutions founded on emergent memories inevitably sparked a backlash in the private
sector. Nine years earlier the revelation of abuse in day care
centers had produced a group called VOCAL—Victims of
Child Abuse Laws—pledged to the support of defendants in
child abuse trials. Now a new coalition, the False Memory
Syndrome Foundation, was organized in defense of those
like George Franklin and Marcos Morales, who were accused of vicious crimes years after the fact. Based in
Philadelphia, the FMSF claimed 4,638 member families,
from all fifty states and nine foreign countries, by July 1,
1993. It comes as no surprise that one of the foundation's
early leaders was a public figure active in VOCAL and
devoted to the notion that most, if not all, emergent
memories are the product of psychiatric "brainwashing."

Minnesota's Ralph Underwager, a Lutheran minister
turned Ph.D., spent two decades dabbling in sex therapy
and psychology before he struck gold in the 1980s as a
professional defense witness for accused child-molesters.
Operating from his home in Minneapolis, he was Johnny-

on-the-spot when charges of ritual abuse rocked Jordan, Minnesota, in 1983 and 1984. Despite a lack of certification in child psychology and child development, Underwager charged into the fray as an expert, insisting that none of the children in Jordan were really abused. Rather, he proposed, they had been brainwashed by a pack of therapists and social workers who searched for nonexistent evidence of sex and Satanism and then whipped up a superstitious frenzy reminiscent of the Salem witch trials. Flush with success in that case, Underwager rolled on to testify in thirty-five states over the next four years, collecting a minimum fee of $1,000 a day for his services. In the New Jersey case of Margaret Kelly Michaels, convicted on multiple felony counts despite Underwager's testimony, the good doctor earned $54,518 for eleven days of work.

The publicity and litigation generated by the FMSF were a mere sideshow to Jan in those days, as she focused on her own delayed recovery with single-minded zeal. The agonizing process of retrieving memories continues to the present day, with shocking images of incest, rape, and violent death emerging when and where they will, without regard to time or circumstances. In July of 1993, for instance, Jan was visiting a friend in Arizona when she found herself compelled to drive along the Gila River. She was barely able to proceed, however, as she was gripped by seizures, dizziness, and sudden panic. Jan believes that she has found another of her father's hunting grounds, and research in an Arizona library has revealed the disappearance of a woman back in 1961, around the time Daddy George was making frequent trips across the Arizona line to hunt deer. The woman's skeletal remains, dispersed by scavengers, were found in 1965, when Georgie had been three years in his grave. The case remains unsolved.

Increasingly, in private sessions with Jim Frey, Jan gives her wounded inner child the opportunity to speak out and communicate her long-ago terror. Little Janice has no voice, but she can write. Jan uses the forbidden right hand, the appendage Georgie threatened to remove if she so much as thought of writing out what he had done. The straggling, childlike script illuminates a world of buried pain: "He puts her in the trunk. The blanket is green, not gray. He opens it up. I see her face. It's my friend Elizabeth. She doesn't have any clothes on. He covers her up and closes the trunk. He smokes and leans on the car. He says I have to help him. This is our little secret. I can never tell my mother 'any of this or I'll kill you you little bitch, do you hear me?'"

Jan heard him and stored the threats away, but in time she remembered everything. She can still hear her father singing as he works. "He cut out messy parts to make her like a paper doll he can call his own," Jan wrote, "'a doll that other fellows cannot steal. And with their flirty-flirty eyes they'll have to realize . . . they'll have to go with dollies that are real.'"

A death-song, echoing across the years. It is the only funeral hymn Beth Short would ever have.

George Knowlton got away with murder for thirty years, but there is truth in the African proverb that human blood is heavy and the man who sheds it cannot run away. Behind the mask of sanity he wore from day to day, George Knowlton was consumed by demons of his own, and in the end they ate him up alive.

The monster lost, because his little girl remembers. She survived.

Notes

1. Thirty-ninth and Norton

pp. 9–10: I interviewed Bill Nash on November 4, 1992. Still lucid at age eighty-four, he recalled the morning of January 15, 1947, in perfect detail. Short's "big smile" and the clump of grass protruding from her vagina were especially clear in his mind. Asked whether he might have seen grass sprouting up between Short's legs rather than inserted in her genitalia, Nash was adamant. "I was right on top of her," he said. "You can't mistake a thing like that." To this day, LAPD refuses to discuss Nash's observations or acknowledge him as a witness in the case, but verification of his report is found in coverage of Short's murder by the *Hollywood Citizen News* dated January 15, 1947. The somewhat garbled front-page story states that "A passing motorist noticed the body lying just off the sidewalk in a vacant lot in a newly developed Southwest Los Angeles residential district. He notified a woman in a nearby house who telephoned police." Further corroboration comes from Mary Shinnerer, a retired Los Angeles teacher, who was informed of the incident by one of Nash's relatives in

January 1947. Ironically, the mother of a student in Shinnerer's class was employed at the L.A. County morgue, and she confirmed Nash's report of grass inserted in Short's vagina.

p. 10: A bizarre and pointless controversy still surrounds the time of Betty Bersinger's anonymous report to the police. Celebrity gossipmonger Kenneth Anger, in *Hollywood Babylon II,* fixed the discovery of Short's corpse at 7:30 A.M. Retired newsman Will Fowler, in his book *Reporters,* changed the time of discovery to 9:05 A.M., still ninety minutes off, but at least Fowler had a reason for departing from the truth. On March 29, 1993, he told me that the timing of events reported in his chapter on the Dahlia case was "not accurate"; the times had been chosen at random "for dramatic effect." This fictional approach to fact may also explain Fowler's placement of Short's autopsy on the wrong day.

pp. 17–21: Our copy of the autopsy protocol on Elizabeth Short was furnished by a former detective with the Los Angeles County Sheriff's Department who copied the document by hand and then typed it. The sheriff's file on Short subsequently disappeared, according to Sergeant Bill McComas of the LASO Homicide Division, and LAPD refuses to release any information on Short's death "until the case is adjudicated in court"—that is, never. Sergeant McComas suggested that an official copy of the Short autopsy protocol could be obtained from the Los Angeles County coroner's office by any citizen willing to pay a fee for duplication of public records. On December 19, 1992, I was informed by Michele Bringier, chief of the coroner's public services division, that "due to the unsolved nature of this case, we have been instructed by the Los Angeles Police Department not to release any copies of the documents retained by the [coroner's] department of this case file." The bureaucratic runaround came full circle when Ms. Bringier referred us to LAPD as a possible source. Ironically, my subsequent request for autopsy files in five other unsolved homicide cases was granted without objection from LAPD, suggesting a strange double standard where the Dahlia case is concerned. Because of LAPD's intransigence and the "unofficial" nature of the autopsy report in hand, the authors are unable to guarantee its total accuracy.

2. Still Small Voice

pp. 36–37: Jan later came to believe that Dr. Thomas Westlake's surgical recommendation was based more on financial considerations than on concern for his patient's welfare. In January 1989, Orange County newspapers reported that Westlake and another surgeon were under investigation for allegations of financial misconduct stemming from reciprocal arrangements made with two L.A.–Orange County hospitals. The press reported that Westlake and his associate "annually produce[d] several million dollars revenue" by referring patients to the hospitals in question, a windfall repaid in kind with generous "research" grants. No charges were filed as a result of that investigation.

p. 53: Kotulak's article, published in the May 28, 1993, edition of the *Chicago Tribune,* includes the quoted opinions of Dr. Coe and Dr. Merzenick. Dr. Charney's opinion is drawn from a *New York Times* interview, published June 12, 1990.

3. New England Gothic

p. 60: Years later, in conversation with her grandchildren, Gladys Knowlton herself described the marital sleeping arrangements. The Knowlton home life is reconstructed here from the firsthand reports of Jan, her sister Prudence, and their great-uncle Arthur Barton, half brother to Gladys.

pp. 64–65: The description of young Frederick Denno was provided by his friend and sometime traveling companion Carl Conrad, who observed in 1990 that Denno "was not a good model to follow."

p. 74: Supervisory Special Agent John Douglas, in charge of the FBI's Investigative Support Service, was kind enough to scan the Bureau's records at my request for any mention of George Frederick Knowlton, but he came up empty. With our positive knowledge of four arrests, including one for nonsupport of family described in Chapter 9, the absence of a federal rap sheet simply reaffirms the allegation that local agencies do not report *all* criminal arrests to Washington.

4. "No Childhood Here"

pp. 76–78: Descriptions of Marge Hatch's parents and early life were gleaned from recollections of Jan Knowlton and her sister Prudence.

p. 78: The conversation with Abe Reles is described by ex-D.A. Burton Turkus in his book *Murder Incorporated* (New York: Farrar, Straus, 1951). Reles went on to testify in a series of New York murder trials, sending several contract killers to the electric chair before his luck ran out on November 12, 1941. Early that morning Reles was thrown to his death from a Brooklyn hotel window, allegedly murdered by corrupt policemen assigned to protect him. The case was written off as "suicide or accidental death." Years later, mob boss Lucky Luciano admitted that NYPD detectives had been paid $50,000 to perform the execution, thus sparing gang leaders Albert Anastasia and Bugsy Siegel from upcoming murder trials.

p. 79: Georgie's style of courtship was described for Prudence by her mother, after the divorce in 1947.

p. 79: The New Hampshire marriage license listed Georgie's occupation as "truck driver," and so he may have been, for a time. At work, as in his choice of victims, he was rather flexible.

p. 85: A few years after the Vermont accident, Georgie's partial disability saved a man's life in Massachusetts. Georgie told his uncle Philip Knowlton that he had argued with his foreman at the latest foundry job and had chased the man, intent on killing him, but ankle pains prevented him from catching his intended victim.

pp. 88–89: More than fifty years after the fact, police in Lynn refuse to discuss the Cochran case with outsiders. Officers in Salem, where much of the manhunt went on, refer modern inquiries to author Joan Noble Pinkham, recognized as a leading expert on the case. Based on her knowledge of the crime and her conversations with Jan, Ms. Pinkham told me in December 1992 that she considers George Knowlton's involvement in the Cochran murder "a distinct possibility."

pp. 90–91: On August 31, 1993, Detective Sergeant Richard Urbanowicz of the Salem Police Department informed me that his department has "no record whatsoever" of Irene O'Brien's disappearance. He described the evidential void as "not unusual," considering the elapsed time.

pp. 98–100: All Short's letters and the answers she received from servicemen in 1944–1946 quoted here and on pp. 133–36 appeared in the Los Angeles *Herald-Express* on various dates in January 1947.

p. 101: There were persistent rumors of other unsolved murders in the Medford-Malden-Stoneham area through the late 1930s and into the 1940s, but I was unable to pin down any details. Police departments in the area uniformly ignored my queries, and newspaper searches were hopeless without some finite starting point. One native of the area, Sue Peterson, remembers her mother being warned by a policeman of a prowling killer in the neighborhood, but once again the crucial details have been lost. She did recall the officer's specific reference to a press blackout, with information on the crimes deliberately withheld from newsmen. As it stands, the rumors constitute another tantalizing mystery, perhaps with no connection to the Dahlia case and Georgie Knowlton's other crimes.

p. 103: As in the earlier case of Irene O'Brien, Salem police have no record of the Shirley Durkee case today. For all intents and purposes, it is the ultimate missing-person file.

5. Open Season

p. 107: After reviewing tapes and photographs of the June 1991 police dig in Westminster, Prudence feels certain that the excavations never reached the site where she remembers seeing open pits in 1946.

p. 110: Nancy Radison, in a private conversation with Jan, confirmed Billy Sexton's affair with George Knowlton. Other family members seem unaware of the relationship, but they remember Sexton fondly as a gay man who was "happy with himself."

p. 119: Confirmation of Short's reputation at the IF Club in Los Angeles was provided by Betty Plunkett, a former patron who saw Short in the bar, during an interview with Jan Knowlton on September 14, 1993.

pp. 119–20: Lee Strasberg described Monroe's foray in prostitution during an interview with *Swank* magazine in August 1980.

p. 121: Tex Driscoll's memories of Georgie were related by his former neighbor, Tina Milburne, in an interview conducted on January 24, 1993.

p. 122: Author Hank Sterling, in *Ten Perfect Crimes,* flatly states that Short and Lynn Martin were turning tricks at the Hawthorn Hotel. To date, no other source beyond Jan's memories has confirmed the specific locale, though former detective Thad Stefan and others corroborate Short's general involvement in prostitution.

pp. 122–23: Retired detective Edwin Hall recalls that a child pornography ring, dubbed "Smut Incorporated" by the press, was active in the neighborhood of Sunset Boulevard around this time. It is conceivable that LAPD knew of Short's link to the netherworld of kiddie porn, a circumstance that may account for Harry Hansen calling her "a bum." In fact, as several sources have confirmed, there seemed to be a common sentiment around Los Angeles, among police and sheriff's deputies, that Short's horrendous death was little more than she deserved.

pp. 131–32: Conflicting viewpoints of the Hubbard-

Parsons conflict are recounted by J. Gordon Melton in *The Encyclopedia of American Religions,* by Arthur Lyons in *Satan Wants You,* and by Bent Corydon in *L. Ron Hubbard, Messiah or Madman?*

6. Paper Doll

p. 140: As noted earlier, Jan's brother often slept in the back room of the garage. Her memories, so far, include no information as to his whereabouts when Short was killed. Jan speculates he may have been allowed to sleep inside the house, since it was winter, and the family was short two children with the death of Marjorie and Sandra. Sister Prudence recalls David suffering from scarlet fever and sleeping inside around this time. He was also hospitalized for an appendectomy, but the exact dates are unknown. David Knowlton seems to have no conscious memory of the event, and he was not interviewed for this account at his—and Jan's—request.

pp. 148–49: Will Fowler, self-styled "first man on the scene" and thus touted as an expert on the case, denies that any saw was used on Short. He bases this contention on his private observation of a "cleanly-severed vertebra"—that is, no fragments chipped off by a saw blade—which, according to the autopsy report, did not exist. Fowler's flat denial also contradicts a string of early front-page stories in the L.A. press, which state that Beth was "cut or sawed" in half. One clipping from a suburban paper quotes an unnamed L.A. medical examiner to the effect that *three* distinct and separate instruments were used to do the job. Meanwhile, we know from records of the Skil Corporation that their hand-held rotary saw was available to the public beginning in 1925. In 1947 it sold for a cool $54.95. Confirmation of George Knowlton owning a Skil saw comes from Nancy Radison, one of his closest friends. George gave the saw to Nancy's husband, Dexter, when the Knowltons moved back east in mid-October 1947. Dexter kept the saw around for several years, until it vanished in the midst of yet another move.

7. Manhunt

p. 162: Despite his frequent on-screen claim that "only the names have been changed to protect the innocent," Jack Webb was not above revising facts if it would help him cast LAPD in a better light. In *Dragnet*'s presentation of the Harvey Glatman case, for instance, Webb—as the intrepid Sergeant Joe Friday, badge number 714—scales a muddy hillside in torrential rain to save a female hostage from the madman who is bent on killing her. In fact, Glatman, an early serial killer from the 1950s, was disarmed by his last intended victim and held at gunpoint while the woman flagged down a California Highway Patrol officer on the Santa Ana Freeway. LAPD took custody of Glatman after the fact, but its detectives played no part in his arrest.

pp. 164–65: Interviewed on March 29, 1993, Fowler insisted that he not only examined Beth Short's body but actually touched her protruding organs. Irresponsible as this may seem, I have no evidence to disprove his statements. The conflicting reports in Jim Richardson's account of the event are worth considering when Fowler's Dahlia chapter is reviewed. Likewise, while Fowler constantly refers to Felix Paegel's photograph depicting Fowler and the severed corpse alone, before police arrived, the photo printed in *Reporters* shows Fowler crouching next to the body, with Harry Hansen and another homicide detective on his left.

pp. 166–67: Richardson's description is from his memoirs, *For the Life of Me* (New York: Putnam, 1954), p. 305.

p. 168: Harriet Manley was not the only witness silenced by the *Examiner*. In San Diego, Richardson likewise ordered Tommy Devlin to muzzle the Frenches. "If it takes dough to shut them up," he commanded, "give it to them." Devlin's reply: "They're shut up. I've seen to that."

p. 169: Will Fowler contradicts Richardson in describing Short's luggage. In Fowler's version there was no trunk, only "a suitcase and some bags." He recalls that "one suitcase in particular" contained dozens of snapshots depicting Beth Short in romantic settings with various men. I have accepted Richardson's account in this regard because it was written closer to the actual events and because of Fowler's tendency to tamper with facts in the interest of "dramatic effect."

p. 173: James Ellroy's comments are drawn from my interview with him on February 23, 1993.

p. 179: Betty Bersinger's name was first revealed by the *Los Angeles Times* on January 24, 1947, suggesting that she was identified by the police the previous day.

p. 180: I interviewed Bill Welsh on December 1, 1992, recording his impression that "someone powerful" had squelched the Short investigation. Niesen Himmel ignored my several letters and telephone calls to the *Times* for reasons unknown, but his opinion of the Dahlia cover-up was recorded for posterity on the syndicated TV program *Murder One,* first broadcast from Los Angeles on February 8, 1992.

pp. 180–81: Detective Harmon's statements on the Dahlia cover-up were recalled by his nephew, Jim Ammerman, whom I interviewed on November 25, 1992. Joe Jasgur was interviewed for this account on March 30, 1993, and Vincent Carter on December 8, 1992. Thad Stefan's original field reports from February 1947 are supported by an interview with Jan Knowlton on July 12, 1993.

pp. 194–95: Richardson is quoted from his memoir, *For the Life of Me,* pp. 310–11.

pp. 195–99: Ben Hecht's column appeared in the Los Angeles *Herald-Express* on February 1, 1947, followed by Steve Fisher's on February 2, the profile by Leslie Charteris on February 5, and that of David Goodis on February 6. I wrote to Charteris in early 1993 at his home in England, hoping to discover what "inside information" he received from LAPD contacts back in 1947, but the aging writer died before he could respond.

p. 201: Richardson is quoted from his memoir, *For the Life of Me*, pp. 311–12.

8. Werewolf at Large

p. 220: Jan Knowlton found Willard Pool in September 1993, still living in Orange County. Predictably, after a lag of forty-six years, he denied any memory of her parents and could offer no explanation as to why Marge Knowlton had kept half of his torn business card for over four decades.

p. 222: Dr. Newbarr's detailed notes on the Mondragon autopsy have not survived, but I was able to obtain a summary of the postmortem findings from the Los Angeles County Coroner's Department in 1993. Again, despite the murder's unsolved status, LAPD offered no objection to the file's release.

pp. 222–23: The murder of Vivian Newton remains unsolved at this writing, but the investigation has apparently been closed by default. In 1993 the San Diego County Sheriff's office confirmed that Torrey Pines Mesa lies within city jurisdiction. Homicide investigators for the San Diego Police Department, meanwhile, were unable to find any record of the case in their files.

9. Bloodlines

p. 232: As of April 15, 1949, when George and Kay purchased the homesite in Saugus, they still were not married. A transfer deed executed on that date lists George F. Knowlton and Kathleen H. Cardran as "joint tenants" of the property, while prior owners Richard and Teresa Crowe are specifically named as husband and wife. Jan surmises that George had married Kay by year's end, but no documents have been unearthed to prove it, and none of her relatives have been willing or able to provide a specific date for the marriage.

10. Tender Prey

p. 243: The later observation of Jan's gynecologist, supporting the belief that she had given birth at some time prior to 1967, is discussed in Chapter 13. The 1985 hysterectomy eliminated any further possibility of scientific proof, unless Jan's child is found alive and willing to submit to blood tests for a DNA comparison. Even that is not impossible, however. See Chapter 13 for evidence that Jan's daughter was alive and seeking her birth mother as recently as 1986.

p. 245: There is a chance, however slim, that Kay Knowlton may not have known about Georgie's later homicides. British serial killer Peter Sutcliffe, a.k.a. the Yorkshire Ripper, murdered thirteen women around northern England without his wife's knowledge. In the United States, John Gacy killed thirty-three victims *at home,* planted twenty-eight of them in the crawl space beneath his house, and convinced his wife and neighbors that the putrid odor emanated from a broken sewer pipe.

p. 258: The exact date of Jan's departure from Maine is unknown. The records from Mechanic Falls High School report her transfer, but without notation of the date. Her "incomplete" grades in all subjects would seem to indicate a stay of short duration, and this is apparently confirmed by a notation from Huntington Beach that a copy of her California records was mailed to Beverly High School on November 4, 1952. And while Beverly High has no record of her enrollment there before December 2, reference to Georgie's known movements indicates that she must have left Maine for Massachusetts in late October or very early November.

p. 258: To this day, Jan cannot recall her horse's name. The painful detail was erased from conscious memory when she discovered George had had him butchered.

11. Killing Time

pp. 264–66: Life with Georgie on Twelfth Street in Seal Beach was so traumatic that Jan repressed even the address for close to forty years. As late as 1992 she believed that George and Kay were living in Garden Grove when she joined them in 1954. It took a review of her transcripts from Orange Coast College, which included the Twelfth Street address, to unleash the halting flow of memories involving incest, rape, and murder. Significantly, Jan's stepsister Lena also has memory blanks for this period. Pressed to describe the two-story house, she can recall its color—white—and a vague layout of the ground floor, but she has no memory whatsoever of the upstairs bedrooms.

pp. 277–78: Detectives in El Monte and L.A. apparently did not discuss the similarity between Ellroy's murder and the death of Laura Trelstad in May 1947. Cotton cords, not further described, were found tied around the neck of each victim. The technique may not amount to a criminal signature, but there is no way to be sure without a meaningful investigation.

pp. 277–78: Dr. Gerald Ridge's autopsy report, number 35339, on Geneva Hilliker Ellroy, was obtained from the Los Angeles County Coroner's Department in 1993. Despite the fact that her murder occurred eleven years after the Dahlia slaying and remains unsolved today, neither the coroner's office nor LAPD opposed my request for release of the file.

p. 278: James Ellroy's comments on his mother's death are drawn from interviews published in the *L.A. Times,* October 4, 1987, and in *People* magazine, December 14, 1987.

p. 280: In fairness to the LAPD Homicide Division, it would have been a tedious procedure to retrieve two cases after thirty-five years had elapsed, when neither the victims' names nor a specific date of the event is known. I faced the same difficulties in my attempt to track the cases down by scanning daily issues of the *L.A. Times* and *Herald-Examiner.* John Austin, meanwhile, has elected to ignore my letters seeking further information on the unsolved crimes.

12. Death Wish

p. 284: Heinrich Pommerenke, dubbed "the Beast of the Black Forest," committed the first of his ten murders and twenty known rapes in 1959 after a viewing of *The Ten Commandments* somehow convinced him that women were the root of all worldly evil. Intent on "teaching them a lesson," he left the theater and walked to a nearby park, where he chose an eighteen-year-old victim, raped her, and slashed her throat with a razor. In October 1960, Pommerenke was sentenced to six life terms in prison, amounting to a minimum of 140 years behind bars.

p. 287: No specific diagnosis of trauma was made in regard to Jan's nose, but a likely cause would seem to be the many beatings she received from Georgie through the years.

p. 290: Ironically, there was another random killer in the neighborhood while George was shuttling Kevin in and out of Boston. The infamous Boston Strangler, later identified as Albert De Salvo, claimed his fourth and fifth elderly victims in mid-August 1962. The murder series began in June 1962 and continued through early January 1964, claiming the lives of thirteen women. Despite detailed confessions, De Salvo was never tried for any of the slayings. Attorney F. Lee Bailey negotiated a plea bargain in 1967, wherein De Salvo accepted a life sentence for unrelated rapes, and the murder charges were dropped. Six years later, De Salvo was murdered by a fellow convict in prison.

p. 295: As late as 1992, Jan still had doubts about her father's death, complete with brooding fears that he might seek her out, despite advancing age, and try to silence her somehow. In fact, while George was certainly cold-blooded enough to let another man die in his place, there is no evidence of such a plot. The brief amount of time between his final pit stop and the fatal crash, together with the presence of a witness at the scene, appears to rule out any possibility that George could have found a stand-in and arranged the crash to dupe authorities.

13. Echoes

pp. 298–99: Hansen's tearful scene at the retirement party was recorded in the *L.A. Times* on January 20, 1975.

p. 299: James Ellroy was told by LAPD officers that the files had been "picked clean." Detective John St. John, in charge of the Dahlia file until March 1993, insisted that sufficient evidence remained for trial, but he acknowledged, in a December 1, 1992, interview, that LAPD retained "very few" of Short's photographs and other personal possessions.

p. 301: Jan did not fly west when George Senior died in early July 1979. She had no conscious reason to avoid the funeral service, which was held ten years before her memories of molestation on Winthrop Avenue emerged, but she now suspects that her reticence was related to the impending anniversary of the Cochran and Shipp murders in Massachusetts.

pp. 316: Prudence now recalls her comment linking George to Beth Short's murder as "a joke," but a letter she sent to Jan in July 1991 suggests otherwise. Describing her reaction to Ellroy's novel, Prudence wrote: "Knowing what a male slut Dad was, I immediately thought he could have done it, and it wasn't long after that I noticed how much [Short] resembled Marian." Prudence also wrote a four-page poem titled "George and the Dahlia," which describes Short's murder as a revenge killing and refers to the "stink of death" on her father's hands. She refused permission to reprint that poem here, but wrote to me on August 21, 1993, that "It was written while trying to figure out a reason why he would kill her, if he killed her, and *before* Jan said she remembered the murder." (Emphasis in the original.) At the same time, Prudence puzzles over strange gaps in her own memory. Her letters speculate on George's role in this and other homicides. Her dreams, meanwhile, are fraught with images that may or may not be precursors of a conscious memory. The fragmentary nature of her early memories is discussed more fully in Chapter 14.

14. Breaking Cover

p. 321: St. John's remark about his senility was made to Milo Speriglio, director and chief of the Nick Harris Detective Agency. Speriglio communicated it to me in a letter dated January 6, 1993.

p. 322: Comments about the Short family's impression of St. John and LAPD were derived from an interview with Valerie Reynolds, Beth's niece and the official voice of her sisters, when we spoke by telephone on November 24, 1992.

pp. 327–28: The revocation of Dr. Beals's license, with reactions from Jan Knowlton and others, was reported in the *Orange County Register* on March 28, 1990.

p. 339: Tiffany subsequently overdosed on drugs and alcohol, spent most of a month in intensive care, and emerged with severe physical and mental damage. After listening to Jan's description of their home life with George, physicians agreed that Tiffany's subsequent seizures might be produced by post-traumatic stress disorder, since their tests failed to reveal substantial organic brain damage.

pp. 341–42: In our March 1993 interview, Fowler emphatically confirmed that he not only measured Short's wounds personally but actually touched the corpse. He recalled Beth's exposed transverse colon as "beautiful."

p. 343: An LAPD internal review of Rothmiller's charges found "no physical evidence" of criminal activity by the Organized Crime Intelligence Division, but Chief Williams admitted he was "not so naive to believe it never occurred."

p. 347: The conviction of Margaret Michaels was overturned on appeal, in 1993. At this writing, authorities have declared their intention to proceed with a new trial on the charges.